Handbook of
FORENSIC
PATHOLOGY

Second Edition

Vincent J.M. DiMaio and Suzanna E. Dana

D0171281

Taylor & Francis
Taylor & Francis Group
Boca Raton   London   New York

CRC is an imprint of the Taylor & Francis Group,
an informa business

CRC Press
Taylor & Francis Group
6000 Broken Sound Parkway NW, Suite 300
Boca Raton, FL 33487-2742

© 2007 by Taylor & Francis Group, LLC
CRC Press is an imprint of Taylor & Francis Group, an Informa business

International Standard Book Number-10: 0-8493-9287-X (Softcover)
International Standard Book Number-13: 978-0-8493-9287-0 (Softcover)

Library of Congress Cataloging-in-Publication Data

Di Maio, Vincent J. M., 1941-
    Handbook of forensic pathology / by Vincent J.M. Di Maio and Suzanna E. Dana. -- 2nd ed.
        p. ; cm.
    Includes bibliographical references and index.
    ISBN 0-8493-9287-X (alk. paper)
        1. Forensic pathology--Handbooks, manuals, etc. 2. Autopsy--Handbooks, manuals, etc. I. Dana, Suzanna E., 1948- II. Title.
        [DNLM: 1 Forensic Pathology--methods--Handbooks. W 639 D582h 2006]

RA1063.4.D525 2006
614'.1--dc22   2006045839

Visit the Taylor & Francis Web site at
http://www.taylorandfrancis.com

and the CRC Press Web site at
http://www.crcpress.com

To my children,
Dominick and Samantha DiMaio

—Vincent J. M. DiMaio

and

To my parents,
Rose and Fieldon Thomas Dana

—Suzanna E. Dana

Preface

In the preparation of this handbook, every effort was made to provide the pathologist-in-training with an up-to-date, concise manual detailing the many varied aspects of forensic pathology. Specialized areas such as forensic anthropology and forensic odontology have been mentioned but not dealt with in detail. The core principles in most other areas of the field are included and are presented in a fashion that allows for rapid assimilation. We have tried to address problems and questions that commonly arise during instruction of pathology fellows, residents, and medical students. It should be kept in mind that the information (descriptions, time periods, processes, etc.) presented in this handbook relates to the most common findings; however, variations will occur.

The field of forensic pathology can be an exciting and fulfilling one, especially if the doctor is well trained. It is our hope that this handbook will provide such instruction.

V. J. M. Di Maio
Chief Medical Examiner
Bexar County, Texas
Professor, Department of Pathology
University of Texas Health Science Center
San Antonio, Texas

S. E. Dana
Forensic Pathologist
Clinical Associate Professor, Department of Pathology
University of Texas Health Science Center
San Antonio, Texas

Acknowledgments

We would like to thank the artists who provided the original artwork used throughout this handbook, especially Donna LaChance Menke of Lytton Springs, Texas. Her careful attention to detail, her patience, and her accessibility were greatly appreciated. Robert B. Lovato of Austin, Texas provided a number of figures as well as digitizing the figures for publication.

We would also like to thank Wanda Beale Austin and Lucretia A. Pierce for typing portions of the handbook. Last, but not least, we would like to thank our mates, Theresa and Miles, for their patience, understanding, and support throughout this endeavor.

Contents

Introduction to Medicolegal Casework

1

I. FIVE CATEGORIES OF MEDICOLEGAL CASES

- Violent deaths, i.e., nonnatural deaths (accidents, suicides, and homicides)
- Suspicious death, i.e., those that may be due to violence
- Sudden and unexpected deaths
- Unattended deaths, i.e., those in which a physician is not in attendance
- Deaths in custody

Individual jurisdictions may modify these categories, either expanding or contracting them.

A. PREVALENCE OF MEDICOLEGAL CASES

1. In most communities, approximately half of all deaths are reportable to a medicolegal office.
2. Of these, half (*approximately 25% of all deaths*) will be accepted as medicolegal cases.
3. The rest are generally unattended deaths of individuals under the care of a physician who is willing to sign a death certificate, e.g., deaths in hospices, at home, etc.
4. Even if a case is not accepted, a written record of the report containing details of the death should be made and retained.

B. THE OBJECTIVES OF A MEDICOLEGAL EXAMINATION OF A BODY ARE:

1. To determine the cause of death
2. To determine the manner of death
3. To document all findings

    4. To determine or to exclude other factors that may have contributed to the death or how the manner of death should be classified

    5. To collect trace evidence from the bodies in criminally related cases

    6. To positively identify a body

C. IN ADDITION, THE PATHOLOGIST MAY SUBSEQUENTLY BE CALLED UPON TO:

    1. Testify in court to the findings

    2. Interpret their significance, how they occurred, and the nature of the weapon used (if any)

    3. Determine time of death

D. A MEDICOLEGAL AUTOPSY DIFFERS FROM A ROUTINE HOSPITAL AUTOPSY IN SEVERAL RESPECTS (TABLE 1.1).

TABLE 1.1   Differences between Hospital and Medicolegal Autopsy

Hospital Autopsy	Medicolegal Autopsy
Requires consent of next of kin	In most U.S. jurisdictions, does not require consent of next of kin
Purpose: To confirm suspected cause of death, as teaching tool, or to assess effectiveness of treatment	Purpose: To determine or document cause of death or to rule out unsuspected cause of death in criminal cases
Identity of deceased usually known	Identity may not be known; information obtained at autopsy may be used to arrive at positive identification
Evidence usually not collected	Evidence collected and preserved for possible use in court proceedings
Time of death usually known	Time of death may not be known, and autopsy findings may be helpful in estimating time of death
Medical records usually available prior to autopsy	Medical records may not be available prior to autopsy
Extent of autopsy may be limited at next of kin request	Complete autopsy is the rule instead of exception and includes head and neck exam
External exam less critical than internal exam	External exam more important than internal exam, as a rule
Photos during exam are optional	Photos **required** to document wounds and findings
Body may be embalmed prior to autopsy	Body should **never** be embalmed prior to exam; embalming destroys evidence, introduces artifacts, affects toxicology
Toxicology usually not helpful; samples usually not taken	Toxicology essential part of exam; results may indicate cause of death
Microscopic sections usually submitted and examined	Microscopic sections taken in select cases only, not as a routine part of the exam

II. CAUSE, MECHANISM, AND MANNER OF DEATH

Deaths can be categorized as to cause of death, mechanism, and manner.

A. The **cause of death** is the disease or injury that produces the physiological disruption in the body resulting in the death of the individual, e.g., a gunshot wound of the chest.

B. It should not be confused with the **mechanism of death,** which is the physiological derangement due to the cause that results in the death, e.g., hemorrhage.

C. The **manner of death** is how the cause of death came about.

1. Manners of death are:
    •   Natural
    •   Accident
    •   Suicide
    •   Homicide
    •   Undetermined
    •   Unclassified

2. A classification of **homicide** does not necessarily indicate that a crime has been committed, as the term *homicide* is not synonymous with **murder.** The term *homicide* just means that one individual killed another.

3. Classification of death as murder is done by a court, not a pathologist.

4. A manner of death is classified as **undetermined** when after an investigation of the circumstances surrounding a death, a postmortem examination, and appropriate laboratory tests, there is insufficient information to classify the death as natural, homicide, suicide, or accident.

5. Some forensic pathologists use a classification of **"unclassified"** when the death does not fall into any of the aforementioned manners of death. An example may be a psychotic individual who decides he can fly and attempts to do so off a 200-foot cliff. Such a death is obviously not natural or homicide, but is it suicide or an accident?

6. Deaths formerly termed **"therapeutic misadventures"** may be listed as unclassified.

7. **Figure 1.1** shows the caseload, broken down by manner of death, for a large metropolitan medical examiner's office (Bexar County, San Antonio, Texas, 2004 statistics). The majority of cases handled are natural or accidental.

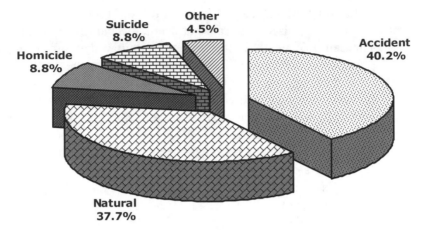

Figure 1.1 ME caseload by manner of death.

III. **THE FORENSIC AUTOPSY VERSUS AN EXTERNAL EXAMINATION**

A. **It is not necessary to perform an autopsy in all medicolegal cases.** The reasons for performing an autopsy are varied. The most obvious ones are:

1. To determine the cause of death when it is not known
2. To document injuries
3. To exclude other causes of death
4. To determine or exclude contributory factors to the death. This last reason is why autopsies are performed in most homicides, suicides, and accidents.

B. In some jurisdictions, autopsies are mandated in certain types of death.

C. Autopsies should be performed on all homicides.

D. The extent of the autopsy

1. A complete autopsy, at a minimum, involves removal and examination of the brain, the larynx and hyoid, and the thoracic and abdominal viscera as well as collection of blood, urine, bile, and vitreous, when available.

2. In certain cases one may want to make an even more extensive examination, e.g., incise the legs looking for the source of a pulmonary embolus.

3. As a general rule, either no autopsy or a complete autopsy should be performed. Exceptions occur. These generally involve autopsies limited to the head and are indicated in cases where there is a well-documented self-inflicted gunshot wound

of the head and the bullet has not exited. The main purpose of the limited autopsy in this case is recovery of the bullet.

    4. All homicides should be completely autopsied.

IV. THREE STEPS OF MEDICOLEGAL DEATH INVESTIGATION

    A. First is an **investigation of the circumstances** leading up to and surrounding the death. One must obtain as much information as possible prior to examining the body.

        1. A postmortem examination of a body should never be conducted until one knows the circumstances of the death.

        2. Investigation of the circumstances of a death may involve:

            a. An investigation of the scene

            b. Talking to witnesses, next of kin, and attending physicians

            c. Obtaining past medical records or police reports

        3. In cases where homicide is suspected, one should talk to the police to find out any special examinations or tests that they may desire.

        4. The circumstances of a death may determine to some degree the extent of the subsequent postmortem examination. Thus, a complete workup for rape would be conducted on the body of a young girl found seminude in an isolated area but not if she was fully clothed and shot while walking home from a store.

    B. Second is the **examination** of the body, whether it be an autopsy or an external examination.

    C. Third is the performance of **laboratory tests** (including but not limited to toxicology, ballistic test firings, etc.).

V. HANDLING OF BODIES AT THE SCENE

    A. It is at the scene that the correct handling of the body begins. If this is not done, physical evidence on the body can be lost or altered and sham evidence inadvertently introduced.

        1. Before the body is touched, its position and appearance should be documented photographically and diagrammatically.

        2. The body should be handled as little as possible so as not to dislodge physical evidence that may be clinging to it.

        3. The hands should never be pried open so as not to dislodge material such as fibers, hair, or gunpowder.

    B. Before transportation of the body to the morgue:

        1. Paper bags should be placed over the hands to prevent loss of trace evidence. Paper bags should be used rather than plastic, because plastic bags promote condensation on their interior as the body goes from refrigerated to heated environments.

2. The body should be wrapped in a white sheet or placed in a clean transport bag. This is done to prevent loss of trace evidence from the body. It also prevents acquisition of bogus evidence from the vehicle being used to transport the body to the morgue, as this vehicle has probably transported numerous other bodies.

VI. HANDLING OF BODIES FROM A HOSPITAL

A. If the deceased did not die immediately and was transported to a hospital, a number of surgical and medical procedures may have been carried out. Because of this:
   1. The complete medical records of the deceased from the time of admission to the time of death should be obtained.
   2. In addition, EMS and ambulance transport records should also be obtained.

B. All hospitals in the area served by the medicolegal system should be informed that in all medicolegal cases:
   1. No tubing should ever be removed from the body after death, e.g., endotracheal tubes, intravenous lines, and Foley catheters.
   2. Injection sites should be circled in ink by the hospital staff to indicate that they are of therapeutic origin and did not antedate hospitalization.
   3. Surgical stab wounds should be labeled or described in the medical records.
   4. If an injury is incorporated into a thoracotomy or laparotomy incision, this should be noted.
   5. If death occurs within a few hours after hospitalization, paper bags should be placed on the hands, just as if the death had occurred at the scene.
   6. Any clothing worn by the deceased should be transferred to the medical examiner's office.
   7. All medical records detailing the procedures performed should accompany the body.
   8. Any blood obtained on admission to the hospital should be obtained for toxicology. Admission blood obtained for transfusion purposes in trauma cases often is saved for one to two weeks in the hospital blood bank. The blood bank should be queried for retained initial blood samples.

VII. HANDLING OF BODIES AT THE MORGUE

A. On arrival at the morgue, the body should be logged in as to:
   1. The deceased's name
   2. The date and time of arrival
   3. Who transported it
   4. Who received it

B. A unique **case number** should be assigned to the body. At the time of the autopsy, an **identification photo** should be taken with the case number prominently displayed in the identification photo.

C. Examination of **clothing** and **external aspect** of the body

1. Before examination by the pathologist, the body should not be undressed, washed, embalmed, or fingerprinted.

   a. The clothing should not be disturbed, as examination of the clothing is as much a part of the forensic autopsy as examination of the body.

   b. Embalming can introduce artifacts, change the character of wounds, and make toxicological analyses impossible or extremely difficult.

2. The pathologist should have **x-rays** taken if they feel that they may be helpful. X-rays should be routinely taken in:

   a. All gunshot wound cases

   b. Deaths of infants and young children

   c. In the case of decomposed, charred, and unidentified bodies

   d. Explosion victims

3. The next step is to recover any **trace evidence** on the clothing or the body.

   a. The body is examined with the clothing still on the body.

   b. The clothing should be examined for the presence of trace evidence.

   c. Following this, the clothing is removed and laid out on a clean, dry surface. The clothing should not be cut from the body except under very unusual circumstances.

   d. Attention is paid as to whether defects in the clothing correspond in location to wounds on the body.

4. The body is then examined without the clothing and without cleaning. One should again search for trace evidence. One may want to take photographs of the uncleaned wounds at this time.

5. The body is then cleaned and reexamined for any other wounds that may have been concealed by blood.

   a. Photographs of the cleaned wounds should then be taken.

   b. The pathologist should go back to the clothing and again correlate any observed trauma to defects in the clothing.

6. The use of a **dissecting microscope** in the examination of both wounds and clothing is strongly recommended.

D. **Photography** of wounds
   1. At least two photographs of each wound should be taken.
      a. One should be a placement shot showing where the wound is in relationship to other body landmarks.
      b. The second should be a close-up showing the appearance of the wound.
      c. Most individuals take a third shot in between the two extremes.
   2. It is helpful if there is a scale and the number of the case in the photograph.
   3. If evaluation of the color of a wound is important, then a color standard/ruler should be included in the photo.
E. Internal examination of the body
   1. In most cases, a **complete autopsy** involving the head, chest, and abdominal cavities should be performed. All viscera should be removed and examined.
   2. Blood, vitreous, urine, and bile should be retained.
   3. In cases of advanced decomposition where these materials are not present, muscle (from the thigh, preferably), liver, and kidney should be retained. These materials can be used for toxicological, serological, or DNA analyses.
F. Laboratory tests
   1. After performing the autopsy, the pathologist may wish to have laboratory tests performed to:
      a. Aid in determining the cause or manner of death
      b. Identify any contributory factors
      c. To exclude other causes of death or contributory factors
   2. The most common tests ordered in forensic autopsies are:
      a. **Toxicology.** Virtually all medical examiner cases should have toxicology performed. Occasionally, such tests will reveal an unsuspected death due to an overdose of drugs.
      b. **Histology.** Histology does not have to be performed on all medicolegal cases, especially those which are traumatic in nature.
      c. **Neuropathology.** In certain cases, the pathologist may wish to save the brain to be cut by a neuropathologist.
      d. **Microbiology** is occasionally helpful in cases where identification of the precise bacterial agent involved is important.
      e. **Serology.** Testing for antibodies to venom may be helpful in anaphylactic deaths.

f. In other cases, **test firings** of weapons may be necessary to make range determinations or to determine if a weapon is defective.

G. Prior to release of the body, **fingerprints** should be taken. It is suggested that at least two sets of prints be made, one for the police and the other for the autopsy file. In homicides, **palm prints** should also be taken.

VIII. **IDENTIFICATION OF BODIES**

In medicolegal cases, positive identification of a body should always be made if possible. Identification methods are discussed in more detail in Chapter 4 and in brief below.

A. **Nonscientific methods** of identification consist of:
1. Identification of a body by relatives or friends
2. Identification based on documents on the body, clothing, scars, or tattoos
3. Identification based on exclusion ("Mary was in the car before it crashed and burned, and only one female body was found in the wreckage")

B. **Scientific methods** of identification include:
1. Fingerprints
2. Dental identification
3. DNA testing
4. Comparison of antemortem and postmortem x-rays

C. In the case of **decomposed or unrecognizable bodies,** scientific methods of identification should be used.

D. If the pathologist is presented with an unidentified body in which attempts at identification have been unsuccessful, prior to its release, the pathologist should:
1. Take identification photos.
2. Chart and x-ray the teeth.
3. Fingerprint the body.
4. Perform total-body x-rays.
5. Retain tissue for DNA analysis.

The Autopsy Report

I. **HEADING OF REPORT SHOULD INCLUDE THE FOLLOWING:**
A. Unique **identification number** for the individual being autopsied, usually generated in the autopsy facility and unique to that facility
B. **Name, sex, age** (with birth date) of the deceased
C. **Date, time and physical location** of the exam

  D. Optional information may include:
    1. Names of persons attending the exam
    2. Date and time of death of the deceased
    3. Authorization information
II. **EXTERNAL EXAMINATION**
  The first section of the forensic autopsy is the **external examination,** in which one gives a general description of the deceased, including:
  A. The age, sex, race, physique, height, weight, and nourishment of the deceased
  B. Congenital malformations, if any
  C. A brief description of the clothing; a simple listing of the articles is usually sufficient. If the death was violent, any significant alterations of the garments as a result of the trauma will be described in further detail in another section of the autopsy.
  D. A general description of the state of the body with, as a minimum:
    1. Degree and distribution of rigor and livor mortis
    2. Hair (length and color), facial hair, alopecia
    3. Appearance of the eyes; the eye color
    4. Any unusual appearance to the ears, nose, or face, e.g., congenital malformations, scarring, severe acne
    5. Presence or absence of teeth or dental plates
    6. Significant scars and tattoos
    7. External evidence of disease
    8. Old injuries unrelated to the death (new injuries or injuries related to the death are described in a separate section)
    9. Evidence of recent medical or surgical intervention
III. **EVIDENCE OF INJURY**
  All recent injuries, whether minor or major, external or internal, should be described in this section. *There is no need to repeat the description of these injuries in the subsequent **Internal Examination** section.* The age of the lesions should be described, if possible, at least in a general way.
  There are many ways to handle the **Evidence of Injury** section.
  A. Excluding gunshot and stab wounds, it is easiest to group the injuries into two broad areas:
    1. The external injuries
    2. The internal injuries
        Some people intermingle the two. They will describe the external evidence of injury to the head and then say, "Subsequent autopsy reveals . . ." and go on to describe the internal injuries of the head. They will then describe the external injuries of the trunk, followed by the internal injuries.
  B. **Gunshot wounds** represent a different situation. In gunshot wound cases, if at all possible, each individual wound should be

described in its entirety (from entrance to exit or point of lodgment) before going on to the next wound.

1. The **entrance wounds** should be assigned an arbitrary number (e.g., gunshot wound #1) and then located on the body (in inches or centimeters) in relation to the top of the head or the soles of the feet and to the right or left of the midline.

   a. They should also be located in regard to a local landmark such as the nipple or the umbilicus.

   b. This latter localization is often of greater value than the former in visualizing the location of the entrance. One can readily visualize the location of a bullet wound described as being 2 inches below the level of the nipples and 1 inch to the right of the midline, in contrast to the same wound described as being located 16 inches below the top of the head and 1 inch to the right of the midline.

2. The features of a gunshot wound that make it an entrance and that define at what range it was inflicted, i.e., the abrasion ring, soot, tattooing, etc., as well as the dimensions of these characteristics, should be described.

   a. The authors recommend that all measurements of the wound itself should be made using the metric system, as this system is easier to use, more suitable for the measurements of small lesions, and less likely to result in inaccuracies.

   b. Pertinent negatives should be noted.

   c. Following this, the course of the bullet through the body should be described.

   d. All organs perforated or penetrated by the missile should be noted.

3. The location of the **exit wound**, if present, should be described, first in general terms, e.g., "the right lower lateral back," and then either in relationship to the top of the head (or soles of the feet) and distance from the midline or in relationship to the distance above or below the level of the entrance and from the midline. It is not useful, but instead very confusing, to assign numbers or letters to exit wounds.

4. In cases where a bullet is recovered from the body at autopsy, one should state:

   - Where it was found
   - Whether it is intact, deformed, or fragmented
   - Whether the bullet is lead or jacketed
   - The approximate caliber of the bullet, if you know

    a. A letter or number should be inscribed on the bullet, and this information should be included in the autopsy report.

    b. The bullet should then be placed in an envelope with the name of the victim, the date, the case number, the location from which the bullet was recovered, the letter or number inscribed on the bullet, and the name of the physician who recovered the bullet.

    c. ***All bullets should be recovered.***

5. After describing the gunshot wound, one should then give an overall description of the missile path through the body in relation to the planes of the body. Thus, one will say, "The bullet traveled from back to front, left to right, and sharply downward." Use of anatomical terminology such as *dorsal, caudal*, etc., is not advisable as most individuals who will read a forensic autopsy report are not physicians and will not understand these terms.

6. In cases where there are dozens of gunshot or fragment wounds, it may not be possible to handle each wound separately, and they may have to be handled in groups. This is of course how one handles shotgun pellet wounds. In the case of buckshot or pellet wounds, it is only necessary to recover a representative number of pellets. All wadding should be recovered and retained.

C. In the case of **stab wounds**, these should be handled the same way as gunshot wounds unless large numbers of wounds in clusters occur. They then can be described in groups.

D. *To aid individuals in better understanding the autopsy report, the physician may wish to make diagrams showing the location of the wounds described. This is of help when the reader is not a physician.*

E. The last part of the **Evidence of Injury** section should concern the clothing. Any disruption of the clothing attributable to the lethal trauma should be given. The presence of gunpowder, soot, and car paint should be described.

IV. **INTERNAL EXAMINATION**

In this section, one systematically describes the major organ systems as well as the organ cavities. One gives organ weights (not necessary for adrenals and pancreas) as well as a brief description of the organs with pertinent negatives. It is not necessary to repeat the description of the injuries.

V. MICROSCOPIC EXAMINATION

Microscopic slides are often not needed in forensic cases, especially in deaths from trauma. They should be made when indicated, however. Samples of tissue from all major organs should be saved for at least 3 years, preferably 5. In most traumatic deaths, microscopic slides, including those of wounds, are not necessary.

VI. TOXICOLOGY

In this section, one lists the tissue tested, the tests performed, the methods of analysis, e.g., gas chromatography, and the results. In all autopsies, blood, urine, vitreous, and bile, as a minimum, should be retained. These materials should be retained for at least 5 years.

VII. FINDINGS

List the major findings in order of importance. One does not have to list every minute or extraneous finding as is done in some hospital autopsy reports.

VIII. OPINION

This should briefly describe the cause of death in as simple language as possible as well as state the manner of death. This section is intended for the public and not for physicians. Thus, for example, one can say, ". . . died of massive internal bleeding due to a gunshot wound of the aorta (the major blood vessel of the body)" or ". . . of a gunshot wound of the heart." Speculation about circumstances surrounding the death should be absent or kept to a minimum.

General References

1. Di Maio, V.J.M. and Di Maio, D.J., *Forensic Pathology*, 2nd ed., CRC Press, Boca Raton, FL, 2001.
2. National Association of Medical Examiners, Forensic Autopsy Performance Standards, 2005.
3. Spitz, W.U., Ed., *Medicolegal Investigation of Death*, 4th ed., Charles C. Thomas, Springfield, IL, 2006.

Physical Evidence

2

I. TYPES OF PHYSICAL EVIDENCE

Physical evidence may be defined as any material that can be used to link a suspect, a weapon, or a scene to a crime. Physical evidence falls into two main categories: **biological** and **nonbiological.**

    A. **Biological evidence** most commonly encountered by the medical examiner is:
        1. Blood
        2. Semen
        3. Hair
        4. Tissue
        5. Fingernails
        6. Bite marks
        7. Saliva

    B. **Nonbiological evidence** is more varied and can be virtually any item. The most common forms that will be encountered by the medical examiner are:
        1. Clothing
        2. Bullets/shotgun pellets, wadding
        3. Fibers
        4. Paint
        5. Glass
        6. Soil

II. PRESERVATION OF PHYSICAL EVIDENCE ON THE BODY

    A. Transport of body

        The medical examiner cannot collect trace evidence from the body if it is lost in transport. Therefore, in order to minimize any loss of trace evidence and to prevent the body from acquiring, in transit, any materials that may subsequently be interpreted as being trace evidence:

1. Place paper bags on the hands at the scene, securing them in place with rubber bands.
2. Wrap the body in a clean sheet.

B. The morgue

When the body is received at the morgue, prior to examination by the medical examiner:

1. It should be handled as little as possible.
2. Identification tags indicating the deceased's name and the case number should be placed on the body.
3. The sheet should not be removed.
4. The body should never be undressed, fingerprinted, washed, or embalmed.

III. **RECOVERY OF PHYSICAL EVIDENCE**

A. The body should be carefully examined for materials adherent to the clothing and skin, such as fibers and hair. Dried blood may be collected from the skin. Fingernail cuttings may be taken as well as swabbings of the mouth, rectum, or vagina. Gunshot residue may be collected from the hands.

B. After recovery of the trace evidence, it should be placed in an appropriate container, which should be labeled with at a minimum:

1. The deceased's name
2. The case number
3. The date of the examination
4. Where the item was recovered from
5. What the item is (or presumed to be)
6. The signature of the medical examiner who collected the evidence

C. In the case of bullets, the case number or some other form of identification should be inscribed on either the base or the tip of the bullet. No inscriptions should ever be made on the side of the bullet, as this may destroy rifling marks necessary for ballistic comparisons.

D. The container with the evidence is then transmitted to a police officer or the Crime Lab.

E. A receipt should be obtained for the evidence in order to maintain chain of custody.

IV. **PROCEDURES FOR COLLECTION OF BIOLOGICAL EVIDENCE**

A. Blood for DNA analysis

1. From the body, collect one tube of blood in a lavender-top test tube (one that uses EDTA as a preservative) and a blood sample card.

2. Dried blood from the surface of the body may be scraped off the surface of the skin with a clean scalpel and placed in a sterile test tube.

3. If the specimen is too small to scrape off, use a sterile gauze pad moistened with saline solution; air-dry and place in a sterile test tube.

4. If the blood is still wet, use a sterile gauze pad and air-dry prior to placing into the tube.

B. Semen
1. Place two cotton-tipped swabs in the vagina and leave in place for 5 minutes. Remove; make two slides from the swabs. Air-dry the slides and swabs and package in appropriately labeled containers.

2. Repeat this process for the rectum.

3. In the case of the mouth, swab between the gums and teeth and then leave the swabs in place for 5 minutes.

4. Suspected material on the surface of the body may be collected with a sterile gauze moistened with saline solution, air-dried, and placed in a test tube.

C. Hair
1. Collect hair adherent to the body and place in envelope, noting area collected from.

2. Control hairs should be taken from the deceased to rule out the possibility that the hair found on the body came from the deceased. In the case of head hair, take samples from multiple areas and **pull** them out to get the roots.

3. In cases of suspected or known rape, the pubic hair should be combed for foreign hair and samples of pubic and head hair pulled and retained.

4. DNA analysis can be performed on hair with roots.

D. Tissue — Collect with clean pickups, place in sterile test tube, and refrigerate.

E. Fingernails
1. Collect any free pieces of fingernail on the body and place in clean envelope.

2. Cut off the ends of the fingernails; place each individually in a clean container and label as to source. (A broken fingernail from a scene or on a body can be matched to its source by either a direct physical match to the broken end or by striae on the undersurface of the nail, which are as individual as fingerprints. Thus, if a portion of a fingernail from the assailant

is recovered from the body, it can be linked to the assailant months later by the striate pattern present.)

   3. If the fingernails are being collected just to determine if there is any material under them, they can be placed in two containers, one for the right hand and the other for the left.

F. Bite marks — Bite mark comparisons are accepted in court roughly equivalent to fingerprints.

   1. If a forensic odontologist is available, have him or her conduct the examination of the bite mark prior to the autopsy or cleaning of the body.

   2. If none is available, swab the bite mark with a sterile gauze pad moistened with saline, followed by a dry cotton swab. Air-dry and place both in sterile tubes. This is done to collect saliva. The material then can be analyzed by STR DNA analysis.

   3. Take photographs of the bite mark with a metric ruler in the photographic field.

   4. If one has access to dental casting material, one should then make a cast of the mark.

G. Saliva — See bite marks. DNA typing can be performed on cells in the saliva.

V. PROCEDURES FOR COLLECTION OF NONBIOLOGICAL PHYSICAL EVIDENCE

A. Clothing

   1. Remove carefully from the body. Do not cut off.

   2. Air-dry if wet.

   3. Wrap each individual article of clothing in clean paper; bag or box the articles.

   4. Label and submit to the Crime Laboratory.

B. Bullets/shot/wadding

   1. Collect from body using gloved fingers or rubber-tipped instruments to prevent marking up the bullet.

   2. Do not remove any foreign material from the bullet.

   3. Inscribe the case number on either the tip or the base of the bullet. No inscriptions are necessary for shot or wadding.

   4. Place in envelope and label as to source.

C. Fibers/paint/glass — These materials can be tested for their physical properties, e.g., chemical composition, refraction index, etc. An analyst can then testify that the materials that you collected from the body are identical in all measurable characteristics to material from a car, house, sweater, etc.

   1. Collect from the body with clean instruments.

   2. Place in individual envelopes, noting source of evidence.

VI. DNA ANALYSIS

DNA analysis can be performed on any tissue or substance that contains nucleated cells. The two most common tissues examined are blood and semen. Less commonly, analysis is performed on hair and saliva.

A. In dealing with DNA identification, two concepts must be understood:
1. If the DNA profile of evidence from a crime scene or victim is different from that of the suspected source, then that evidence **absolutely** did not come from the suspected individual.
2. If the DNA profile of the evidence matches that of an individual, then the **individual is not excluded** as the source of the evidence. One then makes a statistical evaluation as to the odds that the suspect is the source of the evidence.

B. Whenever you perform DNA analysis, there are three possible results:
1. The **specimen is inadequate** in size, degraded, or contaminated, thus resulting in an insufficient amount of DNA for analysis.
2. The DNA profiles are different and one has an **exclusion.**
3. The DNA profiles match.
   If this last situation occurs, the match can indicate that:
   a. The samples come from the same person.
   b. The samples come from different people but an error was made either in the collection of the material or in the laboratory.
   c. Two individuals have the same DNA profile. This could be because they are identical twins or because an insufficient number of tests have been performed so as to differentiate between the two.

C. While it is true that one's total DNA pattern is unique (except for an identical twin), the DNA testing currently being performed involves examination of a very minute portion of one's genetic blueprint.
1. The reason that one concludes that two samples came from the same source (i.e., the same individual) is not because one performs a complete analysis of the genetic structure of an individual but rather because one performs a number of tests in which the DNA profiles from the individual tests are identical.
2. Then, on the basis of probability calculations (i.e., statistics), we say that an individual is the source of the specimen.

D. The nuclei of all cells in the body, excluding sperm and eggs, contain 23 pairs of chromosomes.
1. Each of the 46 chromosomes consists of a **thread** of deoxyribonucleic acid (DNA).
2. This DNA thread is made up of two **strands** of bases held together by a sugar–phosphate backbone arranged in a double helix.
3. The **double helix** has the configuration of a twisted ladder whose steps are formed by the **four bases**: adenine, thymine, guanine, and cytosine. Adenine (a purine) always binds to thymine (a pyrimidine), and guanine (a purine) always binds to cytosine (a pyrimidine).
4. A **gene** is a portion of this DNA **thread** (chromosome) that produces a specific product. The length of this gene can range from a few thousand to tens of thousands of base pairs.
5. The order of the four bases on the thread determines the function of the gene.
6. Genes, however, constitute only a small fraction of the total length of the chromosome. The purpose of the rest of the chromosome is unknown.
7. There is usually more than one form of a gene for each location or locus on the chromosome. The alternate forms are called **alleles.**
E. PCR (polymerase chain reaction)
1. The polymerase chain reaction (PCR) is a method for amplifying or **copying** a **short sequence** of DNA repeatedly, thus, going from a small amount of DNA to a very large amount.
2. In the PCR methodology, **polymerase enzymes** are used to copy specific regions of DNA to obtain numerous copies of these areas to perform typing.
3. PCR-based typing systems allow alleles to be identified as discrete entities.
4. The PCR process
   a. The PCR process is relatively **simple** and easily carried out in the laboratory.
   b. The results are **obtained in a short time** (within a matter of a few days).
   c. Because of the unlimited capacity to reproduce the DNA segments, the PCR-based methods permit **analysis of extremely tiny amounts** of DNA (0.1 to 1.0 ng).
5. The **disadvantages** to this method are:
   a. It is susceptible to contamination.

b.   Most PCR loci have few alleles.
F.   STR (short tandem repeats)
STR is a PCR technique used in forensic labs to make DNA iden-
tifications.
  1.   The repeat unit in this system is **normally two to six base pairs.**
  2.   STR loci occur throughout the genome at an estimated fre-
       quency of 1 STR every 10,000 nucleotides (a base, a sugar, and
       a phosphate).
  3.   While most STR loci have only 6 to 12 alleles, there are a large
       number of such systems that can be exploited for identification
       purposes.
  4.   In combination, they can produce a **high power of discrimi-
       nation.**
  5.   As a general rule, use of 8 to 13 STR loci gives a discriminative
       power of about 1 in 1 billion.
  6.   STR technology:
       a.   Is **rapid** and can be done in 2 to 3 days
       b.   Can be **performed on very small quantities** of DNA
  7.   STR can be performed on wipings from full-metal-jacketed
       bullets that have perforated the body, even if no tissue is visible.
  8.   While STR fragments from different STR loci differ in size,
       they are still very small. Thus, it is possible to run the products
       from several STR loci simultaneously on one gel as long as the
       fragment sizes do not overlap.
  9.   STR analyses are performed by:
       a.   Isolating the DNA
       b.   Replicating the STR fragments by PCR
       c.   Performing gel electrophoresis
       d.   Identifying the fragments using stains, chemilumines-
            cence, or laser techniques
  10. The use of PCR robotics, an automated electrophoresis and
      analysis technology, allows automation of the STR typing.
  11. In the U.S., 13 STR loci are used for DNA identification. Using
      all 13 loci, the average random match probability is rarer than
      one in a trillion among unrelated individuals.
  12. **CODIS** (The Combined DNA Index System) was established
      by the FBI in 1998 as a DNA database for the U.S. The DNA
      profiles of individuals in this database are based on 13 STR loci.
G.   Mitochondrial DNA (mtDNA)
  1.   Mitochondria are located in the cytoplasm of cells.
  2.   mtDNA is inherited strictly from the mother.

3. Siblings and maternal relatives have identical mtDNA sequences.
4. mtDNA is used for forensic purposes only when the biological material to be analyzed is limited or severely degraded.

General References

1. Geberth, V.J., *Practical Homicide Investigation*, 4th ed., CRC Press, Boca Raton, FL, 2006.
2. Sweet, D. et al., An improved method to recover saliva from human skin: The double swab technique, *J. For. Sci.*, 42(2), 320, 1997.
3. Baird, M.L., Use of DNA identification for forensic and paternity analysis, *J. Clin. Lab. Analysis*, 10, 350, 1996.
4. Committee on DNA Forensic Science (National Research Council), The evaluation of forensic DNA evidence: An update, *Nat. Acad. Press*, Washington, D.C., 1996.
5. Karger, B., Meyer, E., and DuChesne, A., STR analysis on perforating FMJ bullets and a new VWA variant allele, *Int. J. Legal Med.*, 110, 101, 1997.

Time of Death—
Decomposition

3

In contrast to what one sees on television and reads in the popular press, determination of the time of death is difficult, imprecise, and often not possible. Whole books have been written on this topic.[1] In spite of this, all that one can give in virtually all cases is a range of time, e.g., "the deceased died 12 to 24 hours prior to the body being discovered." As the interval between the time of death and the body being found increases, so does the inaccuracy of the estimation.

I. **FACTORS USED IN ESTIMATING TIME OF DEATH:**
- Livor mortis
- Rigor mortis
- Temperature of the body
- Potassium level of the vitreous
- Stomach contents
- Environmental factors

A. **Livor mortis** (postmortem lividity) is a reddish, purplish-blue discoloration of the skin due to settling of blood, by gravity, in the vessels of the dependent areas of the body. In dependent areas pressed against a hard surface, the vessels are mechanically compressed by the pressure and blood cannot settle in them. This gives these areas a pale coloration.

1. Livor mortis usually becomes apparent within a half hour of death. In individuals dying of cardiac failure, livor mortis may actually begin to develop prior to death.

2. As time progresses, livor mortis becomes progressively more prominent.

3. As long as livor mortis consists of the intravascular collection of blood, it can **"shift."** By this, one means that it can move from one area to another if the position of the body is changed. Thus, if the body is first facedown, livor will be present anteriorly. If the body is then turned over, the blood will flow to the newly dependent areas and livor will appear on the posterior aspect of the body.

4. After a certain period of time livor becomes **"fixed,"** i.e., changing the position of the body will not cause the livor to shift. This occurs after the blood has hemolyzed and begins to diffuse into the extravascular spaces, i.e., decomposition begins to set in.

   a. The amount of time for livor to become fixed is very variable and depends on how long it takes the body to begin to decompose. Obviously, this is dependent to a great degree on the environment.

5. As livor intensifies, one may get the development of postmortem petechiae due to rupture of capillaries with leakage of blood. This is most pronounced when the dependency is accentuated by additional effects of gravity, i.e., an arm hanging over the side of the bed.

6. Occasionally, livor mortis is misinterpreted by emergency room physicians and EMTs as contusions. At autopsy there should be no problem in differentiating the two. Incising the questioned area will reveal the difference.

   a. In contusions, the bleeding is into the extravascular spaces.
   b. In livor, the blood is within the vessels.
   c. The only time differentiation may not be possible is in livor mortis of the scalp where decomposition has occurred with escape of the degraded blood into the extravascular space.

7. In certain deaths, livor mortis may be an unusual color.

   a. In deaths from carbon monoxide or cyanide, the livor may be a cherry red color.
   b. Prolonged refrigeration of a body or exposure to cold may also cause the same color change.

B. **Rigor mortis** refers to the "stiffening" of the body observed after death due to postmortem muscle contraction.

1. This is due to depletion of adenosine triphosphate (ATP) with resultant development of a stable complex of actin and myosin, thus preventing the muscle fibers from relaxing.

2. Rigor mortis typically begins to develop within 2 hours after death.
3. It appears first in the muscles of the jaw, followed by the face and the upper and lower extremities; disappearance occurs in the same order.
4. It usually takes 6 to 12 hours to develop full rigor mortis.
5. Violent exercise, which depletes ATP, and high body temperatures accelerate the development of rigor.
6. Rigor mortis is lost due to decomposition.
7. In temperate climates, rigor persists 36 to 48 hours. It may disappear in less than 24 hours in hot weather and persist for several days in cold weather.
8. Instantaneous rigor mortis (**cadaveric spasm**), i.e., occurring at the moment of death, is very rare. The authors have seen only two well-documented cases in 30 years. One was secondary to high body temperature and the other due to violent exertion.

C. **Body temperature**[1]
1. This is the most commonly used method of "accurately" determining time of death. It is based on everyone having a "normal" temperature at the time of death and the assumption that the body cools at a uniform rate. Both assumptions are erroneous.
2. Body temperature, determined orally, in apparently normal subjects, may vary from 96.0°F (35.6°C) to 100.8°F (38.2°C).[2]
    a. Body temperature may vary diurnally from a low at 6 a.m. to a high at 4–6 p.m.
    b. Normal temperatures are slightly higher in women.
    c. Strenuous exercise can raise temperatures as can chronic diseases such as congestive heart failure.
3. Body cooling is not uniform and does not follow a linear pattern.
    a. After death, there is often an initial plateau where cooling does not appear to occur or at least is not measurable under ordinary conditions.
    b. Body habitus influences the rate of cooling. Fat acts as an insulator retarding loss of heat.
    c. Infants cool quicker due to their body mass–surface area ratio.
4. The ambient temperature and climate conditions influence the rate of cooling.

    a. Is the ambient temperature higher or lower than the body temperature?

    b. Is there air-conditioning on? What is it set to?

    c. Did the police change the setting as the environment became hotter as more people milled about the scene?

    d. Is there wind, rain, snow?

5. How the deceased was dressed, or covered, has an effect on heat loss. Heavy or multiple layers of cloth (clothing, blankets, etc.) retard heat loss.

6. The surface that the body is lying on may influence heat loss. Is it a good heat conductor, e.g., marble, or will it insulate the body, e.g., a rug?

    In view of the aforementioned problems, the authors cannot recommend temperature determinations for accurate determination of the time of death.

D. Postmortem vitreous potassium levels

    Determination of the time of death based on the level of potassium in the vitreous has been attempted. Sturner and Gantner proposed a formula for making such determinations.[3] This has since been found to be invalid. Unfortunately, the levels of potassium in the vitreous are determined by the degree and rapidity of decomposition rather than the time interval from death. Thus, anything that accelerates decomposition raises the level of vitreous potassium. Time is only one factor. As a result of this, formulas and graphs developed for determination of the time interval since death based on vitreous potassium levels have been found to be unreliable.

E. Emptying of stomach contents

    In cases when the time the last meal was eaten is known, time-of-death determinations have been attempted by trying to determine how long it would take to digest the meal to the state it was found in at the time of autopsy.

1. Radioisotopic studies to determine time of gastric emptying, however, have revealed great variations:

    a. From meal to meal

    b. From person to person

    c. From day to day in the same person

2. In one study where the subjects were given a meal that included meats, seafood, vegetables, soups, salads, desserts, and fluids and allowed to eat as much as they wanted, the half gastric emptying time varied from 60 to 338 minutes with an average of 277 ± 44 minutes.[4]

3. Another factor to be considered in the rate of digestion is **stress.** Individuals under great stress will cease to digest their food. The authors have seen cases where individuals hospitalized a number of days for trauma have come to autopsy with stomachs full of undigested food taken in prior to the trauma.

F. **Environmental markers** include both scientific and nonscientific evidence.

1. **Insect activity** may give one an idea how long an individual has been dead. Different insects are attracted to a body at different times after death. An experienced entomologist may be able to determine how long a body has been dead by determining what insects have preyed or are preying on the body and at what stage in their development they are at in their progress from egg to adult.

2. **Nonscientific markers** consist of things like a pile of newspapers in front of a house, uncollected mail, a dated receipt in the deceased's pocket, etc. In bodies found after years, dates on coins or the type of clothing may narrow down the time of death.

II. **DECOMPOSITION IS DUE TO:**

A. **Autolysis**

1. Defined as the aseptic breakdown of tissue caused by intracellular enzymes.

2. Occurs most prominently in organs that are rich in enzymes, such as the pancreas.

B. **Putrefaction**

1. Defined as the breakdown of tissue due to bacteria.

2. The main source of bacteria in the body is the gastrointestinal tract.

3. Putrefaction is the main cause of decomposition.

4. The process is accelerated by a hot environment and sepsis.

5. **Stages** in decomposition

a. The first sign of decomposition is often greenish discoloration of the skin in the lower quadrants of the abdomen.

b. This is followed by greenish black discoloration of the face and neck, swelling of the features, and protrusion of the eyes and tongue.

c. Decompositional fluid (**purge fluid**) emerges from the nose and mouth. **Purge fluid**, which is reddish in color, is often mistaken for blood with resultant suspicion of trauma.

    d. The body begins to swell due to gas formation, and there is slippage of the skin with marbling and "blister" formation. **Marbling** is manifested by greenish black discoloration along blood vessels due to the reaction of hemoglobin and hydrogen sulfide. The skin color will change to green and then black.

    e. The hair will slip from the scalp.

    f. In bodies exposed to strong sunlight, the skin may become leathery with a gold to black coloration.

    g. Internally, the brain becomes porridge-like with the other organs eventually reduced to the consistency of putty.

6. The rate that a body decomposes is usually determined by the environmental temperature. In hot climates such as Texas, advanced decomposition can occur in 24 hours while it may take a week or two in moderate climates.

7. Skeletonization may take a week or two, months, or years. This is dependent on environmental temperatures and the presence or absence of scavengers.

8. Rarely a body will undergo **adipocere** formation. Here the body's fat is transformed into oleic, palmitic, and stearic acids. Such a change usually requires high humidity or water. Adipocere has a white to brown waxlike appearance.

REFERENCES

1. Henssge, C. et al., *The Estimation of the Time since Death in the Early Postmortem Period*, 2nd ed., Edward Arnold, London, 2002.

2. Mackowiak, P.A., Wasserman, S.S., and Levine, M.M., A critical appraisal of 98.6°F, the upper limit of the normal body temperature, and other legacies of Carl Reinhold August Wunderlich, *JAMA*, 268, 1578, 1992.

3. Sturner, W.O. and Gantner, G.E., The postmortem interval: A study of potassium in the vitreous humor, *Am. J. Clin. Path.*, 42, 134, 1964.

4. Moore, J.G. et al., Influence of meal weight and caloric content on gastric emptying of meals in man, *Digestive Dis. Sci.*, 29, 513, 1984.

Identification of Remains

4

One of the responsibilities of the medical examiner is to determine the identity of the individual upon whom the postmortem examination is to be performed. Ideally, the identification should be **positive**, based on objective scientific evidence, leaving no doubt as to the identity of the deceased. However, in some cases, positive identification cannot be determined due to various factors outlined below. In such cases, either a **presumptive** or **tentative** identification must be made to proceed with investigation of the death and disposition of the remains. In deaths due to homicide, investigation and even prosecution of the case may depend on a positive identification, as oftentimes the identity of the deceased links the victim to his or her assailant.

The positive identification of unknown human remains by the medical examiner is perhaps one of the most satisfying and personally rewarding tasks performed by the medical examiner. In contrast, the inability to establish positive identification can lead to a dead-end investigation of the case by law enforcement personnel, the frustration and displeasure of the family members who believe the deceased is in fact their relative, difficulties in preparation and filing of a death certificate, and, as a consequence, inability to settle insurance claims or estates. For these and numerous other reasons, every possible attempt should be made to establish definitive, positive identification of every individual upon whom a postmortem examination is conducted.

In most cases, the medical examiner will be presented with an intact, nondecomposed body that has been previously identified by a family member or by comparison with a photo ID, such as a driver's license. Regardless of the degree of certainty, the medical examiner should, in **all cases,** obtain:

- A **color facial photo** of the deceased, taken with an identifying case number

- **Two complete sets of classifiable fingerprints,** and palm prints in selected cases
- **Height and weight** of the deceased

Ideally, a noncontaminated sample of the deceased's blood should also be retained for future DNA studies, if needed. Commercially available blood sample cards may be used, which can be stored indefinitely in relatively little space. All, or any, of these items may be needed at a later date, should the identification be questioned.

Upon arrival at the morgue, the remains should be tagged with plastic wrist or ankle tags, on which is written the deceased's name and case number. If the body has arrived at the morgue from a hospital or nursing home with existing tags present, they should be checked to make certain the name on the tag matches the name of the incoming case. Before beginning any postmortem examination, it is the responsibility of the pathologist to check the nametags present on the body and determine if, in fact, they correspond to the name present on paperwork for that case.

I. INTACT, NONDECOMPOSED HUMAN REMAINS
A. Scientific methods used to establish positive identification
1. **Fingerprints.** A system of identification based on the classification of finger ridge patterns. Even today, this method of identification is considered the most desirable for the establishment of positive identity.

   In the United States, the official use of fingerprints for personal identification was adopted by the New York City Civil Service Commission in the early 1900s, followed by adoption of the method by various U.S. agencies including the U.S. armed forces and the FBI. In 1924, fingerprint files from Leavenworth and the Bureau of Investigation were combined, officially establishing a central fingerprint depository. Today, the FBI has the largest collection of fingerprints in the world. To establish identity based on fingerprints, an **antemortem record** of some sort must exist for the deceased. Most individuals in the U.S., over the age of 18, will have been fingerprinted at some time in their lives. Some instances in which fingerprints are obtained include military service, certain governmental positions, licensing for various activities (the practice of medicine, driver's licenses, etc.), and processing of individuals suspected of criminal offenses. Also, today many parents have obtained fingerprint records on their children, as a means of positive identity.

Three fundamental principles of fingerprints exist:[1]
- No two fingers have yet been found to possess identical ridge characteristics.
- A fingerprint will remain unchanged during an individual's lifetime.
- Fingerprints have general ridge patterns that permit them to be systematically classified.

ALWAYS OBTAIN A COMPLETE SET OF FINGER-PRINTS IN FORENSIC CASES, DESPITE THE METHOD USED TO ESTABLISH IDENTITY OF THE DECEASED. In some cases, a set of palm prints may also be needed for comparison to latent prints found at a crime scene. **Latent** prints are invisible prints left on surfaces by the transfer of body oils or perspiration present on skin ridges.

2. **Dental.** The second most reliable means of establishing positive identification, in the absence of fingerprints. Again, however, an antemortem record must exist for comparison, with the most desirable record being that of antemortem radiographs of the teeth.

   a. The establishment of, or the ruling out of, identity based solely on comparison of antemortem **dental charts** with postmortem charts is not recommended, as antemortem charts may be, and often are, incomplete, incorrect, or misleading. However, if antemortem **radiographs** are available for comparison, with or without the presence of metallic fillings, a positive identity can often be established, as distinctive configurations of the bony structures of the jaw, roots of the teeth, and nearby sinuses often exist and are unique for each individual.

   b. To preserve facial structure in nondecomposed bodies, the help of a forensic odontologist may be needed to obtain postmortem radiographs for comparison.

   c. The dentition of all unidentified human remains should at least be charted and ideally radiographed and photographed **before** the body is released for burial. There is nothing more embarrassing, or expensive, than to have to exhume a body, which hopefully was not cremated, in order to compare records that may show up at a later date.

   d. At the very least, examination of the teeth of the deceased may give information as to the age, hygiene, and nutrition of the deceased, all clues to the true identity.

   e. Humans have 20 **deciduous** (baby) teeth:

- 4 maxillary incisors and 4 mandibular incisors
- 2 maxillary cuspids and 2 mandibular cuspids
- 4 maxillary molars and 4 mandibular molars

f. Humans usually develop a total of 32 **permanent** teeth:
- 4 maxillary incisors and 4 mandibular incisors
- 2 maxillary cuspids and 2 mandibular cuspids
- 4 maxillary bicuspids (premolars) and 4 mandibular bicuspids
- 6 maxillary molars and 6 mandibular molars

g. Although a precise determination of age based on dentition requires radiographic evaluation of crown and root development and eruption, an approximation of age may be obtained by evaluation of the eruption pattern alone (**Table 4.1**).

3. **Radiographs.** Individual bones of the body often possess distinctive markings or characteristics that allow for positive identification. Again, antemortem radiographs must exist for comparison, and a diligent search must be made to obtain them. Examples of comparison structures include configuration of the cranial sinuses (especially frontal), prior orthopedic procedures with insertion of orthopedic devices, and distinctive

Table 4.1   Age Determination by State of Dental Eruption

Eruption of Deciduous Teeth (Subadult)		
Tooth	Maxillary	Mandibular
Central incisor	7–8 months	6–7 months
Lateral incisor	8–11 months	8–11 months
Cuspid	17–20 months	16–20 months
First molar	12–16 months	12–16 months
Second molar	20–30 months	20–30 months

Eruption of Permanent Teeth (Adult)		
Tooth	Maxillary	Mandibular
Central incisor	7–8 years	6–7 years
Lateral incisor	8–9 years	7–8 years
Cuspid	11–12 years	$9^{1}/_{2}$ –11 years
First bicuspid	10–12 years	10–11 years
Second bicuspid	10–12 years	11–12 years
First molar	6–7 years	6–7 years
Second molar	12–13 years	$11^{1}/_{2}$ –13 years
Third molar	17–24 years	17–24 years

calcified structures such as a calcified mitral or aortic valve, phlebolith, or granuloma.
4. **DNA.** The evaluation of the DNA pattern of an individual has rapidly become a reliable technique for the determination of positive identity, as each person's DNA is unique, with the exception of monozygotic twins.
   a. The laboratory procedures used have existed for some time in the field of molecular biology but were only used for forensic applications beginning in the mid-1980s.
   b. To establish identity by means of DNA, postmortem samples of whole blood, and if possible hair (including the root bulb), skin, bone marrow, and seminal fluid, should be retained for comparison to antemortem samples.
   c. The samples must contain nucleated cells or mitochondrial DNA to be of value in identification.
   d. Examples of antemortem specimens that may be used for comparison include hair from a comb or hairbrush used solely by the missing person, an old baby tooth or lock of hair from a keepsake album, clothing with stains such as blood, seminal fluid, sweat, or vaginal secretions, or any source of nucleated cells. Even paraffin-embedded tissue taken years before at the time of a surgical procedure, such as tubal ligation, may be a source of antemortem DNA.
   e. **For DNA studies, whole blood obtained at postmortem examination should be preserved in EDTA (and kept at 4°C, until it can be delivered to the appropriate lab for study) or on blood sample cards.**
   f. Other samples, such as hair, seminal stains, bloodstains, or skin, should be dried at room temperature in a sterile container and then placed at 4°C until delivery to the appropriate lab.
   g. Long-term storage at 4°C is not recommended. Therefore, the specimens collected at postmortem exam should be delivered to the appropriate testing lab as soon as possible, where the specimens should be prepared for long-term storage.
B. **Nonscientific** methods used to establish identification, leading to tentative and presumptive identification only
   1. Comparison of **physical attributes**, including sex, age, race, stature, hair color (remember, it could be dyed!), eye color (check for contact lenses), old amputations, etc.

2. Distinctive **marks**, such as tattoos, scars, bony anomalies possibly resulting from occupational wear, or body piercings with or without jewelry.

3. **Visual** identification by a living human, such as a relative or friend.

4. **Circumstantial** evidence, such as papers or cards found on the body, jewelry, clothes, or eyeglasses found on the body, the location in which the body was found (such as a residence or car registered to a specific individual), etc. If dentures are found with the body, and are felt to perfectly fit the mouth of the deceased, and if the name of the deceased is engraved or marked on the inside of the dentures, or if the dentist who made the denture can identify it as belonging to a certain individual, a positive identification can be made, so long as there are no conflicting additional factors in the case.

II. **DECOMPOSED OR CHARRED, NONSKELETONIZED HUMAN REMAINS**

A. **Scientific** methods are the same as for nondecomposed remains, with a few exceptions:

1. **Fingerprints** may often still be obtainable, despite decomposition. Oftentimes the skin from the hands and fingers of a decomposed body will detach in a glove-like fashion and can easily be slipped over the gloved hand of an investigator, and classifiable prints can then be made.

   a. If the fingertips are mummified, or desiccated, they can be clipped from the body and submitted to the FBI for identification. Be sure to place each fingertip into a separate, labeled container!

   b. Even if the epidermis is missing from the fingers, it is oftentimes still possible to obtain a classifiable print from the fingerpad!

2. **Dental** exam, in most decomposed or charred bodies, is more productive due to the absence of jaw rigor mortis, making access to the oral cavity very easy.

   a. The teeth should be charted and removed for radiographs if the body is in such a state as to preclude viewing by the family.

   b. After removal, the jaws may be split down the midline to obtain better lateral films for comparison to antemortem radiographs such as periapical or bite wing views.

     c. If a positive identification can be made, the jaws should be returned to the body for burial, after complete documentation is obtained.

   3. **Radiographs** serve the same purpose as in nondecomposed bodies and are often extremely helpful in identification. In addition, in decomposed and burned bodies, total-body radiographs may reveal foreign objects, such as bullets, and should therefore be performed in all cases where the death is suspicious and the remains are too decomposed or burned to visually rule out the presence of wounds on the body.

   4. **DNA** or serological studies in decomposed bodies may not be productive, due to degradation of the proteins.

     a. However, through the use of sophisticated techniques, some DNA may be detected in degraded remains, and for this reason, postmortem samples of at least muscle and bone with marrow should be retained in plastic bags, kept at 4°C, and delivered as soon as possible to the appropriate lab for study.

     b. Another good source of DNA in decomposed remains is the dental pulp, especially within the molars.

     c. In burned bodies, adequate samples of blood, muscle, and tissues can almost always be obtained for DNA studies.

B. **Nonscientific** methods are the same as in nondecomposed bodies but are usually less available.

   1. Decomposition and maggot activity will usually obscure skin marks such as tattoos. Sometimes, scraping the surface of the decomposing skin will reveal an underlying tattoo.

   2. The use of hydrogen peroxide can reveal or clarify an antemortem tattoo.[2]

   3. Using eye protection, illumination of the body with UV or infrared light can occasionally reveal an antemortem tattoo.

   4. In burned and dismembered bodies, the remains should be carefully examined for jewelry, such as rings. It is often very easy to miss a ring blackened and charred on the burned nub of a finger.

III. **SKELETONIZED HUMAN REMAINS**

When presented with skeletal remains, the first thing the pathologist should do is determine if the remains are human. Intact human bones are usually very distinctive and not easily confused with other animal bones. Problems arise when the bones are from a human fetus, subadult, or juvenile or when the bones are fragmented or charred. In these cases, it is strongly advised that the help of a forensic or physical anthropologist be obtained. If the bones are easily identified as human, then the methods of identification include the following:

A. **Scientific** methods remain the same, with the most reliable being dental and radiographic studies. DNA may be obtainable from bone and teeth.

B. **Semi-scientific** but **nonpositive** means of identifying skeletal remains include the following:

1. Facial reconstruction (by sketch, clay, or computer). This technique may lead to a tentative identification of the remains and subsequent positive identification if antemortem dental records can then be obtained.

2. Photosuperimposition is a technique in which a life photograph of a missing person is superimposed on a photograph of the unidentified skull, or the skull itself, using video equipment. This technique is most useful in **ruling out** a suspected identity.

C. **Nonscientific** means are the same as for fleshed bodies, except in skeletal cases, careful detailing of the clothing is done, to include sizes, brand names, type of clothing (summer versus winter), etc.

1. In all skeletal cases, the sex, race, age, and antemortem stature of the deceased should be determined by standard anthropological techniques.

2. **If the pathologist is not familiar with, or not experienced enough, to determine these parameters, or if he or she has any doubt as to the sex, race, or age of the deceased, the remains should be submitted to a forensic anthropologist for evaluation as soon as possible.**

3. If an error is made in determination of any one of these parameters, the unidentified body may remain unidentified forever!

IV. SAMPLES OR ITEMS THAT SHOULD BE COLLECTED AND RE-
TAINED BEFORE THE RELEASE OF ANY UNIDENTIFIED BODY

Table 4.2   Samples/Items To Be Collected and Retained before the Release of an Unidentified Body

	Nondecomposed Body	Decomposed Body	Burned Body	Skeletal
Color photo of face, with ID number, frontal and profile views	X	X	X	
Color photos of identifying marks (tattoos, scars, piercings, etc.)	X	X		
(2) complete sets of classifiable fingerprints, and palm prints in selected cases	X	X[a]		
Dental chart and dental x-rays	X	X	X	X
Upper and lower jaws		X	X	X
X-rays, total body (especially skull with sinus views)	X	X	X	X
10–20 cc whole blood, in EDTA; blood sample card	X	If available	X	
Hair with root bulb		X		If present
Bone with marrow		X		X
Clothing, jewelry, personal effects, such as eyeglasses, dentures, hearing aids, pacemakers	X	X	X	X

[a] If too decomposed or desiccated, clip fingertips and place in separate containers labeled with the position of the finger, and submit to the FBI.

References

1. Saferstein, R., Fingerprints, in *Criminalistics: An Introduction to Forensic Science*, 8th ed., Prentice-Hall, Englewood Cliffs, NJ, 2003.
2. Haglund, W.D. and Sperry, K., The use of hydrogen peroxide to visualize tattoos obscured by decomposition and mummification, *J. For. Sciences*, 38(1), 147, 1993.

FOR ADDITIONAL READING AND REFERENCE ON IDENTIFICATION:

Fierro, M.F., Ed., *CAP Handbook for Postmortem Examination of Unidentified Remains*, College of American Pathologists, Skokie, IL, 1986. This handbook contains an excellent chapter on the FBI National Crime Information Center (NCIC) unidentified and missing person files and what pathologists can do to help identify unidentified bodies; it contains good appendices with autopsy diagrams, helpful summary charts, tables of proportionate measurements, how to estimate height and weight from children's clothing, growth charts, and other helpful information.

Natural Disease

5

If death has occurred as the result of a natural disease process, in most cases, the medical examiner is not involved in the investigation or certification of the death. For example, an elderly individual with a long history of heart disease is found dead at home, and the local police investigation does not find any evidence of foul play. The deceased's doctor is contacted and agrees to sign the death certificate, based on his knowledge of the deceased's medical history. In many jurisdictions, the death is reportable to the medical examiner, but after review of the information provided by the police, the case is released after a report is made. If the death appears to be natural upon investigation by the local authorities, but no doctor is available who is familiar enough with the deceased's medical history to sign the death certificate, the case is referred to the medical examiner's office for determination of the cause and manner of death. Depending on the medical examiner's office, an autopsy may or may not be performed.

The majority of natural deaths investigated by the medical examiner, therefore, involve cases in which the death has occurred **suddenly**, or **unexpectedly**, without any obvious explanation for why the individual died. These deaths may be witnessed or unwitnessed, occur in the presence or absence of any significant medical history, and occur under suspicious or nonsuspicious circumstances. All ages are represented, from the very young to the very old; however, *sudden, unexpected death due to natural disease is relatively uncommon between the ages of 1 and 30.*

Over the years, confusion as to the true definition of the term **"sudden death"** has occurred, and as a result, it is often used incorrectly. The confusion arises due to the fact that the amount of time between the infliction of trauma, or the onset of symptoms in natural disease, and the physiological death of the individual may vary from seconds, to minutes, and, according to some authorities, up to 24 hours. Even further confusion has resulted due to modern-day emergency resuscitation procedures, where the time interval between collapse and pronouncement of death may be 1 hour to several hours, during which time the individual is comatose but with a reestablished heartbeat and respirations. When death is finally pronounced hours later, has the individual really suffered a sudden death?

For practical purposes, it is best to divide "sudden death" into two categories:

- **True** sudden death (**instantaneous death**) is defined as death occurring within **seconds** of onset of symptoms, or infliction of trauma, or with absolutely no warning. The individual literally "drops dead" in his or her tracks.
- Noninstantaneous **sudden death** is defined as death occurring within **minutes** of the onset of symptoms, or infliction of trauma. If the individual survives for longer than a period of a few minutes, without the aid of medical intervention, then the term "sudden death" is inappropriate.

This chapter will deal with the most frequently encountered causes of natural death in adults, children, and infants seen in most medical examiner offices. It must be kept in mind that the frequencies of some types of death may vary from office to office, depending on the demographics of the local community and the laws governing each office. The causes of sudden death in adults will be discussed first.

Causes of Sudden Natural Death in Adults

I. CARDIOVASCULAR DISEASE

This is the most commonly encountered cause of natural sudden death and, in the U.S., is the leading natural cause of death in men between the ages of 20 and 65 years. In medical examiner cases, the death may not be preceded by classic symptoms such as chest pain or angina but instead by **less classic** symptoms such as abdominal pain or **"indigestion."** It is not uncommon to find antacid tablets in the pockets of individuals dying suddenly from cardiac disease, especially those in their forties and fifties. Other less classic symptoms include back, shoulder, or neck pain. In cases where acute infarction goes unrecognized and progresses to the subacute stage with softening of the wall of the heart, a potential for rupture occurs, and those individuals may well present to the medical examiner's office after sudden collapse and death. Oftentimes, dating of the infarct is necessary for medicolegal purposes. The diseases encountered, according to their frequency, include:

A. Coronary artery disease
   1. Accounts for approximately 75% of all sudden deaths handled by most medical examiners
   2. About 50% die suddenly; 25% die without any preceding history or warning
   3. **Mechanism** of death usually a lethal **cardiac arrhythmia**
      a. Ventricular arrhythmia in approximately 80% of cases
      b. Sudden asystole or bradyarrhythmia in about 20% of cases
   4. Most common anatomic finding — severe coronary artery atherosclerosis, with or without vascular calcification
      a. Usually two vessels significantly involved, but occasionally only one significant plaque is present, usually in the proximal left anterior descending coronary artery or the left main coronary artery.
      b. For death to occur, the degree of stenosis is usually **75%** or greater.
   5. Second most frequent finding — myocardial scarring
   6. **Infrequent** gross findings include coronary artery thrombosis (in less than 15%)[1] and acute or subacute myocardial infarct.
   7. In some cases, it may become necessary to determine the approximate date or time the myocardial infarct occurred. **Table 5.1** describes the general gross and histological changes that may accompany infarcts at various stages of their development. It should be kept in mind that overlap of some findings may occur and that not all findings may be present in all infarcts.
   8. Infarcts less than 24 hours old may contain "wavy fibers" in the area of infarction on microscopic exam. To be significant, the fibers should be stretched and thinner than noninfarcted fibers.[2]
   9. If the mechanism of death is **cardiac arrhythmia**, then the diagnosis is one of exclusion that requires complete autopsy, including examination of the brain and ideally complete toxicology. The finding of severe coronary atherosclerosis does not rule out death due to other causes, such as ruptured berry aneurysm or suicidal drug overdose!
   10. On death certificate, usually designated **arteriosclerotic cardiovascular disease** (ASCVD).
B. Hypertensive cardiovascular disease
   1. In most cases of sudden death, hypertensive cardiovascular disease is usually accompanied by coronary artery atherosclerosis. Pattern of atherosclerosis is usually **concentric**, although focal eccentric plaques may also be present.

TABLE 5.1 Possible Gross and Microscopic Myocardial Changes Following Infarction[a]

Time Period after Infarction	Gross Changes			Light Microscopic Changes							
	Consistency	Color	Other	Necrotic Muscle	Neutrophilic Infiltration	Blood Vessels & Connective Tissue	Removal of Fibers	Pigmented Macrophages	Eosinophils	Plasma cells and Lymphocytes	Collagen
1 day	Sl. soft	Red	Pale, dry	++	+	0	0	0	0	0	0
2 days	Soft	Red	Pale, dry	++++	++	0	0	0	0	0	0
3 days	Soft	Red/yellow	Pale, dry	++++	+++	0	0	0	0	0	0
4 days	Soft	Yellow rim	Possible rupture	++++	++++	0	0	0	0	0	0
5 days	Soft	Inc. yellow	Possible rupture	++++	++++	+	+	0	0	0	0
6 days	Soft	Yellow	Possible rupture	++++	+++	++	+	+	+	+	0
7 days	Soft	Yellow/green	Possible rupture	+++	++	++	+	+	+++	+	0
2 weeks	Soft	Red	+/- Depressed	++	+	+++	+++	+++	++++	+++	+
3 weeks	Soft	Red	+/- Depressed	+	+	+++	+++	++++	+	++++	++
4 weeks	Soft	Red	+/- Depressed	+	0	++++	++	++++	0	++++	++
2 months	Rubbery	Gray	Contracted	+	0	++++	+	+++	0	+++	+++
3 months	Sl. firm	Gray	Contracted	+	0	++++	+	+++	0	+++	++++
4 months	Firm	Gray-white	Contracted	0 to +	0	++++	?	++	0	++	++++
5 months	Firm	Gray-white	Contracted	0 to +	0	++++	?	+	0	+	++++
6 mo to 1 year	Firm	White	Contracted	0	0	++++	?	+	0	+	++++
>1 year	Firm	White	Contracted	0	0	++++	0	+	0	0	++++

[a] Adapted from Mallory, G.K., White, P.D., and Salcedo Salgar, J., The speed of healing of myocardial infarction. A study of the pathologic anatomy in seventy-two cases, *Am. Heart J.*, 18, 647, 1939.

2. **Cardiomegaly** is usually present (consult standard weight tables), in combination with some degree of **symmetrical left ventricular hypertrophy.**
3. Mechanism of death — acute cardiac arrhythmia. Cardiomegaly alone can predispose to cardiac arrhythmia.
4. May or may not have corresponding gross renal changes (fine granularity of cortices), but usually does have some degree of small vessel arteriolar sclerosis on microscopic exam.
5. In some young adults, there may be significant left ventricular hypertrophy without a significant clinical history of hypertension.[3]
6. The diagnosis is usually one of exclusion.

C. **Cardiomyopathies** — diseases characterized by **myocardial dysfunction** of known and unknown etiologies, but not due to arteriosclerosis, hypertension, valvular disease, or infections. There are three general categories:

1. **Congestive or dilated cardiomyopathy (DCM).** Cardiomegaly is present, sometimes massive, with dilatation of the heart chambers. Microscopic interstitial or perivascular fibrosis may or may not be present. In massively dilated hearts, endocardial thrombi are often present. May be primary, without any known cause (**idiopathic dilated cardiomyopathy**), or secondary due to a known cause.

   a. Most common cause of secondary DCM encountered in U.S. medical examiner's offices is **chronic alcohol abuse.**
      1. May be due to toxic effect of alcohol on the myocardium, nutritional deficits present in chronic alcoholism, or toxic effects of alcohol additives, such as cobalt
      2. Typical patient between 30 to 55 years of age, male or female, with history of heavy alcohol consumption for at least 10 years

   b. **Peri- or postpartum cardiomyopathy.** Defined as heart failure occurring during the last trimester of pregnancy or within the first 6 months postpartum. The exact cause is unknown.
      1. In many cases, the enlarged heart returns to normal within 6 to 12 months, but sudden death has been reported.
      2. Tends to occur more frequently in blacks, and in multiparous women older than 30 years of age.
      3. Autopsy reveals an enlarged, flabby heart and usually pulmonary edema. Microscopically, there may be focal

or diffuse myocardial fibrosis, mononuclear infiltrates, degeneration of myocardial fibers, or occasionally fatty infiltrates.

   c. **Chronic, or remote, myocarditis.** Most common suspected etiology being infectious (viral), followed by idiopathic and toxic. Certain drugs, such as *doxorubicin* (Adriamycin), are associated with a direct toxic effect on myocardial tissue, which may result in chronic myocarditis with eventual dilatation, dysfunction, and cardiac arrhythmia. Other causes include radiation, hypersensitivity, and uremia.

2. **Hypertrophic cardiomyopathy.** Heart is always enlarged, but not dilated, with left ventricular hypertrophy, which is symmetrical in 50% of the cases, but asymmetrical in the remaining 50%. In asymmetrical hypertrophy, originally designated idiopathic hypertrophic subaortic stenosis (**IHSS**), or asymmetric septal hypertrophy, the asymmetrically thickened ventricular septum causes obstruction of the aortic outflow tract.

   a. Microscopic sections show **haphazard arrangement** of myocardial fibers of the septum in IHSS and of all walls in the symmetric variety. Other changes include hypertrophied and bizarrely shaped myocardial cells (**Figure 5.1**).

   b. In 50% of cases, it is familial, with *autosomal dominant inheritance*. In remaining 50%, it appears to arise spontaneously, without evidence of the disease in relatives.

3. **Restrictive,** or **infiltrative, cardiomyopathy**. Least common category of cardiomyopathy in Western countries. May be idiopathic, or due to various causes. Represents group of diseases in which myocardial or endocardial abnormalities limit diastolic filling. Causes include:

   a. **Amyloidosis.** Ventricular walls are thickened, rubbery, and firm, with microscopic interstitial, perivascular, or endocardial amyloid deposits present. Infiltration of the conduction system can lead to **arrhythmias** and sudden death.

   b. **Sarcoidosis.** Generalized granulomatous disease that may involve the heart. Sudden death from arrhythmia may occur if the conduction system is involved. Diagnosis is by microscopic examination of the myocardium, including sections of the conduction system, with demonstration of the typical noncaseating granulomas.

   c. Less frequently encountered causes of restrictive cardiomyopathy that may cause sudden death include unsuspected:

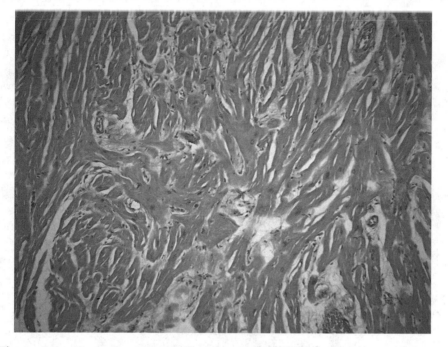

Figure 5.1 (See color insert following page 146) Section of interventricular septum in 19-year-old white male with idiopathic hypertrophic subaortic stenosis (IHSS) demonstrating myofiber hypertrophy and disarray.

1. **Endomyocardial fibrosis** or eosinophilic endomyocardial disease (Loffler endocarditis).
2. **Glycogen storage disease.** Types II (Pompe disease), III, and IV are known to affect the heart, with the usual mechanism of death cardiac failure.
3. **Hemochromatosis,** caused by a genetic defect in iron metabolism that results in multiorgan involvement with excessive deposits of iron in tissues; severity of the heart disease correlates with the amount of iron deposited. On gross exam, the heart is dilated, the walls are thickened, and the myocardium has a conspicuous brown color.

D. Other **coronary artery abnormalities** that may cause sudden death are:
1. **Coronary artery spasm** (Prinzmetal's angina). May lead to transitory myocardial ischemia and arrhythmias. Autopsy usually shows patent coronary arteries, without significant atherosclerosis, and no evidence of infarct.

2. Muscular **"bridging"** of coronary artery. In some cases, instead of running completely within the epicardial fat, a coronary artery (usually the LAD) dips into the myocardium (becoming intramural), and a "muscular" bridge is created over the artery. Theoretically, the bridge may cause compression of the artery during systole or induce coronary artery spasm.

3. **Congenital anomalies** of the coronary arteries. Numerous varieties exist, and many have been reported to cause sudden death. Examples include the following:
   a. Coronary artery hypoplasia
   b. Single coronary artery
   c. Left main coronary artery arising from the right sinus of Valsalva, with passage between the root of the aorta and the pulmonary artery
   d. The right coronary artery arising from the left sinus of Valsalva

Figure 5.2 depicts some of the more commonly encountered coronary artery anomalies that have been reported associated with sudden death.

4. **Acute coronary artery dissection,** in the absence of atherosclerosis (**Figure 5.3**).
   a. May be spontaneous, or due to trauma, and limited to the coronary artery.
   b. May occur as a consequence of aortic dissection extending into a coronary artery.
   c. Most coronary artery dissections limited to the vessel occur in females, especially in the peripartum period.
   d. 75% of the cases involve the LAD, and changes of cystic medial necrosis may or may not be present on microscopic exam.

E. **Valvular diseases** occasionally associated with sudden death
   1. **Floppy mitral valve syndrome.** Caused by **mucinous** or **myxoid degeneration** of the mitral heart valve, which leads to thickened, often voluminous and redundant valve leaflets that can prolapse into the left atrium during systole and in many cases lead to mitral regurgitation.
      a. Myxoid degeneration may also involve the annulus and the chordae tendineae. In a few cases, the myxoid change also involves the tricuspid or aortic valve, while the pulmonic valve is rarely involved.
      b. Nonspecific **symptoms** include fatigue, palpitations, dizziness, atypical chest pain, and anxiety.

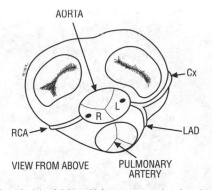

VIEW FROM ABOVE

Normal origin of right and left coronary arteries viewed from above. RCA, right coronary artery; LAD, left anterior descending coronary artery; Cx, left circumflex coronary artery. L-left sinus of Valsalva; R-right sinus of Valsalva.

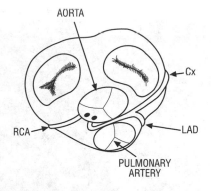

Left coronary artery originating from right sinus of Valsalva.

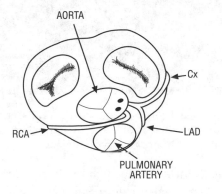

Right coronary artery originating from left sinus of Valsalva.

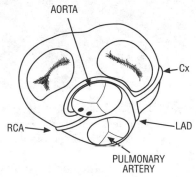

Left coronary artery originating from right sinus of Valsalva and passing behind aorta.

Figure 5.2 Coronary artery anomalies reported in some cases of sudden death.

    c. Heart auscultation usually reveals a *mid to late systolic click* and a late systolic murmur if mitral regurgitation is significant. The abnormal valve may be predisposed to endocarditis.

    d. Although uncommon, sudden death can occur, with the presumed mechanism of death that of ventricular arrhythmia. As in other cases where the mechanism of death is cardiac arrhythmia, all other causes of death must be ruled out by a complete autopsy, including toxicological and microscopic examinations.

    e. The microscopic examination of the affected heart valve(s) usually shows conspicuous myxomatous changes to be present within the valve leaflets.

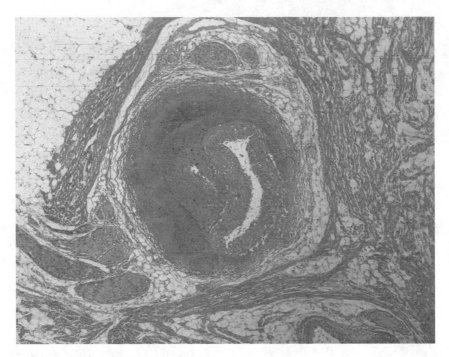

Figure 5.3 (See color insert following page 146) Spontaneous acute dissection of left anterior descending coronary artery in 38-year-old white female. No other significant autopsy findings. No documented history of hypertension.

2. **Calcific aortic stenosis.** Condition in which calcium is deposited in the aortic cusps and valve ring, resulting in marked narrowing of the outlet.
   a. Occurs over a period of years and can involve abnormal as well as normal aortic valves.
      1. **Bicuspid** aortic valves often become calcified with age.
      2. Aortic valves scarred by **rheumatic fever** can, with age, become calcified. With the decline of rheumatic fever in the general population due to appropriate medical therapy when recognized, this condition is becoming less common.
      3. Normal tricuspid aortic valves can undergo degenerative calcification, with artificial fusion of the cusps and eventual stenosis. May begin in the sixth decade of life, and may correlate with systemic calcific atherosclerosis.
   b. Severe aortic stenosis is usually associated with marked cardiomegaly and severe left ventricular hypertrophy, which, if untreated, leads to dilatation and failure.

    c. Deaths due to aortic stenosis presenting to the medical examiner's office tend to involve younger individuals who, for some reason, are undiagnosed and untreated.

  3. **Endocarditis.** Cases presenting to the medical examiner's office are usually bacterial, and either acute or subacute.

    a. In most cases, the patient is an intravenous drug user, with a deformed/scarred right-sided heart valve (usually tricuspid) colonized with various bacteria.

    b. In some cases, the bacterial vegetations are present on the left-sided heart valves (mitral, aortic), instead of the right-sided valves, despite a closed foramen ovale.

F. **Myocarditis** — inflammation of the myocardium by infectious, toxic, or inflammatory agents, or resulting from connective tissue disorders. Some cases are idiopathic. Broad range of presentation, from minor to no symptoms to obvious clinical presentation. Chronic myocarditis, with enlargement of the heart, has already been discussed under the category of cardiomyopathies. Acute myocarditis may or may not lead to enlargement of the heart.

  1. **Infectious myocarditis** is usually caused by a viral agent. Death may occur acutely or remotely as a consequence of myocardial scarring.

    a. In acute cases, the heart may be normal appearing or pale and flabby.

    b. Microscopically, patchy to diffuse areas of necrosis may be present, with interstitial edema and varying degrees of inflammatory infiltrate. The infiltrate may be mostly neutrophils or lymphocytes but may also be mixed, with plasma cells and eosinophils present in varying numbers.

    c. If the individual survives the acute phase, the process may progress to focal or diffuse myocardial scarring with or without subsequent clinical abnormalities such as arrhythmia.

    d. **TO COMPLETELY RULE OUT MYOCARDITIS AS A CAUSE OF DEATH, MULTIPLE MICROSCOPIC SECTIONS OF THE MYOCARDIUM SHOULD BE TAKEN, INCLUDING REPRESENTATIVE SECTIONS THROUGH THE NODAL TISSUE.** In adults, at least six sections from various areas of the left ventricle should be submitted, in addition to at least one section from the SA node and two sections through the AV node and Bundle of His. In infants and children, fewer sections of the myocardium may be submitted, but the same number of sections through the conduction system should be submitted.

   2. Other causes of myocarditis include:

      a. **Hypersensitivity** reactions to various drugs and antibiotics.

         1. The cellular infiltrate is usually predominantly **eosinophils,** admixed with lymphocytes and plasma cells. In contrast to acute infectious myocarditis, the inflammatory infiltrate is usually more prominent than the myocardial cell necrosis.

         2. Involvement of the conduction system is not infrequent, and occasionally the first symptom of hypersensitivity drug reaction may be sudden death.

      b. **Giant cell myocarditis.** Uncommon **granulomatous** degeneration of the heart muscle, with numerous multinucleated giant cells and myocardial cell necrosis. Cause unknown.

         1. Has been seen in association with systemic lupus erythematosus, thymoma, and thyrotoxicosis, suggesting an autoimmune etiology.

         2. May lead to cardiac failure and sudden death.

G. Natural diseases of the **aorta,** which may cause sudden death

   1. **Acute aortic dissection**, with or without preexisting aneurysm. Aortic aneurysms may occur as a result of atherosclerosis, with hypertension present in approximately 50% of cases.

      a. If dissection occurs with rupture into a body cavity or into the pericardial sac, it can result in sudden collapse and death, or delayed death, if untreated.

      b. Occasionally, acute dissection of the thoracic aorta occurs in the absence of a preexisting aneurysm. In such cases, the individual is invariably hypertensive.

      c. At autopsy, intimal tears may be extremely difficult to locate, but the site of rupture through the vessel adventitia is usually easily found.

      d. In most cases, microscopic sections of the aorta, taken in the region of rupture, show cyst-like spaces within the media, filled with a basophilic material, characteristic of the degenerative process **cystic medial necrosis.**

   2. **Syphilitic aortic aneurysms,** also called luetic aneurysms, form as a result of syphilitic aortitis.

      a. May lead to acute dissection and sudden death.

b. Diagnosis may be confirmed by postmortem **serology**, if postmortem blood sample is not significantly degraded.

c. Microscopic examination of the aorta often shows periarteritis and endarteritis of the vasa vasorum, large numbers of plasma cells and lymphocytes in the adventitia, focal necrosis and scarring of the media, and disruption of the elastic lamellae.

II. **CENTRAL NERVOUS SYSTEM DISORDERS**

Central nervous system disorders known to occasionally cause sudden death are less frequently encountered in the medical examiner's office than those due to cardiovascular disease. The most common causes include epilepsy, intracerebral hemorrhage, primary subarachnoid hemorrhage not due to trauma, meningitis, and undiagnosed brain tumors.

A. **Epilepsy,** idiopathic origin. The epileptic individual who dies suddenly, or unexpectedly, is usually young and often found dead in bed in the morning. If the death is witnessed, the individual may or may not exhibit seizure activity prior to collapse.

1. In either case, a complete autopsy is generally negative, and postmortem toxicology reveals either absent or subtherapeutic levels of anticonvulsants to be present. However, therapeutic levels may also be present.

2. Bite wounds to the tongue are found only in 25% of cases, suggesting seizure activity prior to death. However, this is a nonspecific finding, as perimortem seizure activity can accompany other causes of death.

3. The **mechanism of death** is believed to be **cardiac arrhythmia.**

4. If during an epileptic seizure, the individual drowns, or dies as a result of trauma precipitated by the seizure, the death is more appropriately classified as accidental.

5. Gross and microscopic changes in the brain are usually absent. The classic reported finding of *sclerosis of Ammon's horn* is frequently not found.

B. When a seizure disorder occurs secondary to a traumatic injury (**posttraumatic epilepsy**), and the individual dies at a later date from the seizure disorder, it becomes imperative that the initiating cause of the disorder be investigated. For example, if the seizure disorder was caused by a gunshot wound to the head, despite the time interval, the manner of death would depend on whether or not the gunshot wound was due to homicidal, suicidal, or accidental infliction.

C. **Nontraumatic subarachnoid hemorrhage** can occur in varied instances, with the most common being that of a ruptured berry aneurysm of the cerebral vasculature, especially within the circle of Willis. Other causes, according to frequency, include intracerebral hemorrhage with extension into the subarachnoid space and ruptured arteriovenous malformations. Less frequently encountered causes include endocarditis with embolic phenomena, blood dyscrasias, tumors, vasculitis, infections with mycotic aneurysms, and sickle cell hemoglobinopathy.

1. **Berry aneurysms** (congenital intracranial aneurysms)
   a. Reportedly present in approximately 2 to 4% of adults at autopsy, but are rare in infants and children; 90% are silent until rupture.
   b. Are multiple in 15 to 20% of cases.
   c. About two thirds become symptomatic between the ages of 40 and 65; the remaining third cause symptoms at an earlier or later age.
   d. Both **congenital** (maldevelopment of the media at points of arterial bifurcation) and **acquired** (degeneration and fragmentation of the elastica due to age or atherosclerosis) factors are necessary to initiate protrusion; hypertension may play a role in speeding the protrusion and enlargement but cannot by itself cause the initial defect in the media and elastica. Greater than 90% of saccular aneurysms occur at branch points.
   e. The majority of berry aneurysms are found on the anterior portion of the circle of Willis (approximately 80 to 90%), with the remainder found on the posterior aspect (**Figure 5.4**).
   f. Symptomatic aneurysms range in size from 0.5 to 1.5 cm in diameter.
   g. Rupture is not common in aneurysms less than 5 mm in diameter; aneurysms 3 cm or greater act as intracranial masses.
   h. Approximately one third of patients will be engaged in some sort of physical activity, such as heavy lifting, bending, sexual intercourse, or straining during defecation, at the time of rupture. It may be that the transient increase in blood pressure produced by exertion, emotion, or trauma tips the scale in the direction of rupture in an aneurysm about to rupture spontaneously. Therefore, in the majority of cases, rupture occurs spontaneously, while the individual is at rest or engaged in only light, everyday activity.

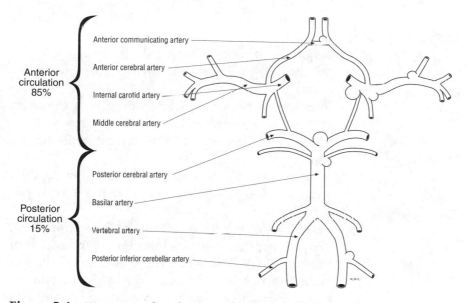

Anterior communicating artery

Anterior cerebral artery

Internal carotid artery

Middle cerebral artery

Anterior circulation 85%

Posterior cerebral artery

Basilar artery

Vertebral artery

Posterior inferior cerebellar artery

Posterior circulation 15%

Figure 5.4 Frequency distribution of congenital cerebral (berry) aneurysms within the circle of Willis.

    i.   In fatal cases of rupture, 60% die immediately after rupture and 80% within 24 hours of admission to a hospital.

    j.   In about one third of patients, the aneurysm will rupture into the brain and ventricles as well as the subarachnoid space.

    k.   At the time of rupture, the patient usually complains of severe, excruciating headache, with immediate collapse into unconsciousness; however, in a small percentage of patients (2%), there is no mention of headache prior to collapse. There may be a history of headache for days or weeks prior to rupture, thought to be due to small, minor leaks from the aneurysm prior to fatal rupture.

    l.   Largest collection of subarachnoid blood is across the ventral aspect of the brain. *In order to visualize the ruptured aneurysm at autopsy, the brain must be examined fresh, after carefully excising the arachnoid membrane and flushing the coagulated blood from the area of greatest concentration. A thorough, exhaustive search should then be made for remnants of the suspected aneurysm.* In approximately 90% of cases, a ruptured aneurysm can be found, while in the remaining 10%, no aneurysm is found. In these latter cases, it is postulated that the aneurysm was so small that the rupture completely obliterated all traces of the aneurysm.

m. Consequences of rupture include the following:

1. Massive subarachnoid hemorrhage in most cases (96%).
2. Intracerebral hemorrhage in about 50% of the cases, with associated intraventricular hemorrhage in 17%.
3. Subdural hematoma in 20%, with most **nonspace** occupying.
4. Infarction in 75% of patients who die after rupture; presumed to be due to vasospasm, as thrombi are seldom found.
5. Vasospasm may lead to infarction. Vasospasm of the perforating arteries arising from the posterior part of the circle of Willis, which supply the midbrain and brainstem, may be a primary cause of the alteration in consciousness that usually follows rupture. Vasospasm may also damage the blood-brain barrier, leading to vasogenic edema.
6. Possible late complication — hydrocephalus, caused by fibrosis and scarring of the subarachnoid space and lining of the ventricles, if intraventricular hemorrhage present, which blocks the pathways of absorption of cerebrospinal fluid.

2. Subarachnoid hemorrhage due to a bleeding **arteriovenous malformation:**

a. Conglomeration of arteries and veins without a capillary bed, located in the cerebral cortex and usually extending into the contiguous white matter.
b. May cause intracerebral or subarachnoid hemorrhage, depending on location.
c. May present clinically as seizure disorder.
d. Majority of AV malformations involve the **central parietal cortex.**
e. **Sturge-Weber** syndrome (encephalofacial angiomatosis) — A rare, nonfamilial congenital disorder characterized by multiple angiomas, including large arteriovenous malformations of the brain, associated with seizures, and vascular nevi (angiomas) of the face or neck. Usually, the facial lesion is unilateral, and called a **port-wine stain.**

D. **Intracerebral hemorrhage** (ICH) can lead to sudden, rapid death.

1. Occurs in 10 to 30% of all strokes.

2. Most common cause is **hypertension** (45% of all ICHs). Usual sites include basal ganglia, thalamus, pons, cerebellum, and subcortical white matter (lobar hemorrhage).
3. Other causes include:
   a. Amyloid angiopathy — usually older patient, with most frequent site occipital cortex, although may be multifocal.
   b. Arteriovenous malformation — usually younger patient; can occur anywhere within the brain matter.
   c. Tumors — cause about 10% of all ICHs.
      1. Metastatic — melanoma, bronchogenic carcinoma, choriocarcinoma, renal cell carcinoma
      2. Primary — glioblastoma, pituitary adenoma
   d. Bleeding diatheses — cause multifocal, widespread, small hemorrhages; causes include thrombocytopenia, disseminated intravascular coagulation (DIC), leukemia. Anticoagulant therapy may cause unifocal, large hemorrhage.
   e. Drug induced — seen in association with cocaine, amphetamine use.
   f. Cerebral vasculitis due to various causes.
4. Prognosis depends on the volume of the hemorrhage and the level of consciousness at presentation.
5. Mortality rate high when the hemorrhage is large and there is extension of the hemorrhage into the ventricles, or subdural space.
6. ICH usually has abrupt onset, usually while the individual is active and awake.
7. Tend to occur more often in males, and more frequently in blacks than in whites, probably due to the higher incidence of hypertension in blacks.
8. Symptoms depend on the location of the hemorrhage within the brain.
   a. Basal ganglia (usually putamen) — slurred speech; gradual weakening of muscles of face, legs, and arms
   b. Thalamus — hemiparesis
   c. Cerebellum — repeat vomiting, occipital headache, vertigo
   d. Pontine (brainstem) — immediate loss of consciousness; if large may be catastrophic with 95% of patients expiring within 24 hours
9. Microscopic brain sections from area adjacent to hemorrhage may show sclerosed, hyalinized arteries or arterioles.

10. Death is due to secondary brain stem compression/herniation or intraventricular hemorrhage.

E. **Cerebral infarction** (ischemic stroke) is less frequent cause of sudden death and therefore is seen less frequently in most ME offices. Ischemic strokes develop more slowly than ICH and are less likely to cause death in less than 24 hours, before adequate diagnosis at the hospital. However, in forensic autopsies, it is not uncommon to find evidence of past cerebral infarctions. There are four main causes of cerebral (ischemic) infarctions:

1. Large vessel disease — infarction occurs as a result of embolism or thrombosis of a large (named) cerebral artery; the resulting infarct involves the territory of the brain supplied by that artery

2. Small vessel disease — usually caused by arteriosclerosis of small penetrating vessels within the basal ganglia or pons
   a. Often associated with hypertension or diabetes mellitus
   b. Resulting small infarcts are called "lacunar infarcts"

3. Global ischemia — caused by a reduction in cerebral blood flow (as in cardiopulmonary arrest from various causes), which results in widespread neuronal necrosis and possible laminar cortical necrosis

4. Venous infarction — least commonly seen
   a. Seen with thrombosis of the main cerebral venous sinuses, which leads to hemorrhagic necrosis
   b. May occur in conditions that predispose to thrombosis, such as polycythemia, dehydration, or spread of infection from nearby structure such as the middle ear or nasal sinus.

F. **Primary,** undiagnosed **brain tumors.** With modern technology and the availability of medical care, very few significant brain tumors go undetected.

1. If the symptoms are not severe enough to require medical attention (i.e., low-grade headache), or the symptoms are misinterpreted as due to a psychiatric disorder, or the symptoms are nonlocalizing, then the tumor may go undiagnosed and progressively enlarge until it causes sudden death.

2. The incidence of such tumors is estimated at 0.16% of all autopsy cases in a medical examiner's office.[4]

3. About 50% of such tumors are in the astrocytoma-glioblastoma category.

4. A varied assortment of other tumors make up the remainder of cases, including oligodendrogliomas, meningiomas, colloid cyst, teratoma, and medulloblastoma.

G. **Meningitis** can cause sudden death in adults as well as infants and children.
   1. The principal organisms involved in acute purulent meningitis are:
      a. *Neisseria meningitidis* and *Streptococcus pneumoniae* in adults
      b. *Streptococcus pneumoniae* and *Listeria monocytogenes* in the elderly
      c. *E. coli*, streptococci, and *Listeria monocytogenes* in neonates
      d. *Haemophilus influenzae* and *Neisseria meningitidis* in children
   2. In adults, meningitis may or may not occur as an extension of meningococcemia. **Meningococcemia** without meningitis can result in rapid, fulminant death (in less than 12 hours from onset of symptoms).
      a. Initial symptom may be mild sore throat, with rapid progression to fever, headache, weakness, prostration, petechial to confluent purpura, intense cyanosis, and cardiovascular collapse.
      b. Autopsy findings in such cases include petechial rash to confluent purpura, internal petechiae, and usually bilateral adrenal hemorrhage (Waterhouse-Friderichsen syndrome).
      c. Postmortem blood cultures may or may not grow the meningococcus, but latex agglutination tests (for the capsular antigen) may be done on postmortem urine and CSF. Postmortem blood may be used if not significantly hemolyzed.
H. **Hydrocephalus** may be a cause of sudden death in adults (and children) with a long-standing history of hydrocephalus, with or without a shunt. In these cases, the patient is relatively stable and dies suddenly, presumably due to a sudden increase in intracranial pressure.
   1. At autopsy, if a shunt is present, it should be inspected for evidence of blockage or malfunction.
   2. If no shunt is present, then the only autopsy finding may be the chronic hydrocephalus. In these cases, all other possible causes of death should be ruled out before the death is attributed to the hydrocephalus.
   3. Occasionally, sudden death occurs as a result of acute intraventricular hemorrhage due to hemorrhage from one of the small vessels that line the walls of the ventricles.

    I.   **Psychiatric disorders** have been associated with sudden death. In most cases, the psychiatric disorder is *schizophrenia*.

III. RESPIRATORY SYSTEM

Sudden death due to respiratory causes is relatively infrequent and comprises approximately 10% of all sudden, natural deaths. The main pulmonary diseases associated with sudden death include those below.

  A. Pulmonary **thromboembolus** — usually results when a lower extremity thrombus becomes dislodged and travels to the heart and pulmonary arterial tree.

    1. The original thrombosis may be due to various causes:

      a. Blood stasis within the lower extremity (caused by immobility and/or bed rest, obesity, intrapelvic tumors, pregnancy and postpartum period for example)

      b. Venous injury, in which case the manner of death may be accidental

      c. Hypercoagulable states, which may be due to inherited coagulation disorders or oral contraceptive therapy

    2. Sudden death usually results from a large, occlusive embolus in the main pulmonary artery. If 60% of the pulmonary vasculature is suddenly blocked, the heart cannot pump blood through the lungs, leading to cardiovascular collapse.

    3. Manner of death thought to be:

      a. Mechanical obstruction of blood flow if a large embolus is involved

      b. Vasoconstriction due to vasospasm if multiple smaller emboli are involved

    4. Symptoms include syncope, chest pain, dyspnea, dizziness due to hypoxia.

    5. If pulmonary emboli are found at autopsy, an attempt should be made to locate their origin. Inspect the pelvic veins, and make incisions into the popliteal fossae and posterior calves. In many cases, no residual thrombi are located.

    6. If the initial cause of the immobilization is due to a homicidal action (i.e., head injury from gunshot wound), and the pulmonary embolus can be shown to be a direct complication of the initial trauma, then the manner of death in such cases would be homicide, despite the length of time occurring between the injury and the death.

    7. **Pulmonary infarcts** occur in less than 10% of cases of pulmonary emboli.

      a. At autopsy, pulmonary infarcts are hemorrhagic, dark red-brown, usually peripherally located, and wedge-shaped.

      b. Pleuritic chest pain may be associated with subpleural in-
farcts, while hemoptysis may be associated with those adjacent to a major bronchus.

    8. Recurrent pulmonary emboli may lead to pulmonary hyper-
tension and sudden death.

B. Other forms of pulmonary emboli (due to embolization of amniotic fluid, fat, bone marrow, air) are discussed more fully in
subsequent chapters.

C. **Bronchial asthma.** Chronic bronchial asthma may be associated
with sudden death in a small percentage ($\approx$5%) of all cases of
chronic asthma.

    1. Sudden death can occur without a prolonged attack (acute
asthmatic paroxysm).

    2. The frequency of sudden death in these cases appears to be
increased at night or in the early morning.

    3. There are several known triggers of asthmatic attacks:

        a. Allergens, both airborne and food (house dust mites, pea-
nuts)

        b. Infections (viral or bacterial)

        c. Occupational exposure to allergens

        d. Certain drugs (e.g., aspirin)

        e. Certain gases (such as sulfur dioxide, ozone)

        f. Psychological stress

        g. Exertion/exercise

        h. Cold air

    4. The mechanism of death is due to reduced air flow, with ven-
tilation-perfusion mismatches that lead to decreased oxygenation of the blood, an elevation in the $_pCO_2$, and right ventricular overload.

    5. Decreased air flow occurs as a result of allergic release of his-
tamine and other vasoactive compounds from inflammatory
cells (eosinophils and mast cells), which in turn causes bronchial smooth muscle contraction; there is also marked intra-
bronchial mucous secretion.

    6. In nonresuscitated individuals, autopsy usually shows hyper-
expanded, puffy, pale lungs, with abundant mucous plugging
of the bronchi (central and peripheral). In cases where CPR
has occurred, the classic findings may not be present.

    7. Microscopic examination of the lungs should show character-
istic changes of chronic asthma, with increased numbers of
eosinophils present in the bronchial mucosa, submucosa, or
peribronchiolar tissue. Representative sections should be taken

from all areas of the bronchial tree (central, mid, and peripheral).

D. **Pneumonia.** Most cases of pneumonia seen in the medical examiner's office are secondary to other causes of death, such as coma due to accidental or homicidal head trauma. Sudden death can, however, occur in cases of primary pneumonia, but this is relatively uncommon, as most individuals with pneumonia are under a doctor's care. Exceptions to this would include individuals who suffer decreased levels of consciousness for various reasons, including alcoholics; drug addicts (heroin); elderly, debilitated, bedridden individuals; and occasionally individuals with mental retardation.

1. At autopsy, there may be lobar pneumonia, or patchy or confluent bronchopneumonia.

2. Occasionally see fulminant, bilateral, undiagnosed tuberculous pneumonitis, especially in homeless people, alcoholics, and immunosuppressed individuals (such as HIV positive patients). These cases may present with exsanguinating bronchial hemorrhage.

E. **Acute epiglottitis** can cause sudden death in both adults and children.

1. The mechanism of death is marked edema of the epiglottis and the upper airway mucosa, leading to mechanical obstruction of the airway.

2. Death can occur very rapidly; occasionally precipitated by pharyngeal examination with a tongue depressor.

3. When airway obstruction occurs, it is a medical emergency, requiring immediate intubation; if this is not possible, emergency tracheostomy should be performed.

4. Most common causative agent is *H. influenzae,* but other bacteria have also been found to be associated with acute epiglottitis, including *S. pneumoniae.*

F. **Massive hemoptysis** may cause sudden death by exsanguination. Causes include:

1. Neoplasms or inflammatory lesions of the nasopharynx

2. Tumor/carcinoma of the bronchus, with erosion into a pulmonary artery

3. Cavitary tuberculosis

4. Cavitary lung abscess (nontuberculous bacterial)

5. Bronchiectasis

6. Aortic aneurysm with erosion and rupture into a pulmonary bronchus or the esophagus (leading to hematemesis)

G. **Spontaneous pneumothorax** is a rare cause of sudden death in adults.
   1. Usually occurs as a result of rupture of an emphysematous bulla.
   2. If suspected before autopsy, a postmortem chest x-ray should demonstrate a large pneumothorax. Can also be demonstrated by flooding the space between the lateral chest wall and the reflected musculature and then stabbing through an intercostal space under water.
   3. May suspect at autopsy if one lung is obviously collapsed and no other cause of death is found. In such cases, the collapsed bulla may or may not be evident.

IV. **GASTROINTESTINAL TRACT**

Sudden death due to GI disorders is very uncommon. Some causes include:

A. Massive **hematemesis** due to:
   1. Esophageal **varices** occurring as a consequence of portal hypertension, usually in relation to advanced hepatic cirrhosis. Ruptured varices may be extremely hard to see or demonstrate at autopsy, due to their collapsed state.
   2. Mallory-Weiss syndrome, with gastroesophageal lacerations caused by repeat, violent vomiting.
B. Massive **GI hemorrhage** due to gastric or duodenal ulcer that has eroded into artery. May also cause death by development of peritonitis and sepsis.
C. Strangulated hernias (inguinal, umbilical), which may lead to bowel infarction, peritonitis, and sepsis.
D. **Pancreatitis** can, on occasion, be a cause of sudden death.
   1. Usually of the fulminant, hemorrhagic type, with a very short prodromal period
   2. May or may not be associated with prior alcohol consumption
   3. Mechanism of death usually overwhelming fluid and electrolyte abnormalities
E. Occasionally, **diabetes mellitus** may have an acute onset, with the initial presenting symptom that of diabetic coma ending in death.
   1. The postmortem blood glucose level is **not** a reliable indicator of the antemortem blood glucose level and should never be used to diagnose antemortem hyperglycemia.
   2. Postmortem blood acetone levels may or may not be increased in ketoacidosis and are usually not increased if death has resulted from hyperosmotic coma. An increase in the postmortem blood acetone level may also be seen in cases of malnu-

trition and starvation and is therefore not a specific indicator of diabetes.

3. **The most reliable indicator of antemortem hyperglycemia is elevation of the vitreous glucose level (above 200 mg/dl).**

4. One cannot diagnose hypoglycemia by evaluation of the vitreous glucose. The vitreous glucose level can fall to zero within an hour after death, even with a normal antemortem blood glucose level.

V. **HEPATIC DISORDERS**

   Although uncommon, some hepatic disorders may cause sudden death in adults.

   A. Most commonly associated with alcoholic liver disease. Usually, two subtypes are seen:
      1. Massive **"fatty metamorphosis"** of the liver (**Figure 5.5**), usually associated with chronic alcohol abuse, has been found in association with sudden death. The exact mechanism of death is unknown but has been postulated to be due to metabolic cause or electrolyte imbalance.
      2. Advanced **cirrhosis**
         a. May be the only finding present in cases of sudden death

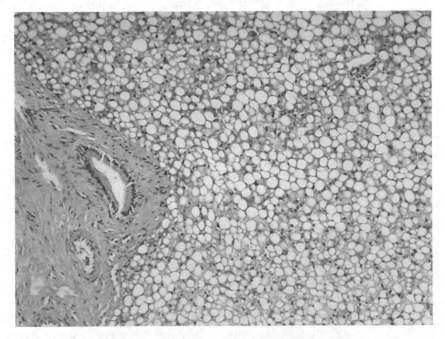

Figure 5.5 (See color insert following page 146) Liver with marked fatty metamorphosis in 40-year-old alcoholic, found dead in bed, without any other significant autopsy findings.

     b. May occur with or without significant ascites

     c. Mechanism of death postulated to be possible hepatic failure, metabolic disorder, electrolyte imbalance, delirium tremens, or cardiac arrhythmia

B. Massive, nontraumatic intra-abdominal hemorrhage has been found in some cases of sudden death.[5]

    1. The intra-abdominal hemorrhage is great, as much as 2 to 5 liters in most cases.

    2. A site for the hemorrhage is rarely found at autopsy.

    3. Occurs in association with advanced micronodular cirrhosis.

    4. Postulated cause is disseminated intravascular coagulopathy.

VI. ADRENAL DISORDERS

Rarely cause sudden death primarily. Some causes include:

A. **Pheochromocytomas.** With minor trauma, or abdominal manipulation during a physical exam or surgery, sudden catecholamine release from the tumor may precipitate adrenal crisis with cardiac stimulation and death.

B. Chronic adrenal insufficiency (**Addison's disease**) may occasionally present as sudden death. The primary cause of Addison's disease is felt to be due to an autoimmune process. Other causes include tuberculosis, fungal infections, or chronic infection. At autopsy the adrenal glands are markedly shrunken and atrophic, and on microscopic exam they may be reduced to fibrous strands of tissue with associated chronic inflammatory infiltrate.

VII. SPLENIC DISORDERS

Relatively few splenic disorders are associated with sudden death.

A. Undiagnosed leukemia can lead to splenic rupture and sudden death.[6]

B. Absence of the spleen can predispose an individual to pneumococcal infections, septicemia, and bilateral adrenal hemorrhage.

C. Splenic rupture is an uncommon complication of infectious mononucleosis.

VIII. MISCELLANEOUS CAUSES OF SUDDEN DEATH IN ADULTS

A. **Sickle cell** trait has been found associated with sudden death.

    1. Infection, hypoxia, dehydration can precipitate sickling and result in sudden death.

    2. Has been reported in young athletes with hemoglobinopathies.

    3. The autopsy in such cases is usually negative for other causes of death.

    4. Microscopic exam usually shows sickled red blood cells in various organs (kidney, brain, spleen). This may occur postmortem and is therefore not considered evidence of antemor-

tem sickling but rather only evidence of the presence of an abnormal hemoglobin.

    5. The presence of an abnormal hemoglobin in such cases can be confirmed by postmortem blood electrophoresis.

B. Occasionally, an unsuspected **ruptured tubal pregnancy** may lead to rapid intraperitoneal hemorrhage and sudden death. A ruptured cystic ovarian tumor or hemorrhagic corpus luteum may cause sudden death by similar means.

C. Undiagnosed malignant tumors with widespread metastasis may be found occasionally at autopsy. The most common primary tumors involved are those of the lung, bowel, and breast.

Causes of Sudden Natural Death in Infants and Young Children

A large number of differing diseases or disorders may cause sudden natural death in infants and children (**Table 5.2**). Only the more commonly encountered ones will be discussed. Many of the disease processes are similar to those that cause sudden death in adults, such as epiglottitis and meningitis, but the causative agent may be different.

    I. **SUDDEN INFANT DEATH SYNDROME (SIDS)**

    (SIDS) is also referred to as cot or crib death.

      A. SIDS was originally defined in 1969 at the Second International Conference on Causes of Sudden Death in Infants, as "the sudden death of any infant or young child, which is unexpected by history, and in which a thorough postmortem examination fails to demonstrate an adequate cause for death."[7]

      B. The definition was revised in 1989 by the United States National Institute of Child Health and Human Development Group, as "the sudden death of an infant under one year of age which remains unexplained after a thorough case investigation, including performance of a complete autopsy, examination of the death scene, and review of the clinical history."[8]

      C. Incidence — Estimated at approximately 2 per 1,000 live births in the United States; most common cause of death, in Western countries, of infants between 1 week and 1 year of age.

      D. The greatest number of deaths occurs between 2 and 4 months of age.

      E. Male predominance.

**TABLE 5.2   Diseases That May Result in Sudden, Natural Death in Pediatric
Population**

Cardiac	Infections (myocarditis, endocarditis, rheumatic fever)
	Congenital cardiac defects
	Cardiomyopathies
	Valvular abnormalities (aortic stenosis, mitral valve prolapse)
	Subaortic stenosis
	Tumors (rhabdomyoma, fibroma, myxoma)
	Conduction system disorders
	Endocardial fibroelastosis
	Emotional stress
Vascular	Aortic abnormalities (coarctation, supravalvular stenosis, cystic medial necrosis, aortitis)
	Coronary artery abnormalities (anomalies, hypoplasia or aplasia, arteritis, Kawasaki disease)
	Total anomalous pulmonary venous drainage
	Vascular malformations (especially cerebral AV malformations)
	Pulmonary hypertension
	Marfan's disease
Respiratory	Bronchial asthma
	Upper airway obstruction (congenital deformities, infections)
	Bronchopulmonary dysplasia
	Acute bronchopneumonia
	Massive pulmonary hemorrhage
	Idiopathic pulmonary hemosiderosis
	Tension pneumothorax
Central nervous system	Tumors (primary, metastatic)
	Epilepsy
	Infections (meningitis, encephalitis)
	Bleeding diatheses
	Tuberous sclerosis
Hematological	Hemoglobinopathies (sickle cell, CS disease)
	Lymphoma, leukemia
	Coagulation disorders (inherited and acquired; bleeding diatheses and hypercoagulable syndromes)
	Congenital asplenia
	Splenic rupture (Western countries — infectious mononucleosis, leukemia)
Gastrointestinal	Gastroenteritis with electrolyte abnormalities
	Intestinal obstruction (intussusception or volvulus with associated bowel infarction, sepsis)
	Late-presenting congenital diaphragmatic hernia
	Anorexia nervosa/malnutrition
Genitourinary	Primary renal disease (pyelonephritis, glomerulonephritis)
	Ovarian torsion
Metabolic/ endocrine	Fatty acid oxidation disorders (MCAD, LCAD)
	Carbohydrate disorders (galactosemia, glycogen storage disease)
	Amino acid disorders
	New onset diabetes mellitus
	Adrenal hypoplasia
	Reye syndrome
Miscellaneous	Chromosomal disorders (Down, fragile X, Turner syndrome)
	Anaphylaxis (food related — nuts, eggs, milk)

F. Higher occurrence in winter months of the year and in countries with colder climates.

G. Premature infants are at a higher risk, but in the majority of cases, the infant is full-term.

H. Maternal risk factors include:
    1. Low socioeconomic status
    2. Age less than 20 years at first pregnancy
    3. Cigarette smoking during and after pregnancy
    4. Use of illicit drugs (cocaine, heroin) during pregnancy

I. No apparent association between maternal caffeine or alcohol consumption during pregnancy and subsequent SIDS has been demonstrated.

J. Can occur at any time of the day, but the peak time is between midnight and the early morning hours.

K. In many cases, there is a history of minor respiratory or gastrointestinal illness in the days prior to death.

L. Sleeping position is alleged to play a role in the causation of SIDS.[9] Thus, the "Back-to-sleep" campaign. This concept may not be valid.[10]

M. Death usually occurs during sleep, without evidence of distress or a struggle.

N. May occur anywhere, including cribs or beds, automobiles, daycare centers, strollers, even in the arms of an adult.

O. **Diagnosis of SIDS is one of exclusion and cannot, therefore, be made without a complete autopsy, including microscopic and toxicologic testing.** In approximately 15% of cases where the initial impression is that of SIDS, another cause of death is found at autopsy.

P. Nonspecific gross findings which may be present include:
    1. Blood-tinged edema fluid at the nostrils or between the lips
    2. Hands clenched, with fingers curled to palms; occasionally fibers from the bedding may be found in the hand

Q. **Nonspecific** autopsy findings may include:
    1. Thymic, pleural, and epicardial petechiae; present in 70 to 95% of cases
    2. Congested or edematous lungs with edema froth in the tracheobronchial tree
    3. Sparse or focal submucosal chronic inflammation of the airways
    4. Gliosis of the brain stem

R. Scene investigation should be conducted in all cases of suspected SIDS. The investigation should include questions regarding:

1. Age of the infant; prior birth and medical history, including immunization history
2. The last time the infant was seen alive, and the time found deceased or unresponsive
3. The last time the infant was fed, amount and matter, and by whom
4. How the infant was put down (position and bed coverings), and how the infant was found
5. Whether the infant was sleeping alone
6. The type and condition of the bed and mattress
7. Temperature of the room
8. Whether resuscitation was attempted
9. The recent health of the infant (sniffles, cold, etc.)
10. Whether the infant was currently taking any medications, prescription or nonprescription
11. Whether any other family members had been sick
12. History of any other SIDS deaths in the family

S. In theory, the occurrence of repeat SIDS in the same family may be due to undetected or undiagnosed inherited metabolic disorders. Homicidal asphyxia (see Chapter 11) is more likely.

T. The exact cause of sudden infant death syndrome is unknown, despite many theories that have been proposed through the years. Multiple factors are probably involved. Some of the more popular theories proposed include:

1. Older theory of status thymolymphaticus — death thought to be due to enlarged thymus gland, in association with arterial and adrenal hypoplasia. This theory became obsolete when it was documented that the thymus is normally enlarged in healthy infants.

2. More recent theories
   a. Related to diphtheria-pertussis-tetanus (DPT) inoculations. Recent studies have disproved this theory.
   b. Idiopathic apnea — most cases subsequently proven to be due to repeat smothering episodes (Munchausen syndrome by proxy)
   c. Mechanical upper airway obstruction due to anatomical abnormalities such as narrow nasal passages, short mandibular rami, etc.
   d. Defective or immature brain stem respiratory or cardiac control centers
   e. Activation of the "diving" reflex
   f. Anaphylaxis

g. Adrenal insufficiency

h. Hyperthermia

i. Vitamin or trace metal deficiency

j. Gastroesophageal reflux leading to bradycardia and apnea

II. **OTHER DISORDERS ASSOCIATED WITH SUDDEN DEATH IN INFANTS AND CHILDREN**

A few of the entities listed in Table 5.2 are discussed in more detail below.

A. **Myocarditis** in infants and children is usually due to a viral agent (with the more common one being coxsackie B virus); can also be caused by certain bacteria and fungi.

1. In order to make the diagnosis, there should be an inflammatory infiltrate **and** myocyte necrosis.

2. The degree or amount of inflammation that may be present is variable and not always widespread.

B. **Conduction system disorders**

1. *Long QT syndrome (LQTS)*, characterized by syncope or sudden death occurring during physical activity or emotional distress

a. May be as frequent within the population as 1 in 5,000 children

b. May be inherited or acquired

i. The inherited form has two main varieties:

a. Romano-Ward variety, with normal hearing; autosomal dominant

b. Jervell and Lange-Nielsen syndrome with severe congenital deafness; autosomal recessive

ii. The acquired form may be seen with the use of certain medications, including erythromycin, antihistamines, epinephrine, amitriptyline, and others.

2. *Wolff-Parkinson-White syndrome* characterized by supraventricular tachycardia.

C. **Respiratory infections**

1. Acute **epiglottitis** in children is usually due to *H. influenzae*, type B, but cases due to pneumococcus, staphylococcus, and streptococcus have been reported. The postmortem blood cultures are positive in 50 to 75% of cases.

2. **Bacterial pneumonia.** The severity of the pneumonia may be masked in infants and children until the sudden development of respiratory distress. Ninety percent (90%) of the cases in children are due to *S. pneumoniae*.

3. **Interstitial pneumonitis** is usually due to a virus but may also be due to mycoplasma, rickettsia, or chlamydia. It can be ex-

tremely difficult to determine if the degree of peribronchial chronic inflammation present is greater than that which can be present in normal lungs and is therefore significant and a possible cause of death.

4. **Bronchiolitis** may cause sudden death due to apnea and respiratory arrest.
   a. Usually due to respiratory syncytial virus (RSV), in infants less than 6 months of age.
   b. Microscopic exam should show diffuse peribronchial and peribronchiolar chronic inflammatory infiltrate, which spills into the surrounding tissue; the lumina of the bronchi are usually obstructed by necrotic debris, mononuclear cells, and mucus.

D. **Spontaneous pneumothorax of the newborn** is known to occur in approximately 1 to 2% of live births, usually while the infant is still in the hospital nursery. The condition is usually benign and resolves without any severe sequelae. However, in some cases, the pneumothorax can cause sudden death and therefore should be suspected in any case where an apparently healthy newborn dies suddenly and unexpectedly. The diagnosis is easily made with a postmortem chest x-ray.

E. **Meningitis** may develop due to direct extension from a middle ear infection.
   1. Neonates and children rarely show classic signs of meningitis. They will usually have a vague history of poor appetite, irritability, and vomiting.
   2. At autopsy, the brain may be swollen and may or may not have an obvious purulent exudate.
   3. The middle ear should be opened and checked for possible infection.

F. **Gastroenteritis** can cause sudden death, if there is associated severe dehydration and electrolyte imbalance. In these cases, the vitreous electrolytes should be measured. A diagnosis of antemortem dehydration can be made if the vitreous sodium is greater than 155 mmol/l, the vitreous chloride is greater than 135 mmol/l, and the vitreous urea is greater than 40 mmol/l.

G. **Reye syndrome** — metabolic disorder of childhood of unknown etiology
   1. Characterized by acute onset of encephalopathy, associated with hypoglycemia and/or hyperammonemia, liver dysfunction, and fatty change of the viscera (liver, heart, kidney).
   2. Usually occurs in children less than 10 years of age.

  3. Often follows a viral illness (chicken pox, influenza).
  4. Symptoms include vomiting, irritability, lethargy, convulsions, coma.
  5. Consumption of aspirin (salicylate) is associated with an increased risk of the development of Reye syndrome.
  6. At autopsy, the liver may appear enlarged and yellow on cut section; brain may show marked cerebral edema.
  7. Microscopic exam shows hepatic steatosis characterized by microvesicular lipid deposition.
  8. Can be differentiated from other causes of hepatic steatosis by electron microscopy, if tissue preservation is good.
H. Autopsy findings that may suggest the presence of an inborn error of metabolism are:
  1. A family history of similar sudden death, especially in siblings
  2. An enlarged liver, heart, or spleen
  3. Dysmorphic features
  4. Pallor of the liver, heart, or muscles
  5. Cerebral edema
  6. Microscopic fatty change in the liver, heart, or smooth muscles

References

1. Di Maio, V.J.M. and Di Maio, D.J., Incidence of coronary thrombosis in sudden death due to coronary artery disease, *Am. J. For. Path. Med.*, 14(4), 273, 1993.

2. Bouchardy, B. and Majno, G., Histopathology of early myocardial infarcts. A new approach, *Am. J. Path.*, 74, 301, 1974.

3. Wagner, B.M., Left ventricular hypertrophy and sudden death, *Hum. Path.*, 17(1), 1, 1986.

4. Di Maio, T.M. and Di Maio, D.J., Sudden deaths due to colloid cysts of the third cerebral ventricle, *NY State Med. J.*, 74(10), 1832, 1974.

5. Di Maio, V.J.M., Sudden unexpected deaths due to massive non-traumatic intra-abdominal hemorrhage in association with cirrhosis of the liver, *Am. J. For. Med. Path.*, 8, 266, 1987.

6. Nestok, B.R., Goldstein, J.D., and Lipkovic, P., Splenic rupture as a cause of sudden death in undiagnosed chronic myelogenous leukemia, *Am. J. For. Med. Path.*, 9(3), 241, 1988.

7. Beckwith, J.B., The sudden infant death syndrome, *Curr. Prob. Ped.*, 3, 1, 1973.

8. Willinger, M., James, L.S., and Catz, C., Defining the sudden infant death syndrome (SIDS): Deliberations of an expert panel convened by the National Institute of Child Health and Human Development, *Ped. Path.*, 11, 677, 1991.

9. Taylor, B.J., A review of epidemiological studies of sudden infant death syndrome in Southern New Zealand, *J. Paediatrics & Child Health*, 27, 344, 1991.

10. Malloy, M.H. and MacDorman, M., Changes in the classification of sudden unexpected infant deaths: United States, 1992–2001, *Pediatrics*, 115(5), 1247, 2005.

General References

1. Di Maio, V.J.M. and Di Maio, D.J., *Forensic Pathology*, 2nd ed., CRC Press, Boca Raton, FL, 2001.

2. Byard, R.W. *Sudden Death in Infancy, Childhood and Adolescence*, 2nd ed., Cambridge University Press, Cambridge, UK, 2004.

Blunt Force Injury

6

I. DEFINITION

An injury produced by a blunt object striking the body or impact of the body against a blunt object or surface.

    A. The severity, extent, and appearance of the injury produced by blunt trauma is determined by:

        1. **Nature** of the weapon — A weapon with a flat surface, such as a board, diffuses the energy over a broader area, resulting in a less severe injury than one caused by a narrow object, such as a pipe, delivered with the same amount of energy. A weapon, which is easily deformed or broken upon impact, will deliver less energy to the impacted surface.

        2. **Amount of body surface** over which the force is delivered. The greater the area over which the force is delivered, the less severe the wound, as the force is dissipated. A blow delivered to a rounded portion of the body (i.e., head) will cause a more severe injury than one delivered to a flat surface (i.e., the back), where a larger area of contact leads to a dispersion of the force.

        3. **Amount of force** delivered to the body by the blow.

        4. **Time** over which the force is delivered. In general, if the period of time over which a force is delivered is *increased*, a less severe injury will result than if the same force was delivered in a *shorter* period of time.

        5. **Region** of body impacted by the blow.

    B. The injuries caused by blunt force trauma include:

        1. Abrasions

        2. Contusions

        3. Lacerations

        4. Fractures of the skeletal system

II. ABRASIONS

An abrasion (scrape) is caused when the superficial (epithelial) layer of the skin is scraped away, destroyed, or detached due to contact of the skin with a rough surface, by a sliding motion and/or occasionally by compression or pressure.

    A. Abrasions usually heal without significant scarring, but this is dependent upon the depth of injury.

    B. *Antemortem* abrasions appear reddish-brown, in contrast to *postmortem* abrasions, which usually appear yellow and/or translucent, due to a lack of blood flow. Postmortem insect bites, caused by ant or cockroach activity after death, can mimic true abrasions, and are often misinterpreted as such by inexperienced physicians and law enforcement personnel.

    C. Abrasions are *not* always produced by blunt force injury, despite direct contact of the skin with the blunt object or surface. Rarely, a portion of the skin scraped free may remain attached to the body, at the edge of an abrasion, thus indicating the direction in which the scrape occurred.

    D. Types of abrasions:

        1. **Scrape** (or brush) abrasions caused by a scraping-type of injury. May denude the epithelial layer only or extend deep into the dermis. Examples include linear abrasions, or **scratches**, **sliding** abrasions seen on lower extremities of pedestrian struck by motor vehicle, **dragging** abrasions (may be ante- or postmortem).

        2. **Brush burn** abrasion is a term commonly used to describe a scraping injury over a *large* area of the body, such as the back; such injuries, when dry, may be very firm, even though no true "scab" is present (**Figure 6.1**).

        3. **Impact** (pressure) abrasions are caused when the force is delivered perpendicular to the skin, so that the skin is crushed by the force, usually over a bony prominence. Impact abrasions may occur as a body collapses to the ground, or is thrown against a flat surface, at the time of death (perimortem), or immediately after death (postmortem).

        4. A **patterned** abrasion is a variation of the impact abrasion, where the pattern of the object, or pattern of an intermediary object such as clothing, is imprinted on the skin underlying the point of impact (**Figure 6.2**).

           a. Patterned injuries should be photographed from various angles, and directly with a scale, for size comparison, in the picture.

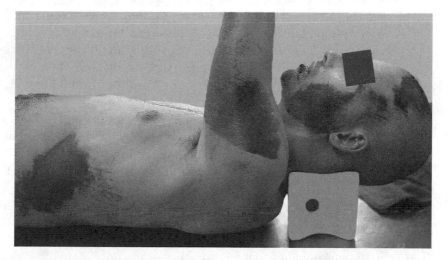

Figure 6.1 (See color insert following page 146) Motor vehicle passenger, ejected during collision with fixed object. Large brush burn abrasions from sliding across pavement.

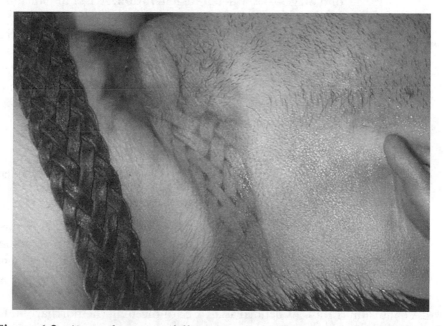

Figure 6.2 (See color insert following page 146) Patterned abrasion of neck produced by braided belt used as ligature.

b. The use of alternative light sources, such as UV light, may reveal, in some cases, patterned injuries not readily apparent with visible light.

E. **Stages in the healing** of abrasions. Healing proceeds in a fairly orderly and predictable manner, but the exact time and/or changes outlined below can vary greatly, depending upon numerous factors, including the preexisting physical or medical state of the victim, the severity of the injury, the location of the injury, secondary infection, and repeat trauma to the same area.

1. First Stage — **Scab** Formation. If fibrin, serum, and red blood cells accumulate on the surface of the abrasion, this is usually interpreted as "survival" following the injury.
   a. From *2 to 6 hours* after the injury, polymorphonuclear cells may infiltrate in a perivascular fashion.
   b. By *8 hours*, a zone of infiltrating polymorphonuclear cells is seen underlying the area of epithelial injury.
   c. At *12 hours*, collagen in the area of injury may stain abnormally.
   d. From *12 to 18 hours* post injury, the wound is progressively infiltrated by polymorphonuclear cells.

2. Second Stage — **Epithelial Regeneration**. Arises in hair follicles, and at the edges of the abrasion.
   a. May appear as early as *30 hours* post injury in superficial scrape abrasions
   b. Clearly visible by *72 hours* post injury in most abrasions

3. Third Stage — **Subepidermal Granulation**. Becomes prominent during *days 5 to 8*.
   a. Occurs only after epithelial covering of an abrasion.
   b. Perivascular infiltration and chronic inflammation is prominent.
   c. Overlying epithelium becomes more and more thickened with new keratin.
   d. Most prominent at *9 to 12 days* post injury.

4. Fourth Stage — **Regression**. Begins at about *12 days* post injury. Epithelium becomes thinner and occasionally atrophic. New collagen fibers are now prominent. Definite basement membrane is present, and vascularity of the dermis decreases.

III. CONTUSIONS

A contusion (bruise) is defined as an area of bleeding (hemorrhage) into the skin or soft tissue as a result of rupture of blood vessels due to blunt force injury, or pressure.

A. May be present on the skin, but can also occur within internal organs.

B. Focal *collection of blood* within an area of contusion is commonly referred to as a **hematoma**.

C. Extent and severity depends upon amount of force applied and the structure and vascularity of the tissue injured.

D. May or may not be **patterned**.

E. The site of the contusion does not necessarily correspond with the impact point, as bleeding within soft tissue will often follow the path of least resistance, or occur along fascial planes, i.e., the **Battle sign** where bleeding from a basilar skull fracture pools or appears behind and below the ear.

F. *Deep contusions* may not become visible externally until hours after infliction; after death, they may only be discovered, or demonstrated, upon incision of the skin and soft tissue in an area of suspected trauma.

G. May be difficult to see or demonstrate in dark-skinned individuals.

H. When present, a contusion indicates blunt force has been applied to a certain area, or the vicinity of the bruise (see E. above); however, a contusion, or other injury, does not always result from blunt force. Severe, forceful, sudden blunt force impact to the abdomen, and occasionally the chest, may cause massive damage to internal organs without producing any external injury.

I. Factors which may influence the *size* of a contusion:
   1. Amount of force applied; may or may not be directly proportional.
   2. Age of victim. Children and the elderly bruise more easily. **Senile ecchymoses on the upper extremities of elderly individuals may be caused by minor blunt trauma, or may occur spontaneously. They should *not* be interpreted as evidence of assault, unless they occur in an assaultive pattern (Figure 6.3).**
   3. Sex. Women tend to bruise more easily than men.
   4. Condition and health of the victim.
      a. *Obese* individuals, especially females, tend to bruise easier. Deep contusions in obese victims may not be readily apparent.
      b. *Muscular* individuals are less likely to bruise.
      c. Bleeding diatheses lead to easy bruising; i.e., alcoholics with cirrhosis, individuals taking aspirin or coumadin, platelet deficiencies, clotting disorders.
   5. Site and type of tissue injured or impacted. Loose, lax, or soft tissue is more easily bruised than firm, supported tissue.

J. Although rare, contusions may be *produced* postmortem if a severe blow is delivered to a body within a few hours after death.[1] They are most commonly seen in skin and/or soft tissue overlying bone or bony prominences. Microscopic examination of a contusion,

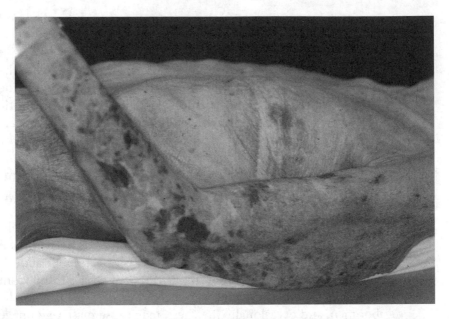

Figure 6.3 (See color insert following page 146) Multiple senile ecchymoses on upper extremity of elderly individual, associated with multiple hypopigmented scars.

in order to determine if it is ante- or postmortem, is usually nonproductive, unless obvious evidence (such as inflammatory infiltrate) is present. The presence of white blood cells in an area of contusion *must be interpreted with caution*, as some white blood cells may be deposited in the area of contusion by the mechanical disruption of blood vessels, and do not, therefore, represent a "vital reaction" to the injury.

K. Artifactual contusion-like injuries may be caused by postmortem removal of corneas or whole eyes for transplant and/or research purposes.

1. If removed very shortly after death, and if the head of the body is not elevated after removal, blood may flow into the thin, lax tissue of the eyelids and orbits, and on occasion produce "raccoon eyes."

2. Such postmortem artifacts may be difficult to explain to funeral directors or family members. They may be avoided by elevation of the head of the body immediately *after* removal.

L. Artifactual scleral hemorrhage or contusion may occur after postmortem removal of the vitreous fluid, especially when taken shortly after death.

M. **Color changes** in resolution of a contusion

1. Not always reliable as indicator of age of bruise

2. General color progression:
   a. Initially (minutes to hours) may be red, violaceous, purple, or dark blue.
   b. As the hemoglobin is broken down, may change to green, dark yellow, then pale yellow.
   c. Length of time for resolution may vary from several days to months.
   d. If photographed for documentation, a color scale should be included in the photo.
3. Consistent, reliable microscopic dating of contusions is not possible. Occasionally, microscopic examination of contusions may lead to false assumptions if this fact is not considered.

IV. LACERATIONS

A laceration is a tear in tissue produced by blunt force injury, such that tissue is stretched, crushed, sheared, or avulsed (**Figure 6.4**).

A. General features:
   1. Occur most commonly over bony prominences.
   2. Internal organs, and other structures such as mesentery, can be lacerated as well as skin.
   3. Characterized by strands of **"bridging"** tissue within the laceration; this feature is used to differentiate a laceration (tear)

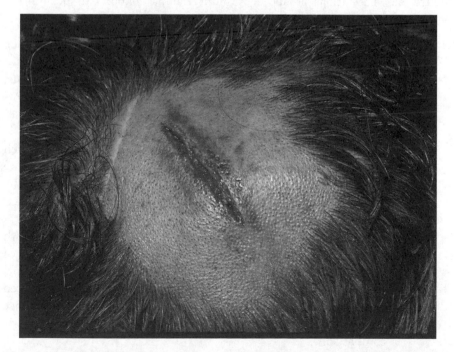

Figure 6.4 (See color insert following page 146) Simple laceration of posterior scalp.

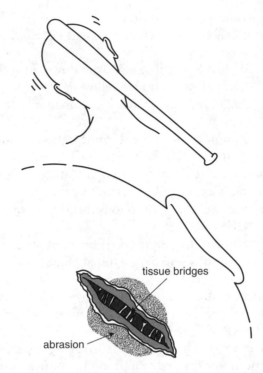

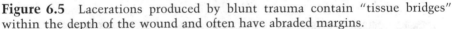

Figure 6.5   Lacerations produced by blunt trauma contain "tissue bridges" within the depth of the wound and often have abraded margins.

from an incised wound (cut) which lacks "bridging" tissue (**Figure 6.5**).

4. As a general rule in blows to the head, long, thin objects (bats, pool cues, pipes) tend to produce linear or elongated lacerations, while flat objects (or surfaces) tend to cause irregular, or Y-shaped lacerations.

5. A tangential or angled blow may produce a laceration which shows undermining of the tissue on one side or edge, with the other edge abraded or beveled. If present, the direction of the blow is from the abraded, beveled edge toward the undermined edge.

B. Edges and depth of laceration should be examined, if possible with a dissecting microscope or magnifying lens, for the presence of foreign matter such as wood splinters, paint chips, glass fragments or metal fragments, which may have been deposited or transferred from the weapon to the wound. If found, this trace evidence should be retained, labeled, and preserved for later evaluation or comparison.

C Age determination of lacerations is difficult, unless there are clear signs of healing, such as granulation tissue, fibroblast ingrowth, or organizing infiltrate.

V. COMBINATION INJURIES

In many cases of blunt trauma, abrasions, lacerations, and contusions will occur in combination with each other (**Figure 6.6**).

VI. BLUNT FORCE INJURY TO THE CHEST (THORAX)

A. Severe, sometimes massive, injury may occur to the intrathoracic organs in the *absence* of external evidence of injury. This may be due to:
   1. Clothing (type and thickness) worn.
   2. Age of victim may determine how pliable and deformable the chest wall is; children and young adults may have severe internal injuries without rib or sternal fractures, while these are more frequently found in older individuals.

B. **Rib** injuries
   1. Four classes or types of rib fractures exist:
      a. *Spontaneous*, or pathologic, rib fractures may occur with primary or metastatic tumors of the bone.

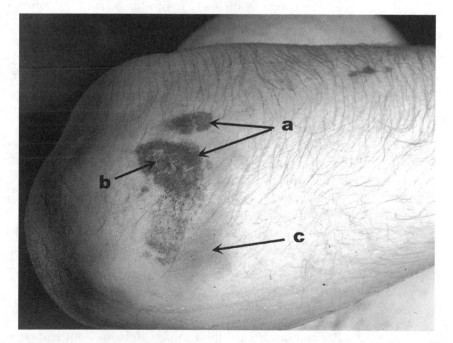

Figure 6.6 (See color insert following page 146) Abrasions, lacerations, and contusions may occur together in some cases. **a** — abrasions; **b** — laceration at center of an abrasion; **c** — contusion.

    b. *Therapeutic* (iatrogenic) rib fractures may be caused by cardiopulmonary resuscitation, especially in elderly individuals:
1. May be accompanied by sternal fractures, mediastinal and substernal hemorrhage, and pneumothorax.
2. Tend to be more left-sided than right, but can be bilateral, or only right-sided.
3. If present, the pathologist should be certain that CPR *was* administered before determining the fractures were due to resuscitation.

    c. Rib fractures due to *direct,* localized trauma:
1. May be simple, displaced, or compounded with projection through the pleura.
2. Usually lie immediately beneath the point of impact.
3. If compounded, may puncture underlying organs, leading to hemo- or pneumothoraces.
4. Fractures of ribs 1–3 are frequently associated with severe injuries of the trachea, and great vessels of the upper chest (aorta, vena cava, subclavian veins).
5. Fractures of ribs 10–12 may be associated with injuries of the spleen, liver, and diaphragm.

    d. Rib fractures due to *indirect* trauma. Compression, or squeezing, of the chest can cause rib fractures.
1. If compression is *front to back* (anteroposterior), lateral rib fractures may result.
2. If compression is *back to front*, the ribs tend to fracture near the spine.
3. If compression is *side to side*, the ribs may fracture near the spine and sternum.

  2. Complications of rib fractures:
    a. **"Flail chest"** — Collapse of the chest wall, making breathing impossible. Usually the fractures are extensive (2–9), and bilateral, both anterior and posterior. Flail chest also leads to a decreased blood return to the right atrium.
    b. Lacerations of the intercostal vessels leading to hemothorax.
    c. Lacerations of the lungs, leading to pneumothorax or hemopneumothorax.
    d. Pneumonia due to "splinting," with or without empyema.
    e. Impaling wounds of the heart.

C. **Sternal fractures:**
  1. Due to *direct* trauma:

      a. Are usually transverse
      b. Are found usually in body of sternum
      c. May occur from severe injury to the anterior chest or from severe anterior-posterior compression
   2. May be iatrogenic, due to CPR. These sternal fractures usually occur at the level of the third or fourth interspace (mid-level of body of sternum).
  D. **Heart** and **pericardium:**
   1. Cardiac injury can result from:
      a. *Direct* force to anterior thorax (blows, automobile crashes where driver, usually unrestrained, is thrown against steering wheel or passenger impacts dashboard, falls from great height, etc.)
      b. *Deceleration* forces
      c. *Compression* (crushing) of heart between sternum and vertebral column
      d. *Blast* injury to the chest
      e. *Indirect* force, such as sudden forceful compression of the abdomen, or lower extremities causing a rapid return of blood to the right heart leading to high right intraventricular pressure and possible cardiac damage
      f. A combination of any of the above mechanisms
   2. Nature of injury to the heart depends on:
      a. The severity of the localized trauma
      b. Whether or not the heart is filled with blood at impact
      c. Whether or not the force is severe enough to compress the heart between the sternum and vertebral column
   3. **Myocardial contusion** results from sufficiently severe direct trauma to the heart.
      a. The force is usually directed from front to back, resulting in contusion of the anterior ventricles or interventricular septum. If the heart is driven against the vertebral column, a posterior contusion may occur.
      b. *Recent* contusions are dark red, hemorrhagic, predominantly subepicardial; larger contusions may be transmural.
      c. May grossly simulate myocardial infarction, but are usually more hemorrhagic, and transition from normal to injured tissue is more abrupt upon microscopic exam. Should be associated with evidence of trauma to the anterior chest wall, but not always.

d. Areas of subendocardial hemorrhage may be caused by open heart massage and should not be confused with antemortem contusion.

4. **Myocardial laceration** occurs more frequently if the heart is filled with blood at the moment of impact, as a result of bursting force within the chambers.

 a. Lacerations may involve ventricles, atria, interatrial and interventricular septa, valves, and papillary muscles, either singularly or in combination.

 b. If cardiac laceration occurs in the absence of pericardial laceration, **cardiac tamponade** may result.

  1. As little as 150 cc of intrapericardial hemorrhage may cause death.

  2. More likely to result in death if laceration occurs in thin-walled chambers such as the atria or right ventricle.

  3. Cardiac tamponade causes death by increasing the intrapericardial pressure and producing progressive external compression of the heart, with subsequent inadequate filling of the chambers. Intrapericardial hemorrhage can also cause mechanical interference with ventricular myocontractility.

 c. Cardiac **valvular lacerations** are uncommon with severe blunt force injury, but are known to occur in approximately 5% of cases, and are usually associated with other severe cardiac injuries.

  1. Mitral valve most commonly lacerated.

  2. Tricuspid and pulmonary valves are rarely ruptured.

  3. Diseased valves are more likely to be injured than non-diseased valves.

  4. If initial injury was incomplete, latent rupture may occur several days later.

  5. Lacerations of valve cusps, leaflets, chordae tendineae or papillary muscles usually result in rapid cardiac failure.

5. **Cardiac concussion** can occur after a sudden, forceful impact directed at the mid-anterior chest wall in the region of the heart.

 a. Also called "commotio cordis."

 b. The trauma is usually of insufficient force to cause gross or microscopic cardiac damage, although chest wall, and/or substernal hemorrhage may be present, occasionally accompanied by sternal fracture.

    c.   Mechanism of death is ventricular fibrillation or asystole.

6. **Pericardial lacerations:**
   a. Can be superficial (nontransmural), penetrating or perforating
   b. Can be single or multiple
   c. Can vary in length from less than one centimeter up to several centimeters
   d. Tend to be linear and not stellate
   e. Can occur alone, but are usually associated with cardiac and/or intrapericardial great vessel injury
   f. If transmural, depending on location of laceration, lead to right or left hemothorax or hemomediastinum

E. **Aortic** injuries caused by blunt trauma tend to be lacerations.
   1. Occur most commonly as a result of vehicular accident, and less commonly in falls.
   2. Lacerations tend to be transverse and may be associated with rib and/or vertebral fractures.
   3. In motor vehicle accidents, impact is usually frontal but can also be found in side impacts.
   4. Most common site of laceration is in the descending thoracic aorta, just distal to the origin of the left subclavian artery.
      a. Arch of aorta is anchored by the great vessels arising from the arch, and by the *ligamentum arteriosum.*
      b. Usually seen in acceleration-deceleration incidents, such as motor vehicle accidents, suggesting the heart and great vessels are forcefully pulled away from the posterior chest wall where the descending thoracic is anchored, leading to incomplete laceration or complete transection.
   5. Bursting lacerations in the root of the aorta, ascending aorta, or aortic arch may be caused by sudden compression of the heart with subsequent sudden increase in intra-aortic pressure. These lacerations are usually not circumferential, but are usually rapidly fatal.
   6. Nontransmural (usually intimal) lacerations:
      a. May heal without sequelae, resulting in a fibrous intimal scar which may be found incidentally at autopsy
      b. May slowly erode through the vessel wall, leading to delayed extra-vascular hemorrhage or exsanguination
      c. May progress to form a "false aneurysm" which may stabilize or subsequently rupture

        d. May cause a post-traumatic aortic dissection (also termed post-traumatic dissecting aortic aneurysm)

    7. Traumatic laceration/rupture of the aorta should not be confused with spontaneous rupture due to natural disease, such as cystic medial necrosis, atherosclerosis, or syphilis.

        a. Microscopic examination should disclose features of natural disease.

        b. Presence of other traumatic injuries supports traumatic origin of aortic laceration.

        c. Although natural aortic disease may be present, aortic rupture/laceration may still be due to trauma, but the possible predisposition to rupture created by the natural disease may be a contributing factor to the rupture.

F. **Diaphragmatic** injuries caused by blunt trauma:

    1. Are usually lacerations due to rupture

    2. May be unilateral or bilateral, anterior or posterior

    3. Caused by blunt force to lower anterior chest which causes an overstretching and twisting of the leaflets

    4. Frequently associated with rib fractures and injuries of the thoracic and abdominal organs

    5. Can also be caused by severe, sudden blunt abdominal trauma with increased intra-abdominal pressure and upward displacement of abdominal viscera

    6. Ruptured/lacerated diaphragm may allow displacement of abdominal organs into the thoracic cavities:

        a. More common on the *left*, where stomach, spleen, intestine, and/or omentum is displaced into the chest cavity, with or without accompanying hemorrhage.

        b. On the right, due to its size, the liver is less likely to be displaced, unless extensively lacerated, and/or the diaphragmatic laceration is large.

G. **Pulmonary** (respiratory tract) injuries caused by blunt trauma:

    1. Displaced rib fractures may puncture (lacerate) lung tissue, leading to various **complications**:

        a. Pneumothorax, hemothorax, or hemopneumothorax

            1. Pneumothorax is most often of the "tension" type, leading to mediastinal shift, lung collapse, and downward bowing of the diaphragm on the side of tension.

            2. *Tension pneumothorax* can lead to severe cardiac arrhythmias and rapid asystole if not decompressed.

    b.   Emphysema (subcutaneous, interstitial, mediastinal). *Subcutaneous emphysema* can be massive and may be *only* external sign of significant intrathoracic injury.

    c.   Intraparenchymal hemorrhage

    d.   Air embolism

    e.   Late sequelae, including infection with or without abscess

    f.   If intercostal vessels or internal mammary arteries are lacerated, significant hemothoraces may result

2. Pulmonary contusions and lacerations:

    a.   May result from sudden, violent chest compression, or a forceful blow to the chest, especially if the glottis is closed at the time of impact.

    b.   May be gross or microscopic; focal or diffuse.

    c.   May be located centrally or peripherally or both.

    d.   A pure, simple pulmonary contusion usually resolves rapidly without scarring. Improvement occurs within 48 h, with near complete resolution a few days later.

3. Occasionally, old pleural adhesions may be stretched and lacerated by blunt chest trauma. If the adhesion is very vascular, significant intrapleural hemorrhage may result.

4. Preexisting pulmonary disease (emphysema, tuberculosis, infection with abscess) can predispose the lungs to damage by blunt trauma of less severity than that necessary to produce a similar injury in a healthy, elastic lung.

5. Rupture of the intrathoracic trachea and bronchi requires a severe compressive injury of the chest.

    a.   Not commonly seen.

    b.   Most usual site of rupture is within 2.5 cm of the carina.

    c.   Combined injury of trachea and bronchi is infrequent.

    d.   In 30% of the cases, fractures of the second and third ribs are also present.

VII. BLUNT FORCE INJURY TO THE ABDOMEN

If blunt force is directed at the anterior or lateral abdominal walls, the force is readily transmitted to the internal organs, as the abdominal walls are relatively compressible and lax in most individuals. Tensing of the abdominal muscles may prevent internal injuries, if the blow is anticipated.

    A. The *severity* of the injury is dependent on:

       1. Force of the impact

       2. Site of impact

       3. Size, and to some degree the consistency and shape, of the blunt object

4. The organ injured, and its condition at the time of injury (i.e., a spleen enlarged and swollen by infectious mononucleosis may rupture with less trauma)

    a. Organ consistency. Solid organs (liver, spleen) are more readily lacerated than hollow organs (such as the empty stomach or intestines).

    b. Organ mobility. A fixed retroperitoneal duodenum is more readily injured than a movable, displaceable ileum or jejunum.

    c. Organ distention. As a rule, the more distended a hollow viscus (such as the stomach or urinary bladder), the greater the likelihood of rupture with blunt force.

B. ABSENCE OF EXTERNAL INJURY TO THE ABDOMINAL WALL DOES NOT EXCLUDE INTERNAL, SOMETIMES MASSIVE, INJURY.

    1. Probably due to compressive, absorbable nature of abdominal wall

    2. May be also due to presence of clothing

C. Abdominal trauma may be diffuse and generalized, or localized, such as when an individual is kicked in the abdomen. (Most homicides attributed to blunt abdominal trauma involve *localized* injury.)

D. Rarely, hepatic lacerations, sometimes with intra-abdominal hemorrhage, can be caused by misplaced, aggressive CPR. The amount of intra-abdominal bleeding is small. Resuscitative injuries of other abdominal organs, including the spleen, are uncommon.

E. **Hepatic** injuries:

    1. The liver is the most frequently injured, by blunt trauma, of the abdominal organs.

    2. The liver is partially protected from trauma by the lower ribs and sternal xiphoid process.

    3. Blunt force hepatic injuries may be classified as:

        a. Transcapsular (both capsule and parenchyma are lacerated)

        b. Subcapsular (capsule intact, underlying or deep parenchymal lacerations present)

    4. Preexisting disease, such as severe fatty infiltration, may make the liver more susceptible to blunt trauma.

    5. Right lobe injured more than left (5 to 1).

    6. Most injuries occur on convex (domed) surfaces.

    7. A *subcapsular hematoma* may result from blunt trauma:

        a. May resolve without further complications

       h. May continue to enlarge, and possibly rupture, sometimes days after the initial trauma, leading to fatal intraperitoneal hemorrhage

  8. Complete separation of the right and left lobes of the liver may result from a severe, crushing force applied to the anterior aspect of the liver, such that the liver is crushed between the anterior abdominal wall and the vertebral column.

  9. Injuries of the portal vein, hepatic artery, and inferior vena cava may occur, but isolated injuries of these vessels are extremely rare.

10. The amount of energy necessary to produce hepatic injury was explored experimentally by Mays.[2] He reported:

    a. Energy in the range of *27 to 34 ft lb* produced tears and lacerations of the capsule, but no damage to the vascular and biliary trees.

    b. Energy in the range of *106 to 134 ft lb* creviced the liver externally, occasionally disrupted a small bile duct or hepatic artery, but still did not injure the major vascular or biliary trees.

    c. Energy in the range of *285 to 360 ft lb* burst and pulped the liver, causing severe disruption of tributaries of the portal vein, bile ducts, and hepatic artery, but the major vessels and ducts remained mostly intact.

11. Isolated traumatic rupture of the **gallbladder** is uncommon:

    a. Isolated rupture is reportedly more common in children and young adults.

    b. Leakage of bile into the abdomen may cause a chemical peritonitis.

F. Blunt force injury of the **spleen:**

  1. More protected, and, therefore, less frequently injured than the liver.

  2. Force is directed at left upper abdomen or left inferolateral chest wall.

  3. Injuries may range from small superficial capsular tears up to massive rupture, with pulpification, and virtual disintegration.

  4. Can see parenchymal laceration without capsular injury.

  5. Subcapsular hematoma may occur as in liver, with similar outcome (see E.7 above).

  6. Normal spleens do not rupture spontaneously. Certain diseases which render the spleen susceptible to rupture after relatively minor trauma include:

    a. Infectious mononucleosis

      b.   Malaria

      c.   Typhoid fever

      d.   Hemophilia

      e.   Leukemia

G. **Pancreatic** injuries due to blunt trauma can occur, but are encountered less frequently than those of the liver or spleen. This is in part due to its relatively protected location in the retroperitoneum and relative fixation to the posterior abdominal wall.

  1. Severe, direct force to the upper mid abdomen can injure the body of the pancreas as it crosses the vertebral column in the vicinity of the second lumbar vertebra. Lacerations, contusions, and occasionally transection can occur.

  2. Isolated injuries of the head or tail of the pancreas occur much less frequently, unless massive abdominal trauma has occurred.

  3. Lacerated pancreatic ducts can exude pancreatic secretions into the abdominal cavity resulting in a severe chemical peritonitis as well as mesenteric and omental fat necrosis.

  4. Pancreatic contusion can cause thrombosis of the splenic artery or vein, with subsequent splenic infarcts if the individual survives.

  5. Late complication of pancreatic trauma may be formation of a pseudocyst.

      a.   The pseudocyst can be peripancreatic or intrapancreatic;

      b.   Majority of pancreatic pseudocysts are due to pancreatitis, and not trauma.

H. **Gastrointestinal tract** injuries due to blunt trauma:

  1. Esophageal injury secondary to blunt trauma is unusual, unless the trauma is massive and diffuse, as in vehicular accidents.

  2. **Mallory–Weiss** Syndrome — Repeated, violent retching (vomiting) can cause lacerations and/or perforations of the lower esophagus at or near the gastroesophageal (GE) junction.

      a.   The lacerations are usually single, longitudinal, and located on the lateral or posterior wall of the esophagus.

      b.   Lacerations may be superficial (mucosal) or more extensive (transmural).

      c.   Most frequently seen in alcoholics after bouts of prolonged vomiting.

      d.   Rupture may progress to mediastinal emphysema, bilateral hydrothorax, hydropneumothorax, or massive hemorrhage. If the individual survives the acute rupture, a potentially lethal complication is fulminant mediastinitis.

3. Gastric injuries due to blunt force trauma are generally due to a localized, directed force to the epigastric region or left upper abdominal quadrant, as the greater part of the stomach (fundus and body) is protected by the ribs.
   a. At impact, stomach may be crushed between anterior abdominal wall and vertebral column.
   b. Can be contused, lacerated, ruptured.
   c. In most cases of rupture, the stomach is distended with food and/or fluid, and the *anterior* wall is most often the site of rupture.
4. The phenomenon of **esophagogastromalacia** is occasionally seen in individuals who die within hours or days after receiving severe head trauma with cerebral injury (comatose), and has also been reported in debilitated individuals.
   a. Due to autodigestion of the lower esophagus and/or stomach with thinning, and disruption of the wall.
   b. Stomach usually more often involved than esophagus.
   c. Stomach contents spilled into left chest cavity or left subphrenic area as a result of disruption of the lower esophagus or stomach.
   d. Involved tissue is grayish white to black in color, and extremely friable.
   e. No microscopic evidence of inflammation.
   f. May occur immediately prior to death or shortly after death.
   g. Of no clinical significance, but may be misinterpreted at autopsy as significant antemortem injury if not recognized as an agonal or postmortem artifact.
5. **Small bowel** injuries due to blunt force
   a. Duodenal injuries:
      1. Most common site injured is in the area of the ligament of Treitz, at or near the duodenojejunal flexure.
      2. Injury ranges from contusion, to perforation, to transection if the bowel is crushed between the anterior abdominal wall and vertebral column.
      3. Contusion may progress to perforation if tissue is significantly devitalized. Delayed perforation may occur hours to days after the initial impact.
   b. Small bowel distal to the duodenum (jejunum and ileum) may be crushed between the anterior abdominal wall and vertebral column or pelvis by severe abdominal impact.

         1. Resulting injuries include contusions, lacerations, transections, perforations (blowouts).
         2. Dependent on severity of force and area over which it is applied (diffuse versus directed).
         3. Contusion and/or subtransmural laceration may progress to a delayed perforation and peritonitis.
         4. Transection of the jejunum, if present, usually occurs just distal to the ligament of Treitz.

    6. **Mesenteric** injury can result from severe blunt abdominal trauma.
        a. Injuries range from contusion to laceration, to avulsion.
        b. May be multiple or singular, large or small.
        c. Mesenteric laceration can be, and often is, accompanied by intraperitoneal hemorrhage. **Laceration of a single large mesenteric blood vessel (usually artery) can result in death, even in the absence of other significant injuries, with the mechanism of death massive intraperitoneal hemorrhage.**

    7. **Colonic** injuries:
        a. The large bowel, in general, is less exposed to blunt injury by virtue of its position in the body.
        b. The mid portion of the transverse colon may be injured as it is crushed between the anterior abdominal wall and the vertebral column.
        c. Injury ranges from contusion, to laceration (mucosal or transmural), to transection.
        d. Rupture of the colon due to an externally applied blunt force is unlikely, due to the potential large intraluminal volume present. If, however, fecal impaction is present, or volvulus, leading to overdistention of the bowel proximal to the blockage, rupture is much more likely if blunt force is applied.

I. Blunt force injury to the **kidneys** is uncommon, but can occur.
    1. May be seen in motor vehicle mishaps, falls from great heights, and if blunt force is directed to the side or flank region of the body.
    2. Children and young adults are more likely to suffer renal injury than older individuals.
    3. Most common injury is contusion.
    4. May find small transverse lacerations with insignificant hemorrhage, and an intact capsule.

5. Massive injury (fragmentation, transection, avulsion) is uncommon but, when present, is usually associated with massive injury of the other abdominal organs or body (i.e., plane crashes, parachutists).

6. Spontaneous rupture of a normal kidney does not occur.

7. Multiple renal infarcts may develop as a result of renal artery thrombosis secondary to blunt abdominal trauma.

J. The **adrenal glands** are susceptible to blunt trauma directed in the vicinity of the kidneys.

   1. Adrenal injuries can range from contusion, to laceration, to rupture, with or without peri-adrenal hemorrhage.

   2. *Unsuspected* adrenal injury, especially with hemorrhage, necrosis or infarction of the cortex and/or medulla, can lead to numerous clinical abnormalities.

K. Severe blunt trauma to the lower abdomen and pelvis can lacerate and/or rupture the **urinary bladder.**

   1. In adults, the empty urinary bladder is protected by the pelvic bone. When distended, the bladder rises into the lower abdominal cavity.

   2. Two types of rupture are possible, depending upon the volume of urine in the bladder at the moment of impact;

      a. *Extraperitoneal* rupture occurs when the bladder is empty or filled with only a small amount of urine;

         1. Usually associated with fractures of the pelvis

         2. May occur without pelvic fracture if force is directed downward into the lower abdominal wall, behind the pubic bone

      b. *Intraperitoneal* rupture occurs if the bladder is expanded, or significantly distended, with urine at the moment of impact.

         1. Bladder is compressed against sacrum, leading to over-expansion and rupture.

         2. Ruptures produced usually occur in the superior or posterior aspects of the bladder.

   3. Bladder rupture can lead to hemorrhage with primary shock, and rapid death. If the individual survives the acute phase, late complications include sepsis, peritonitis, and ascending renal infection.

VIII. **BLUNT FORCE INJURY TO THE GENITALIA (INTERNAL AND EXTERNAL)**

A. Male genitalia

1. Forceful blows to the male *external* genitalia can cause total or subtotal amputation. Blows of less force cause abrasions and lacerations (penile or scrotal), and contusions with or without scrotal hematomas.
2. A wide range of injuries can occur to the male *internal* genitalia.
   a. Injury produced depends on the severity of the blow and the structure injured.
   b. Injuries include contusion, laceration of ductal structures and parenchyma, testicular hematomas, interstitial hemorrhage.
3. In rare cases, a kick or blow to the scrotal region can cause immediate death, due to cardiac asystole:[3]
   a. Blow to the testicles initiates simultaneous stimulation of the vagi.
   b. Hypervagal stimulation is presumed to cause cardiac standstill.
4. In cases of assault, deaths during altercations with law enforcement personnel, or any unusual sudden death, the genitalia should be carefully examined. If no external injuries are present, small posterior incisions into the scrotum should be made in order to rule out internal injury.

B. Female genitalia
   1. Injuries to the *external* female genitalia, due to blunt force, if present, are usually due to sexual assault.
      a. Injuries include contusions, lacerations, and/or abrasions.
      b. If present and possibly related to sexual assault, the injuries should be extensively photographed (with and without comparison scale) *before* proceeding with collection of trace evidence which may be present, or internal manipulation.
   2. Blunt force injury of the *internal* genitalia in a nonpregnant female, can occur, but is rare.
   3. Blunt force injury to the *pregnant* uterus and/or fetus occurs more often, especially as a result of vehicular accidents, and less commonly due to falls or assaults.
      a. Mechanism of fetal death is placental separation with rapid or delayed intrauterine death.
      b. Following intrauterine death, labor usually begins within 48 hours, but may be delayed for as long as a few weeks.
      c. If pelvic fractures result from the blunt trauma, direct fatal injury is possible.

IX. SKELETAL FRACTURES DUE TO BLUNT FORCE TRAUMA
A. Bone fractures are caused by *direct* and *indirect* trauma.
  1. *Direct* trauma is subdivided into three types, depending on the amount of force applied and the size of the area impacted:
    a. *Focal* (tapping) fracture — produced by small force striking a small area:
      1. Usually transverse
      2. In regions where two bones lie adjacent to each other, usually only one bone is fractured
    b. *Crush* fracture — produced by a great force striking a large area:
      1. Usually comminuted
      2. Usually accompanied by soft tissue injury
    c. *Penetrating* fracture — produced by a great force striking a small area (i.e., gunshot wound).
  2. *Indirect* trauma is produced by a force acting at a location removed from the fracture site. Subdivided into (6) categories:
    a. *Traction* fracture — bone pulled apart
    b. *Angulation* fracture — bone is bent until it snaps; usually a transverse fracture is produced
    c. *Rotational* fracture — bone is twisted, producing a spiral fracture
    d. *Vertical compression* fracture — produces an oblique fracture of the body of long bones; in the femur, this produces a T-shaped fracture at the distal end of the bone
    e. *Angulation* and *compression* fractures are usually curved, not transverse
    f. *Angulation, rotation,* and *compression* fractures
B. Vertebral column fractures are usually *indirect*, except for those produced by gunshot wounds, which are direct.
  1. Vertebral column mobility is greatest in the *cervical* region, least in the *thoracic* region, and intermediate in the *lumbar* region.
  2. Most common spinal fracture is *anterior compression* fracture of the vertebral body at or near the thoracic/lumbar junction; this fracture is most common in individuals of middle age or older, and can follow minor trauma in older individuals with osteoporosis.[4]
C. Pelvic fractures
  1. Are caused by *direct*, or *indirect* (through force applied to lower extremities) trauma
  2. Usually require great force to be produced

   3. Can be subdivided into (3) major types:[4,5]
      a. **Open-book** fracture — produced by anterior-posterior compression with fracture separation of symphysis pubis;
      b. **Lateral compression** fractures:
         1. If lateral force is applied to the iliac crest, usually the ipsilateral pubic rami are fractured and the ipsilateral sacroiliac joint is impacted; less frequently, there may be fracture of the contralateral pubic rami, or fracture of all (4) pubic rami.
         2. If the force is to the femoral head such that it is driven into the acetabulum, then usually acetabular fractures result as well as fractures of the ipsilateral pelvic rami and disruption/impaction of the sacroiliac joints.
      c. **Vertical shear** fractures are produced by an extremely severe force vertically displacing one hemipelvis in relation to the other:
         1. Anterior disruption of symphysis and/or pubic rami
         2. Posterior gross disruption of the sacroiliac joints or fractures of adjacent sacrum or ilium
         3. Usually accompanied by massive hemorrhage
   4. To evaluate pelvic fractures at autopsy, soft tissue should be scraped away in the area of suspected fracture, so direct visualization of the fracture is possible.
   5. Most frequent complication of pelvic fracture is hemorrhage, and in severe fractures, severe hemorrhage almost always occurs.
      a. The fatality rate from hemorrhage associated with pelvic fracture, with current management techniques, ranges from 5 to 20%.[6]
      b. In cases of severe pelvic fracture, it is not uncommon to see a two to three liter hemorrhage from small vessel venous and arterial sources.
      c. **Massive intraperitoneal and retroperitoneal hemorrhage resulting from severe pelvic fracture may be the only finding, and, therefore, the cause of death, in some traumatic deaths.**
D. Fractures of the extremities will be discussed below in Section X.
E. Occasionally, the presence of certain specific fractures may provide a clue as to the mechanism of injury. Some examples include:
   1. A fall on the outstretched hand can cause a fracture of the distal radius (i.e., *Colle's* fracture).

   2. Fractures of the metacarpal bones occur most commonly by striking the closed hand (fist) against a firm surface ("boxer" fracture).

   3. Fractures of the heels (calcaneal) can occur in falls from a great height, when landing on the feet in a relatively upright position.

X. EXTREMITY INJURIES DUE TO BLUNT FORCE TRAUMA

May be superficial (skin and subcutaneous tissue) or deep (involving muscle, blood vessels, bone, nerves).

   A. **Lower extremity** injuries may be

     1. Abrasions, contusions, lacerations

     2. Avulsive injuries, as in auto-pedestrian mishaps; may be superficial or deep, with creation of blood and crushed fat filled subcutaneous pocket beneath intact skin

     3. Fractures:

       a. **"Bumper" fractures** may be produced by the front end of a moving vehicle (i.e., automobile or truck) striking an upright individual.

         1. The severity of the injury depends on:

           a. Speed of the vehicle

           b. Shape of the bumper

           c. Age of the pedestrian

           d. Amount of clothing covering the area of the body impacted

         2. If fractures result, bone fragments may or may not be displaced, and the skin opposite the site of impact may be lacerated.

         3. If the impact creates a wedge-shaped bone fragment at the point of impact, the apex of the fragment usually points in the direction the vehicle was traveling.

         4. *If lower extremity fractures are present at autopsy, the distance of the fractures (or any patterned abrasion or contusion) above the heel should be measured and recorded.*

       b. Ankle fractures may be found in autopsies performed on drivers of motor vehicles (or occasionally their passengers) or pilots. These fractures suggest the feet were braced or firmly applied to regulating devices (such as brake or accelerator pedals, or rudders) at impact. The soles of the shoes should be examined for patterned marks corresponding to the object the foot was pressed against.

    c.   Patellar, femoral fractures (open or closed) may be found in automobile/truck mishaps where the knee and lower extremity impact the dashboard.

4. Possible complications of lower extremity injuries:

    a.   Hemorrhagic shock due to massive soft tissue crush injury or lacerated/transected major artery.

    b.   Pulmonary embolus may result in delayed death.

    c.   Fat embolization may result in the **fat embolization syndrome.**

        i.   Classically, the syndrome of fat embolization has (3) main symptoms or signs:

           a.   Pulmonary distress — present in 75% of cases.

           b.   Cerebral signs — occur in 86% of cases, vary from confusion, lethargy, convulsions, to coma.

           c.   Petechial rash — 50% of cases. Rash is on mucous membranes and/or skin of the anterior chest and neck.

       ii.   The symptoms become manifest 24 to 48 hours *after* injury.

      iii.   The incidence of the syndrome increases as the number of fractures increases.

      iv.   The syndrome is more likely to occur after pelvic or lower limb fractures, and is seldom seen with isolated fracture of an upper limb.

      v.   The syndrome is *rare* in children.[7]

      vi.   At autopsy, gross evidence of cerebral fat embolization may appear as multiple punctate hemorrhages (petechiae) on the cut surfaces of the brain, mostly within the white matter.

      vii. At autopsy, the diagnosis of fat embolization may be made by demonstration of fat globules in capillaries of the lung, brain, kidney, and skin, usually through a fat stain. If fat embolization is suspected, frozen portions of lung, brain, and kidney should be retained for fat stain, such as Oil Red O.

      viii. In some cases, small fragments of bone and bone marrow will be readily apparent in pulmonary vessels with routine stains. These emboli can also be seen following aggressive resuscitation, which may make differentiation as to their source difficult.

    d.   Infection — more common in open wounds than in crushing injuries with intact skin

      c. Rhabdomyolysis resulting from *severe* crush injury

B. **Upper extremity** blunt force injuries may occur in vehicular accidents, falls, or assaults.

  1. **"Defense"** wounds to upper extremities include contusions, abrasions, lacerations of the backs of hands, forearms, or upper arms, fractured fingers and/or fingernails.

  2. **"Offensive"** wounds are mostly to the hands, and include abrasions, contusions of knuckles, or fractures of metacarpal bones.

  3. Potentially lethal complications of upper extremity injuries are mostly infection (if open wounds are present), and occasionally exsanguination if a major artery is lacerated or severed (i.e., brachial artery) with or without amputation.

XI. **HEAD INJURIES CAUSED BY BLUNT FORCE TRAUMA**

A. The *scalp* may be contused (with or without hematoma), abraded, or lacerated (with or without avulsion).

  1. Possible significant complications include hemorrhage and infection.

  2. **In cases of homicide with head trauma, always retain a sample of the victim's head hair, pulled from an area adjacent to the area of trauma.** This sample may become a very significant part of the investigation, should a possible weapon or impact surface be found at a later date.

B. Skull fractures

  1. The *probability* that a skull fracture will occur with blunt impact is dependent on:

    a. The severity of the blow (velocity at impact)

    b. The object impacted, or impacting the head (weight, shape, consistency)

    c. The amount and thickness of the hair at the impact site

    d. The thickness of the scalp at the impact site

    e. The thickness and shape of the skull at the impact site

    f. The age of the victim (elasticity, brittleness of the bone)

  2. The presence of a linear skull fracture does not always correlate with significant cerebral injury or loss of consciousness. The reverse is also true — death due to severe brain injury can occur in the absence of a skull fracture.

  3. Skull fractures produced by blunt force trauma begin at the impact point, radiating outward.

  4. If the skull impacts a hard, unyielding surface, *33 to 75 ft lb* of energy is needed to produce a single linear fracture of the skull. For example, a 6-foot-tall man with a 10 lb head free falling onto his back generates 60 ft lb of energy. With the velocity of

the head at impact about 20 ft/sec or 13.5 mph, there is ample energy to produce a posterior linear skull fracture. If the skull impacts a soft, yielding surface, *268 to 581 ft lb* of energy is required to produce a skull fracture, with the impact velocity about 29 to 45 mph.[8]

5. Skull fractures can result from low-, intermediate-, and high-velocity blows or impacts.
   a. High-velocity impacts usually cause penetrating or depressed fractures.
   b. Flat impacts usually cause linear, nondisplaced fractures.
C. Intracranial hemorrhages or hematomas due to blunt impact
   1. **Epidural** hemorrhage/hematoma. The epidural space is a *potential* space between the inner skull and the dura.
      a. **Acute epidural hematomas**
         i. Are relatively infrequent.
         ii. Seen most often as a result of a fall or motor vehicle accident.
         iii. Occur infrequently in the very young or elderly.
         iv. In 90 to 95% of cases, a fracture is present at the site of impact, with most fractures involving the squamous portion of the temporal bone.
         v. Hemorrhage is from lacerated meningeal vessels, with the most common the *middle meningeal artery*.
         vi. Are disc-shaped, and centrally thickened.
         vii. Are usually unilateral.
         viii. Epidural hematoma due to venous bleeding is rare, and usually due to laceration of the meningeal veins, diploic veins, and dural sinuses.
         ix. Symptoms usually occur within 4 to 8 hours after injury, but in 25 to 30% of cases, there is immediate loss of consciousness.
         x. Mechanism of death is displacement with subsequent herniation.
      b. **Chronic epidural** hematomas (defined as identification or presentation greater than 48 to 72 hours after injury) are rare.
         i. May or may not be associated with skull fracture
         ii. Tend to occur in older children and young adults
   2. **Subdural hematomas**. The subdural space is an *actual* space between the brain and dura. Subdural hemorrhage is caused by a shearing/tearing force acting upon the parasagittal bridging veins during acceleration-deceleration injuries.

    a. May occur on ipsilateral or contralateral side of impact, or be bilateral.

    b. May or may not be accompanied by other cerebral injuries.

    c. May or may not be associated with a skull fracture; if a skull fracture is present, it may be ipsilateral or contralateral to the hematoma.

    d. Subdural hematomas are more common in elderly individuals and alcoholics.

    e. Most (75%) are due to falls or assaults.

    f. Can be:
1. *Acute* — symptoms occur within 72 hours of injury; becomes life threatening at about *50 ml* size in an adult
2. *Subacute* — symptoms occur between 3 days and 2 to 3 weeks post injury
3. *Chronic* — becomes manifest greater than three weeks after injury

    g. Organization occurs over a period of time, initiated by cells from the dura, with complete resorption possible; eventually, only a thin yellow-gold colored membrane may remain adherent to the dura (**Table 6.1**).

    h. A chronic subdural hematoma can rebleed, either spontaneously or as a result of relatively minor trauma.

    i. When present at autopsy, the subdural hematoma should be photographed and measured (volume or weight) in order to provide objective rather than subjective evidence in possible later court proceedings.

3. **Subarachnoid** hemorrhage is the most common intracranial finding after blunt head trauma.

    a. May be diffuse or focal and patchy.

    b. May be minor or severe.

    c. Hyperextension injury of the neck may lacerate or overstretch the vertebral arteries or basilar artery, leading to ventral subarachnoid hemorrhage.

    d. A blow to the *lateral neck* may damage a vertebral artery, producing massive ventral subarachnoid hemorrhage. This is best illustrated or evaluated postmortem first by angiography, and lastly by neck dissection.

4. **Intracerebral** hemorrhages/hematomas may result from blunt force injury.

    a. Most are located in the frontal and temporal regions and are often associated with skull fractures.

TABLE 6.1   Stages in Organization of Subdural Hematoma

Time Period Following Injury	Status of Clot	Possible Microscopic Findings	
		Side of Membrane Facing Dura	Side of Membrane between Clot and Arachnoid
24 hours	Fresh red blood cells	Thin layer of fibrin between dura and clot	
48–72 hours	Fresh red blood cells	Rare fibroblast (spindle cell) at interface	Fibrin only
4–5 days	Rbc begin to break down	2- to 5-cell-thick layer of fibroblasts	Occasional spindle cell within fibrin
5–10 days	Red blood cells are laked; fibroblasts may extend into clot; early capillary formation	3- to 14-cell-thick layer of fibroblasts; occasional small capillaries may be present; pigment-laden macrophages present	Layer still mostly fibrin with some fibroblasts
10–20 days	Few rbc remain; capillary formation continues	Fibroblast layer 1/3 to 1/2 as thick as dura; capillaries & pigment-laden macrophages present	Early fibroblastic membrane is evident
3–4 weeks	Nearly liquefied	Membrane equal to dura in thickness; pigment-laden macrophages present	Fibroblastic membrane about 1/2 as thick as dura; occasional pigment-laden macrophages
5 weeks	Large capillaries present	Membrane well-formed	Membrane well formed
1–3 months	Large (giant) capillaries may be present; may be secondary hemorrhage (rebleed)	Hyalinization of membrane	Hyalinization of membrane
3–6 months		Hyalinized membrane	Hyalinized membrane

    b. Development may be "delayed" by several hours, or days
        after the initial traumatic insult.
  D. **Cerebral contusions** are bruises of the cortical (outer) surface of
     the brain, which can extend into the white matter as a triangular-
     shaped lesion.
    1. Various types of cerebral contusions exist:
        a. **Coup** contusion — occurs at the point of impact; classi-
            cally associated with a blow to the stationary head;
        b. **Contrecoup** contusions — occur on the brain *opposite* the
            point of impact.
            1. More common than coup contusions
            2. Occur most commonly in frontal and temporal lobes

3. Classically associated with falls

c. **Fracture** contusions — result from overlying fracture

d. **Intermediary coup** contusions — hemorrhagic contusions of the deep brain structures

e. **Gliding** contusions — occur in the dorsal surfaces of the cerebral hemispheres, usually the frontal lobes

f. **Herniation** contusions — caused by herniation of brain matter (medial temporal lobes or cerebellar tonsils) against or through the foramen magnum usually secondary to cerebral edema or a space-occupying hematoma

2. Cerebral contusions occur most frequently in the frontal and temporal lobes.

3. In severe open fractures of the cranial vault, contusions may be, and usually are, absent.

4. Cerebral contusions may resolve/heal, forming a depressed, yellow glial scar (*plaque jaune*).

E. **Cerebral lacerations**

1. May result from a displaced skull fracture, or occur in the absence of any skull fracture.

2. When severe cerebral lacerations are present, usually massive skull trauma is also present.

3. Cerebral lacerations are usually bloodless, despite antemortem infliction.

4. In young infants (5 months or less), blunt head trauma results more frequently in cerebral laceration than contusion.

a. Grossly visible lacerations may occur in the white matter of the frontal and temporal lobes, while microscopic lacerations may occur in the superficial cortex.

b. When evaluating suspected lacerations in brains of young individuals or infants, it is important to remember that artifactual linear defects can occur in these brains as a result of removal, due to their extremely soft, gelatinous nature! Microscopic exam may not help in the determination of significance, as cellular reaction to the injury may not be evident until 36 hours post injury.[9]

5. Unlike cerebral contusions, the location of a cerebral laceration, in relation to the point of impact, is not indicative of the mode or mechanism of injury (fall versus blow).

F. **Diffuse axonal injury** (DAI) of the brain is used to describe a condition characterized by immediate prolonged coma (greater than 6 hours) occurring after head trauma, not associated with an intracranial hemorrhage or mass lesion.

1. Produced by sudden acceleration-deceleration motion of the head which causes stretching and/or shearing of nerve fibers which results in axonal dysfunction and/or necrosis.
2. May be mild or severe. The degree of injury is dependent on:
   a. *Direction* of movement; DAI is most severe in *coronal* head motion, and mild in sagittal head motion
   b. The *magnitude* of the acceleration-deceleration movement
   c. The *time span* over which it occurs; acceleration over a long period of time (as in vehicular accidents) is more likely to result in DAI than in subdural bleeds
3. The axonal injuries of DAI are not visible by light microscopy until about 12 hours post injury with H & E stains.
4. DAI may be seen 2 to 3 hours after injury by use of beta-amyloid precursor protein (APP) immunohistochemical stain. The axonal injury is not specific for trauma, however.

G. **Cerebral concussion** can follow blunt head trauma, and varies from mild to severe.
   1. *Mild* concussion — no loss of consciousness, and amnesia may or may not be present
   2. S*evere* concussion — transient loss of consciousness (less than 6 hours), usually accompanied by amnesia (transient or prolonged); occurs probably as a result of diffuse brain injury resulting in mostly physiological disturbance of neuronal activity

H. **Cerebral swelling** can occur as a complication of blunt head trauma. The swelling may be diffuse, focal, adjacent to a specific area of brain injury (such as a contusion or laceration), or one sided, following removal of a subdural or epidural hematoma.
   1. The swelling may be due to:
      a. An increase in the cerebral intravascular blood volume due to vasodilation
      b. An absolute increase in the water content of the brain tissue (termed *cerebral edema*)
   2. Significant *delayed* brain swelling is rare.
      a. Usually associated with less severe forms of brain trauma.
      b. Usually diffuse.
      c. The most severe form of delayed brain swelling occurs more commonly in children (4 to 10 years of age).[10]
   3. Brain swelling can cause symmetrical or asymmetrical herniation of the brain.

XII. NECK INJURIES CAUSED BY BLUNT FORCE TRAUMA

A. *Indirect* injuries are usually the result of blunt head trauma, which causes an alteration in the normal alignment of the cervical vertebral column; these include:

1. **Hyperflexion** (chin on chest) injuries. May result in posterior atlanto-occipital fracture/dislocation. In order to best demonstrate this injury at autopsy, a *posterior* neck dissection should be performed; may see hemorrhage without obvious fracture, or gross separation and/or fracture, with or without hemorrhage.

2. **Hyperextension** injuries (head/chin forced backwards); may result in rupture of anterior ligament, or discs, crushing up posterior aspects of the vertebrae, or marked dislocation/subluxation injuries.

3. **Compressive** injuries (as in landing on top of head); may cause bursting fractures of vertebrae, especially C1.

4. **Torsion** injuries consist of a combination of fractures and/or ligamentous lacerations.

5. **Elongation** (stretching) injuries, as in judicial hangings; there is vertical separation of the vertebral column with partial or complete spinal cord transection. These same findings are rarely found in suicidal hangings, which usually lack the "drop" necessary to produce critical elongation of the vertebral column.

B. The most frequently injured cervical bone is the axis (C2), followed by C5 and C6, followed by the atlas (C1).

C. Whenever external evidence of head trauma is present (especially if the intracranial injuries are relatively minor), a thorough neck exam must be performed, as significant cervical injuries may be present in the absence of external neck trauma.

D. Cervical spinal cord blunt traumatic injuries include contusions, lacerations, crush injuries, and transections. Spinal cord injuries may occur without associated fractures, having been produced by *transient* dislocation of the vertebral column at the moment of impact.

References

1. Robertson, I., Antemortem and postmortem bruises of the skin: Their differentiation, *J. For. Med.*, 4, 2, 1957.

2. Mays, E.T., Bursting injuries of the liver. A complex surgical challenge, *Arch. Surg.*, 93, 92, 1966.

3. Adelson, L., Homicide by blunt violence, in *The Pathology of Homicide*, Charles C. Thomas, Springfield, IL, 1974, p. 487.

4. Day, L.J., et al., Orthopedics, in *Current Surgical Diagnosis & Treatment*, 9th ed., Way, L.W., Ed., Appleton and Lange, Norwalk, CT, 1991, p. 987.

5. Di Maio, V.J.M. and Di Maio, D.J., Wounds due to blunt trauma, in *Forensic Pathology*, 2nd ed., CRC Press, Boca Raton, FL, 2001, p. 114.

6. Iverson, L.D. and Swiontkowski, M.F., Fractures of the pelvis, sacrum, and coccyx, in *Manual of Acute Orthopaedic Therapeutics*, 4th ed., Little, Brown & Company, Boston, 1995, p. 207.

7. ten Duis, H.J., The fat embolism syndrome, *Injury*, 28(2), 77, 1997.

8. Di Maio, V.J.M. and Di Maio, D.J., Trauma to the skull and brain: Craniocerebral injuries, in *Forensic Pathology*, 2nd ed., CRC Press, Boca Raton, FL, 2001, p. 149.

9. Ibid., p. 161.

10. Snoek, J.W., Minderhoud, J.M., and Wilmink, J.T., Delayed deterioration following mild head injury in children, *Brain*, 107, 15, 1984.

Wounds Produced by Pointed, Sharp-Edged, and Chopping Implements

7

Sharp-edged or pointed weapons leave distinctive wounds on the body, depending upon the type of weapon used. These wounds may be divided into three types: stab wounds, incised wounds, and chop wounds.

I. STAB WOUNDS

By definition, these are wounds produced by a pointed instrument (i.e. knife, ice pick), in which the depth of penetration into the body is greater than the length of the wound on the skin. Stab wounds, therefore, consist of an outer, visible skin wound (**external component**) and a deeper, inner wound (**internal component**).

   A. A distinguishing characteristic of stab wounds is the absence of "bridging tissue" in the depth of the wound. If connecting tissue strands are present in the base of the wound, it is more likely the wound was produced by a blow with a blunt object, and not a stab with a sharp-edged implement, as the latter would cut through, not tear, the tissue. Therefore, **the terms laceration and stab wound (or cut) should never be used interchangeably.**

   B. A **knife** is the most common weapon used to produce a stab wound. Other instruments which can cause stab wounds are **ice picks, scissors, forks, pencils or pens, screwdrivers, knitting needles,** or any similar device with a relatively pointed end capable of penetrating the skin.

   C. In this country, most knives used for assault tend to have a *single* sharp edge, and a three to five inch long blade.

107

D. The size and shape of a stab wound on the skin (external component) is dependent upon:
   1. Shape of the weapon (**Figure 7.1**):
      a. A sharp weapon tends to produce a regular, linear wound without abraded margins.
      b. The external skin wound produced by a *single-edged* weapon should have a squared-off or blunted margin (produced by the dull edge, or back of the blade) and a V-shaped margin (produced by the sharp edge of the blade).
      c. Both margins of the external skin wound produced by a *double-edged* weapon should appear V-shaped.
      d. Scissors tend to produce linear wounds if closed, but paired perforations if open.

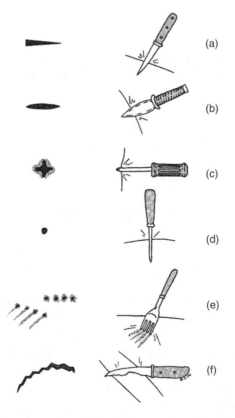

Figure 7.1   Skin wounds produced by different pointed or sharp-edged weapons: (a) single-edged knife; (b) double-edged dagger; (c) Phillips screwdriver; (d) ice pick; (e) four-pronged dinner fork; (f) serrated knife, with tangential angle of attack to the skin.

    e. A Phillips screwdriver may produce a circular wound with four equally spaced cuts or abrasions.

    f. A serrated knife may leave a saw-tooth cut on the body, if the blade of the knife encounters the skin at an oblique or shallow angle; usually, no markings are present.

2. The angle of thrust.

3. Movement of the blade within the wound, or movement of the individual stabbed as the blade is withdrawn from the body. In either case, the resulting wound may be Y- or L-shaped.

4. The state of tension or relaxation of the skin stabbed.

5. **Langer's lines**. Bundles of collagen and elastic fibers in the dermal layer of the skin are mostly arranged in parallel rows. The direction of these rows is referred to as the lines of cleavage, or Langer's lines. In the extremities, these lines tend to run longitudinally; in the neck and trunk, these lines tend to run circumferentially.

    a. If a stab wound is made parallel to the lines of cleavage, the wound will tend to be narrow, slit-like, or thin.

    b. If a stab wound is made perpendicular to the lines of cleavage, the fibers in the skin will tend to pull the edges of the wound apart, causing an open, gaping wound.

    c. If a stab wound is made diagonally across the lines of cleavage, a curved or semilunar wound may result.

E. The force needed to penetrate the body, when stabbed, is dependent on:

1. The configuration of the tip of the weapon (sharp vs. dull).

2. The amount and composition of clothing covering the body in the area stabbed. For example, clothing items made from leather (jacket, belt) are more difficult to penetrate than items composed of soft material, such as a nylon nightgown.

3. The toughness or thickness of the skin in the area stabbed. Skin within the same individual varies in thickness depending upon the body location. Other factors that affect the skin thickness/toughness include preexisting medical conditions which affect the skin, age, and sun exposure.

F. The **length of the wound in the skin** (external component) may be equal to, greater than, or less than the **width** of the knife blade. The **depth of the stab wound** (internal component) may be equal to, less than, or greater than the **length** of the knife blade.

G. If a stabbing victim has been stabbed multiple times, and assuming only one knife (or multiple knives with similar dimensions and characteristics) was used to inflict all of the wounds, it may be

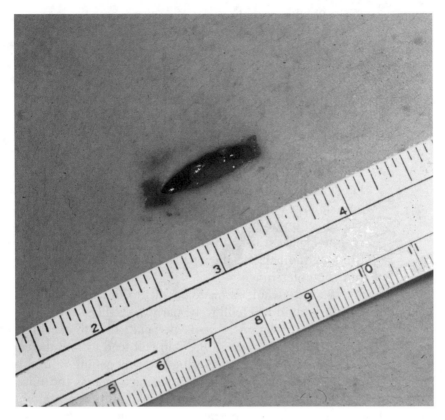

Figure 7.2 (See color insert following page 146) Stab wound with abrasion and contusion due to guard, photographed with ruler for documentation of size.

possible to arrive at an approximation of the length, width, thickness, and configuration (single vs. double edged) of the weapon.

H. A patterned skin abrasion or contusion may be produced by the **guard** (**Figure 7.2**) of the knife contacting the skin if the weapon is driven into the body with great force. The guard on a knife is a separate piece of metal which is perpendicularly attached to the blade, between the blade and the handle, which keeps the hand away from the blade while cutting (**Figure 7.3**).

I. Single-edged weapons may produce skin wounds in which both ends are squared-off or blunted, if the weapon has been driven in up to the guard. This happens because in most knives, a short section of the blade (ricasso) immediately in front of the guard is unsharpened on both edges (**Figure 7.4**).

J. If the knife or stabbing weapon encounters bone, the tip of the weapon may break off, and remain in the body. For this reason,

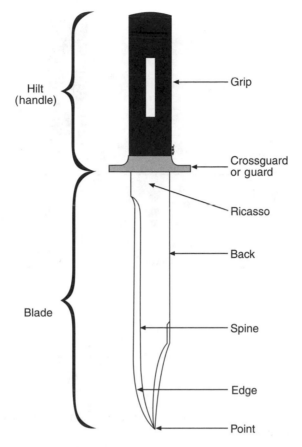

Figure 7.3   Parts of single-edged knife.

victims stabbed multiple times, or having stab wounds into bone, should be radiographed prior to autopsy. If the x-rays reveal a fragment of metal retained within the body, this fragment should be recovered in the same fashion as a bullet, taking care to preserve any toolmarks that may be present, as it is possible to match the metal fragment found at autopsy with the weapon, if it is recovered. If a portion of the weapon is broken off within the body, this information should be communicated to the investigating officers, as it may aid in ruling in or out certain suspect weapons.

K. Stab wounds may be homicidal, suicidal, or accidental:
   1. In suicidal stabbings:
      a. The wounds are usually multiple and to the mid or left anterior chest, with most of the wounds superficial or barely breaking the skin (**"hesitation wounds"**).

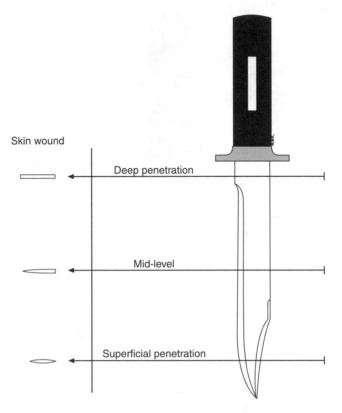

Figure 7.4   Differing skin wounds produced by same knife, at three different depths of penetration.

       b. The stab wounds do not usually go through the clothing, consistent with the individual pushing aside or pulling up the clothing prior to stabbing him/herself.

       c. Stab wounds to the neck or head do occur occasionally, but these are much less common than those to the chest; suicidal stab wounds to the abdomen are very rare.

  2. In homicidal stabbings:

       a. Multiple wounds are usually present, with most penetrating deep into the body.

       b. Most fatal chest wounds involve injury to the heart or aorta. A stab wound to the heart that severs the left anterior descending artery can cause rapid death.

       c. The abdominal organs may be injured by stab wounds to the abdomen or lower chest; fatal stab wounds of the abdomen usually involve the liver and/or a major blood vessel. Abdominal stab wounds may cause delayed death due to peritonitis, and sepsis.

    d. Wounds of the head and neck are less common than wounds to the chest or abdomen.

        1. Stab wounds of the **neck** cause death acutely by exsanguination, air embolism, or asphyxia by compression of the neck organs if massive soft tissue hemorrhage is present.

            a. Delayed death may occur from cellulitis, or arterial thrombosis leading to cerebral infarction.

            b. **If stab wounds are present in the neck, a postmortem radiograph of the chest should be made prior to autopsy, as an aid in demonstrating an air embolus (Figure 7.5).**

        2. Fatal stab wounds of the head are uncommon. When present, they may cause injury of the skull or brain.

            a. The thinner areas of the skull are more likely to be penetrated (orbit, temporal bones).

            b. Intracranial hemorrhage resulting from a stab wound may be subarachnoid, subdural, intracerebral, or a combination of these.

    3. Accidental stabbings:

        a. Can occur, but are very rare

        b. Usually involve an individual being impaled after an accidental fall onto a sharp or pointed object, or by a moving sharp object striking the individual

L. **"Defense stab wounds"** occur usually to the hands, extensor or ulnar aspects of the forearm, or backs of the upper arms of an assault victim. These wounds are produced as the victim attempts to defend him/herself from the assailant.

    1. Defense wounds are rarely fatal by themselves.

    2. Defense wounds of the lower extremities can also occur, but are much less common than those of the upper extremities. These wounds result from the victim being assaulted while lying down, usually face up, as he/she kicks at the assailant.

M. It is not uncommon for a stabbing victim to be transported to the hospital trauma unit, especially in large metropolitan areas, where various **artifacts** may be introduced.

    1. Stab wounds resulting from the assault may be altered or destroyed by medical personnel. For example, a chest tube may be placed through a preexisting stab wound, thus altering the dimensions and characteristics of the wound, or a chest wound

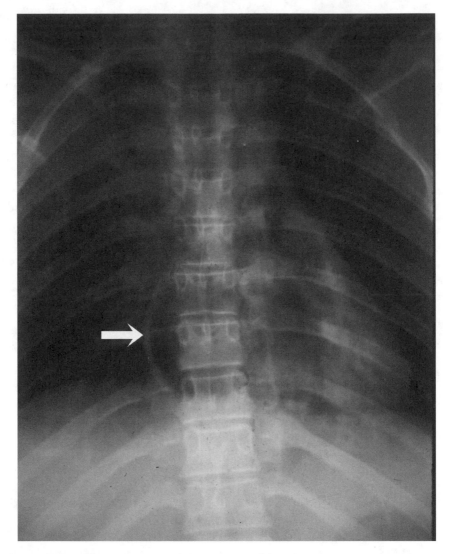

Figure 7.5   (See color insert following page 146) Postmortem chest radiograph demonstrating air in right side of heart in victim with incised wound of neck. Air within the right-sided heart chambers allows clear delineation of the wall of right atrium (arrow).

may be totally obliterated when the surgeon incorporates it into a thoracotomy incision.

2. Surgical stab wounds may be made to the body for the placement of drainage tubes. If the tubes are then removed prior to the body being released to the morgue, it becomes extremely difficult to separate assault stab wounds from surgical stab

wounds, especially if the medical records are incomplete or poorly annotated at the time of autopsy.

3. An open surgical cut-down made on the wrist or ankle may appear identical to a primary incised wound, especially if the catheter inserted was removed (or never inserted) from the wound prior to transfer of the body to the morgue.

N. If the knife, or sharp weapon, used to inflict the stab wounds is still present in the victim's body when found, the handle of the weapon should be processed for fingerprints, preferably at the scene, before the body is moved. If this is not possible, great care should be taken to preserve the evidence, for later processing. A paper bag may be used to loosely cover the weapon. A plastic bag should never be used for such a purpose, as condensation may occur within the plastic bag, which may interfere with subsequent examination for fingerprints. **Never pull an embedded weapon from a body prior to determining if the weapon has been fingerprinted.**

O. Whether or not a victim is capable of movement or physical activity after being stabbed is dependent upon several factors:
1. The size of the blood vessel severed or cut
2. The vascularity of the organ stabbed
3. The total amount of blood lost (internal and external)
4. The rate at which the blood loss occurs

P. The presence or absence of the stabbing weapon at the scene of the death does not necessarily help establish the manner of death (homicide vs. suicide vs. accident). A weapon may not be present at the scene of a suicide, as it may have been removed by family members, or by the victim prior to total incapacitation, in an attempt to disguise the death as a homicide. The reverse is also true — the stabbing weapon may be left at the scene of a homicide, possibly in an attempt to make the death appear as a suicide.

Q. When stab wounds are present, the clothing should always be examined to see if defects corresponding to the body wounds are present in the clothing. The location of the clothing defects may suggest a struggle, or if absent, may suggest the body was dressed after the attack.

R. **Postmortem stab wounds** are usually yellow to tan in color, due to the absence of tissue perfusion. Stab wounds inflicted shortly before, or at the time of death (antemortem or perimortem), may also appear relatively bloodless, if significant blood loss has already occurred and lowered the blood pressure. If several bloodless, yellow stab wounds are present, in addition to the obvious lethal wound, this is a clearer indication that some wounds were inflicted after death, and therefore, after the victim had ceased to struggle, or "put up a fight."

II. INCISED WOUNDS

An incised wound is defined as a wound produced by a sharp-edged weapon or instrument, which is longer on the skin than it is deep. In other words, the length of the wound on the outer aspect of the body (external component) is greater than the depth of the wound track within the body (internal component).

- A. Incised wounds are usually not fatal. However, fatal incised wounds can occur, which usually involve the neck or arms.
- B. Like stab wounds, incised wounds will lack "bridging tissue" within the depth of the wound.
- C. Sharp-edged weapons produce clean, sharply incised wounds without associated abrasions or contusions of the wound edge. A dull-edged weapon may produce an irregular incised wound with abraded or contused edges. However, even in these wounds, "bridging tissue" should not be present in the base of the wounds.
- D. Suicidal incised wounds:
  1. Are usually to areas of the body accessible to the individual.
  2. As with stab wounds, clothing may be open, or pulled away from the injured area, providing good evidence that the wound is in fact a suicidal one.
  3. Fatal incised wounds of the arms (wrists, antecubital fossae) are almost always suicidal, unless the scene clearly indicates an accidental manner of death.
     - a. The wrist and arm wounds are usually to the anterior (flexor) surface of the wrist or forearm.
     - b. Right-handed individuals tend to cut the left wrist or forearm, while left-handed persons tend to do the opposite. Occasionally, cuts are present on both arms or wrists.
     - c. In the investigation of a possible suicide by other means, such as overdose, the pathologist should always carefully inspect the anterior arms and wrists for the presence of superficial linear scars, which may have resulted from a prior suicide attempt.
  4. "Hesitation" marks or wounds may be present, and are commonly found in association with incised wounds of the wrists or neck. These are very superficial cuts, usually multiple, parallel to each other, and found in association with a deeper, fatal incised wound of the neck or wrist. It is important to remember, **similar superficial "hesitation" marks or wounds may be**

present in deaths due to homicide, in association with incised wounds of the neck. In these cases, the wounds may be caused by the victim struggling and/or pulling away from the assailant, or possibly are due to hesitancy on the part of the assailant to cut the throat of the victim.

E. Accidental incised wounds are rare, but do occur. The majority of these cases involve glass fragments accidentally injuring a major blood vessel, leading to exsanguination, or air embolus.

F. Homicidal incised wounds, when present, are usually associated with multiple stab wounds. Lethal homicidal incised wounds are usually to the neck.

   1. If the incised neck wound is inflicted from **behind**, the resulting wound usually begins behind or near the victim's ear opposite to the hand holding the knife, continues across the anterior neck in a somewhat horizontal fashion (deepest wound), and ends on the opposite side of the neck, usually at a point lower than the initial point of injury.

   2. If the incised wound is inflicted from the **front**, the resulting wound is usually short and angled, but occasionally horizontal wounds are seen. An assailant holding a knife in his right hand and slashing at a victim from the front will tend to produce incised wounds of the victim's left neck, and vice versa.

   3. Extremely deep incised wounds of the neck can completely transect the trachea or larynx, and extend to the vertebral column, producing near decapitation. These wounds are almost always inflicted from behind.

G. The mechanism of death in incised wounds of the neck is exsanguination, and/or air embolus.

H. **"Defensive incised wounds"** usually occur to the upper extremities, as the victim assumes a defensive posture, with his/her upper extremities thrown up between the weapon and their body, or as the victim attempts to grab the offending weapon and encounters the blade of the knife. Therefore, defensive incised wounds should occur on the palms, or the backs of the hands, forearms, or upper arms (**Figure 7.6**).

III. CHOP WOUNDS

Chop wounds are caused by heavy instruments, or weapons, which have at least one sharp, cutting edge. Examples of such weapons include axes, hatchets, meat cleavers, and machetes (**Figure 7.7**).

A. A chop wound consists of an incised wound with an associated groove or cut in the underlying bone.

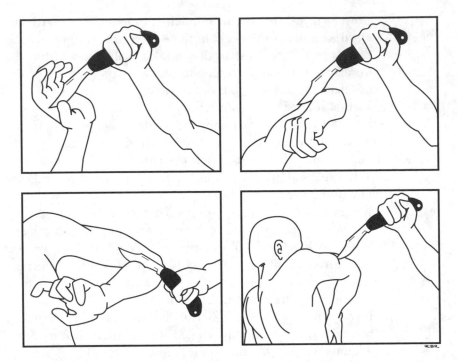

Figure 7.6   Various ways in which "defense wounds" may be received.

Figure 7.7   (See color insert following page 146) Multiple chop wounds produced by attack with machete.

B. If the chopping blow is tangential, then a disk-shaped portion of bone or skin and soft tissue may be cut away.

C. Dull-edged chopping weapons (such as a heavy shovel) may cause more crushing than incision of the tissue and may, therefore, result in a wound more consistent with a laceration than an incised wound.

D. Moving propellers (boat or airplane) may cause severe chop-like wounds.

E. The presence of soft tissue hemorrhage associated with a chop or incised wound is generally considered good evidence the wound occurred prior to death. Prolonged immersion of a body in water can cause hemorrhage initially present in the wound to be leached out, giving the wound a postmortem appearance, and making the determination of its true nature difficult.

Gunshot Wounds

8

I. **TYPES OF SMALL ARMS**
   A. There are five types of **small arms**:
     1. Handguns
     2. Rifles
     3. Shotguns
     4. Submachine guns (machine pistols)
     5. Machine guns
     All of these weapons, except for shotguns, have rifling of the interior of the barrel.
   B. **Rifling** is a series of parallel spiral **grooves** cut the length of the bore of the barrel.
     1. The metal left between the grooves is the **lands** (**Figure 8.1**).
     2. The number of grooves can vary from 2 to 20 with the direction of the rifling either clockwise (right) or counterclockwise (left).
       a. Virtually all handguns have five or six grooves with a right-hand twist. Colt has a left-hand twist.
       b. In centerfire rifles, virtually all weapons have a right-hand twist with the number of grooves varying from four to six.
       c. .22 rimfire weapons generally have a right-hand twist with four, five, or six grooves.
     3. Rifling imparts a rotational spin on the bullet as it travels down the barrel. The spin imparted to the bullet stabilizes its flight through the air, preventing it from tumbling.

II. **FIREARMS**
   A. Handguns can be divided into two general categories:
     1. Revolvers — cartridges are carried in a cylinder which is rotated by pulling the trigger (**Figure 8.2**)

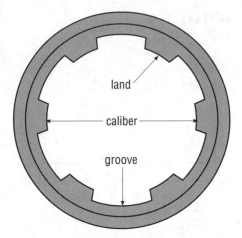

Figure 8.1   Cross-sectional diagram of a rifled barrel showing lands and grooves.

      2. Autoloading pistols (automatics; semiautomatics) — cartridges are kept in a magazine; the first round has to be manually loaded into the chamber (**Figure 8.3 and Figure 8.4**)

  B. Rifles and shotguns

      Shotguns and rifles are meant to be fired from the shoulder.

      1. Shotguns differ from rifles in that the bore is smooth and contains no rifling.

      2. A shotgun is designed to fire multiple pellets down a barrel, while a rifle is intended to fire a single missile down the barrel.

      3. An assault rifle:

         a. Is a self-loading rifle

         b. Is capable of full automatic fire

         c. Has a large magazine capacity (20 rounds or more)

         d. Is chambered for an intermediate powered rifle cartridge (a cartridge intermediate in power between a standard rifle cartridge and a pistol cartridge)

  C. A submachine gun (machine pistol) is a weapon capable of full automatic fire which is chambered for a pistol cartridge.

  D. A machine gun fires a rifle cartridge and is capable of full automatic fire.

  III. CALIBER

    A. The caliber of a rifled weapon is supposed to be the diameter of the bore measured from land to land (**Figure 8.1**). This policy is not strictly followed and some of the caliber designations are essentially arbitrary. In the metric system used in Europe, the caliber identifies the bullet diameter and the cartridge case length

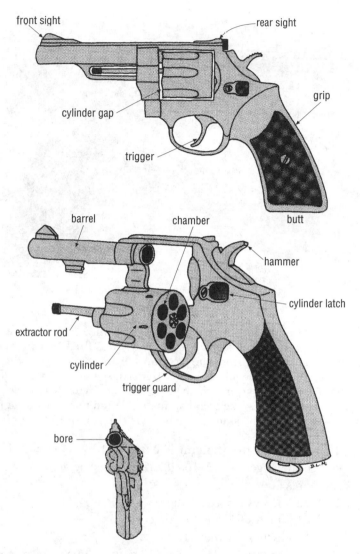

Figure 8.2   Parts of a revolver. Revolver depicted at the center has the cylinder unlatched and swung out for loading and unloading of cartridges. In hard contact wounds, an image of the muzzle end with the configuration of the barrel and the front sight may be transferred to the skin.

in millimeters. Thus, a 7.62 x 39 mm cartridge fires a bullet 7.62 mm in diameter from a cartridge case 39 mm long.

B. The term **Magnum** in reference to a handgun or rifle refers to an extra powerful loading of a cartridge such that a bullet is propelled at a greater velocity. In shotguns, the term *Magnum* refers to an increase in the weight of the pellet charge with the velocity generally not increased.

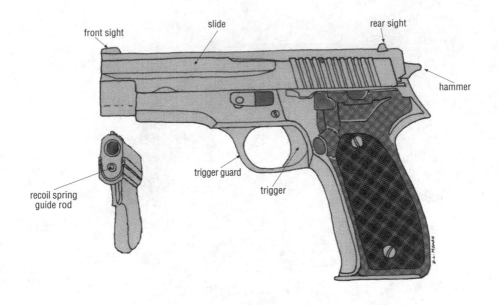

Figure 8.3   Parts of a semiautomatic pistol. The slide is a separate piece of metal around the barrel which slides back as the gun is fired, causing the empty cartridge case to be expelled from the ejection port near the top of the weapon on the right side. As the slide moves forward, it strips another cartridge from the top of the magazine, places it into the firing chamber (Figure 8.4), and cocks the hammer. In contact wounds, the recoil spring guide rod may produce a punched out or round abrasion on the skin associated with an imprint of the muzzle.

   C. The caliber of the shotgun is expressed by its gauge. The most common gauges are 12, 16, 20, and .410. The actual diameters of the bores are:
       1. 0.729 inches for a 12 gauge
       2. 0.615 inches for the 20 gauge
       3. 0.410 inches for the .410
   D. Whether a shotgun is 12, 16, or 20 gauge, the pellets are propelled at approximately the same velocity. The only difference is that a 12-gauge shell can contain more pellets than a 16 gauge, which contains more pellets than a 20 gauge.
IV. **AMMUNITION**
   A. Ammunition for rifled weapons is divided into two categories — centerfire or rimfire — depending on the location of the primer (**Figure 8.5**).
       1. In **rimfire** cartridges the primer composition is in the rim of the cartridge case with the propellant in contact with the primer.

Figure 8.4 Sectional diagram of autoloading pistol. The magazine is also referred to as a "clip."

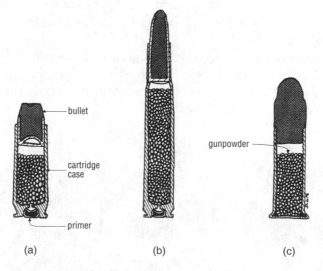

Figure 8.5 Categories of rifled weapons depend on location of primer. (a) centerfire handgun cartridge; (b) centerfire rifle cartridge; (c) rimfire cartridge.

      a.   On firing, the firing pin crushes the rim of the cartridge case, detonating the primer composition, igniting the powder.

      b.   Current rimfire ammunition is limited to four calibers — 22 Short, 22 Long Rifle, 22 Magnum, and 17 Magnum.

      c.   Rimfire ammunition may be fired in either handguns or rifles.

   2. Most ammunition is **centerfire**. In centerfire cartridges, the primer complex is located in the center of the base of the cartridge. On firing, the firing pin strikes the center of the primer igniting the primer composition, which in turn ignites the powder.

B. **Cartridge cases** are usually made of brass, though aluminum and steel cases may be encountered.

   1. On firing, the cartridge case contains the gases from the ignition of the powder.

   2. Most handgun cartridges have a straight design while rifle cartridges are bottlenecked.

   3. In commercial ammunition, the caliber and the name of the manufacturer is stamped on the base of the cartridge.

   4. In military ammunition, the plant that manufactured the ammunition (either by letters or by code numbers) and the year of manufacture are stamped on the base of the cartridge.

C. The **powder** used in the cartridge case is smokeless powder, a nitrocellulose compound, to which nitroglycerin may or may not be added. The physical forms of the powder in the United States are generally:

   1. Disk (flake) or ball in handguns and shotguns

   2. Either cylindrical or ball powder in rifles

D. The **bullet** is the part of the cartridge that leaves the muzzle on firing the weapon (**Figure 8.6**).

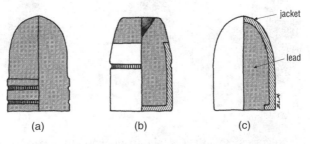

Figure 8.6   Types of bullets. (a) all lead; (b) partial metal jacketed; (c) full metal jacketed.

1. Because of their high velocities, centerfire rifle bullets have to have either a full or partial metal jacket.
   a. This jacket is usually copper or copper alloy but may be steel.
   b. The core is usually lead but in the case of military bullets may be mild steel or a combination of steel and lead.
2. In full-metal-jacketed ammunition, the jacketing covers the tip and sides of the bullet.
3. All military ammunition, even handgun ammunition, has to be full metal jacketed.
4. In semi-jacketed ammunition, there is a lead core with a copper jacketing that covers the sides, and usually the base, of the bullet with the core exposed at the tip.
5. Traditionally, all lead bullets were used in revolvers; full-metal-jacketed bullets in autoloading pistols.
6. Most handgun ammunition is now loaded with semi-jacketed bullets, usually of hollow-point design, whether intended for use in revolvers or autoloading pistols.
7. .22 Short and Long Rifle ammunition is loaded with lead bullets; .22 Magnum ammunition either full metal jacketed or semi-jacketed; 17 Magnum ammunition is loaded with jacketed bullets either hollow point or with a colored polycarbonate tip.
8. The configuration of the bullet is variable (**Figure 8.7**).
   a. Handgun ammunition tends to be:
      1. Round nose
      2. Hollow point
      3. Wad cutter (cylindrical shaped)
   b. Centerfire rifle ammunition is either:
      1. Full metal jacketed

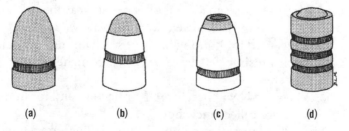

| (a) | (b) | (c) | (d) |

Figure 8.7   Bullet shapes. (a) all lead, round nose; (b) round nose, semi-jacketed; (c) hollow point, semi-jacketed; (d) lead wad cutter.

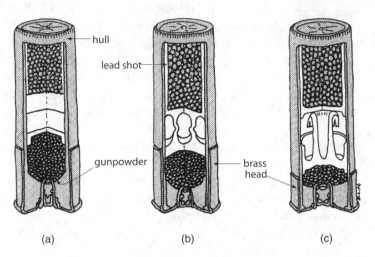

Figure 8.8   Cross-sectional views of three types of shotgun shells. (a) Winchester birdshot shell with cardboard wads and thin plastic shot collar; (b) Remington birdshot shell with one-piece plastic wad; (c) Federal birdshot shell with plastic wad and plastic shot cup.

      2. Semi-jacketed

      3. With a spitzer point or a round nose

  E. Virtually all shotgun shells are manufactured with a plastic hull and a brass head with the end of the shell crimped closed (**Figure 8.8**).

      1. Underneath the crimped end are the pellets (the shot), then wadding and then powder.

      2. Different manufactures use different wad materials and designs of wadding. It is possible to identify the gauge and manufacturer of the ammunition from a recovered wad (**Figure 8.9**).

      3. Federal and Remington use plastic wads while Winchester typically uses wads made out of paper and cardboard. Some Winchester rounds, however, do use plastic wadding.

      4. Pellets used for hunting birds or small animals are called **birdshot**. Birdshot pellets vary from .05 inches to .18 inches in diameter.

      5. Pellets used by police, for self-protection and for hunting large game are called **buckshot**.

        a. The most common buckshot loadings are #4 and 00.

        b. #4 buckshot measures .24 inches in diameter.

        c. 00 measures .33 inches in diameter.

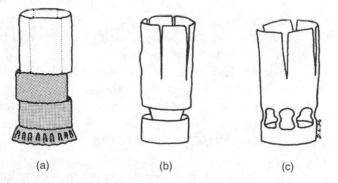

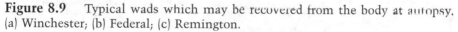

Figure 8.9   Typical wads which may be recovered from the body at autopsy.
(a) Winchester; (b) Federal; (c) Remington.

Figure 8.10   Types of shotgun slugs. (a) Foster slug; (b) Brenneke slug; (c) sabot
slug.

     d.   Typically, buckshot is loaded packed in a white granulated
           plastic material, which on firing will be expelled in addi-
           tion to the buckshot and wadding.
   F. While most loadings for shotgun shells contain either birdshot or
     buckshot, some shells are loaded with **shotgun slugs** (**Figure 8.10**).
     1. A shotgun slug is really a large lead missile. It may be:
        a.   Bullet-shaped like the **American Foster slug**
        b.   A European **Brenneke slug** which resembles the Foster
            slug but has a cardboard wadding literally screwed into the
            base
        c.   Hourglass-shaped like the **sabot round**
     2. A number of angled ribs and grooves run down the surface of
        both the American Foster and the Brenneke slug.

3. These slugs range in weight from approximately 350 to 490 grains depending on the gauge.
4. The sabot slug has an hourglass configuration and is enclosed in two pieces of plastic.
    a. The whole complex, the two pieces of plastic enclosing the slug and the slug, go down the barrel.
    b. As they emerge, the two pieces of plastic fall away and the hourglass missile continues on its path to the target.

V. **BALLISTIC COMPARISON OF BULLETS**
A. The bullet
    1. When a bullet is fired down the barrel, the rifling imparts two types of markings to the bullet:
        a. Class characteristics
        b. Individual characteristics
    2. **Class characteristics** are those of the make and model of the gun, i.e., the number of lands and grooves; the rate of twist; the depth of the grooves and the direction.
    3. **Individual characteristics** are marks made on the bullet by imperfections in the barrel which are individual for only that barrel. These markings are used by a firearms examiner to identify a bullet as having come from a specific gun.
B. The cartridge case
    1. Cartridge cases also have markings on them from the firing pin, the breech face, the ejector, the extractor and even the magazine.
    2. These also can be used to identify a cartridge case as having come from a specific weapon.
    3. Occasionally, fingerprints may be recovered from fired cartridge cases.
C. Fingerprints on weapons, especially if they are handguns, are relatively rare. Thus, while fingerprinting of a weapon is recommended, usually no benefit is obtained.

VI. **THEORY OF WOUNDING**
A. The severity of a gunshot wound is determined by two factors:
    1. Disruption of the tissue caused by the **mechanical interaction** between the bullet and the tissue
    2. The effects of the **temporary cavity** produced by the bullet
B. Once a bullet enters the body, the spin imparted from the rifling is insufficient to compensate for the increased density of the tissue.
    1. The bullet then begins to yaw, or wobble along its projected path. The **yaw** is the angle between the projected path and the longitudinal axis of the bullet.

2. As the bullet travels through the tissue, the yaw increases. If the path is sufficiently long, the yaw will reach 90°, thus exposing maximum surface area.

3. If the bullet continues its travel, it will eventually make a complete 180° flip and end up traveling backwards.

C. In addition to the mechanical disruption of the tissue, a moving bullet displaces tissue just the way a speedboat displaces water as it travels across a lake.

1. The greater the kinetic energy the bullet possesses, the more energy that it loses, and the greater the displacement of tissue will be.

2. The tissue is flung away from the path of the bullet creating a temporary cavity (**Figure 8.11**).

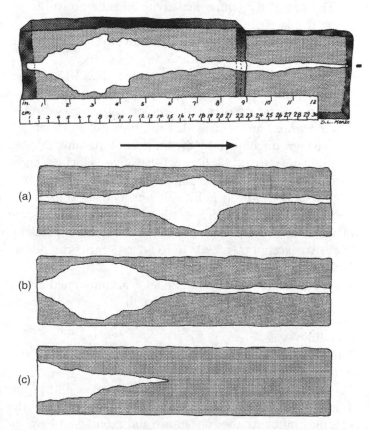

Figure 8.11   Temporary cavity demonstrated in gelatin block. The top figure is a sketch of high-speed photography of the passage of a bullet through a gelatin block (left to right) demonstrating the temporary cavity created. The lower three diagrams represent the shape and appearance of the temporary cavities created by (a) full-metal-jacketed rifle bullet; (b) hunting rifle bullet; (c) shotgun pellet.

3. This cavity is temporary in nature lasting only 5 to 10 thousandths of a second.
   a. From initial growth until collapse, it undergoes a series of gradually smaller pulsations and contractions before it disappears, leaving the permanent wound track.
   b. The temporary cavity can be as much as 11 times the diameter of the bullet.
   c. The maximum point of expansion of the cavity in a nondeforming, nonfragmenting bullet would be at the point the bullet is traveling sideways.
4. The temporary cavity is especially destructive in regard to gunshot wounds of the head. Here the rigid structure of the skull can only relieve pressure by bursting.
5. The size of the temporary cavity and the pressures produced by displacement of the tissue play very little, if any, role in wounding with handgun bullets, due to the fact that handgun bullets possess relatively little kinetic energy.
6. This is different with centerfire rifle bullets which by virtue of their high velocity possess a tremendous amount of kinetic energy. Large cavities and large pressure waves can be generated which can actually disrupt, rupture, and even shred organs not directly hit by the bullet, but are only in close proximity to its path. **Tables 8.1–8.3** give velocities and kinetic energy of various types of ammunition.

D. Hollow-point and soft-point rifle bullets tend to break up in the body causing much more severe wounds than if they remained intact. In contrast military rifle bullets tend not to break up in the body. An exception is the M16 (5.56 x 45 mm) cartridge.

VII. GUNSHOT WOUNDS

Whenever a gun is fired, the exiting bullet is accompanied by:
- A jet of flame, 1 to 2 inches in length, having a temperature of approximately 1400°F
- A cloud of gas
- Burning and unburnt grains of gunpowder
- Carbon, or soot, from burnt gunpowder
- Vaporized metal from the bullet, cartridge case and primer

Depending on the range between the muzzle of the gun and the body, these materials may influence the appearance and extent of the wound (**Figure 8.12** and **Figure 8.13**).

Based on their appearance, and thus their range, gunshot wounds can be divided into four broad categories:
- Contact

TABLE 8.1 Velocity and Kinetic Energy of Centerfire Handgun Cartridges

Caliber	Type of Bullet[a]	Bullet Weight (grains)	Muzzle Velocity (ft/sec)	Kinetic Energy (foot-pounds)
25 Automatic	FMJ	50	760	65
7.62 mm Tokarev	FMJ	87	1390	365
32 S&W	lead	88	680	90
32 S&W long	lead	98	705	115
32 Automatic	FMJ	71	905	130
380 Automatic	FMJ	90	1000	200
9 x 18 mm Makarov	FMJ	95	1000	258
9 mm Luger	FMJ	115	1155	340
9 mm Luger	FMJ	123/125	1110	340
9 mm Luger	FMJ	147	990	320
38 Special	SJHP	110	945	220
38 Special	lead WC	148	710	165
38 Special	lead	158	755	200
357 Magnum	SJHP	110	1295	410
357 Magnum	SJHP	125	1220	415
357 Magnum	SJHP	150/158	1235	535
357 Sig	SJHP	124	1387	530
40 S&W	JHP	155	1140	447
40 S&W	JHP	180	985	388
10 mm Automatic	SJHP	155	1125	436
10 mm Automatic	SJHP	180	1030	425
44 Rem. Magnum	SJHP	180	1610	1035
44 Rem. Magnum	SJHP	210	1495	1040
45 Automatic	FMJ	230	830	355

[a] FMJ — full metal jacket; SJ — semi-jacketed; JHP — jacketed hollow point; SJHP — semi-jacketed hollow point; WC — wad cutter.

- Near contact
- Intermediate
- Distant

A. In **contact wounds**, the muzzle of the gun is against the skin at the time of discharge.

   1. If the gun is pushed "hard" against the skin, indenting it, and thus guaranteeing a complete seal between the muzzle and skin on discharge, this wound is called a **hard contact** (**Figure 8.14**).

      a. In hard contact wounds, all the material exiting the muzzle of the gun goes beneath the skin.

      b. The edges of the wound will be seared (burnt) and blackened by a combination of burning from the flame exiting the muzzle, as well as impregnation of soot in this area of burning.

TABLE 8.2   Velocity and Kinetic Energy of Rimfire Ammunition

Cartridge Type	Bullet Weight (grains)	Muzzle Velocity (ft/sec)	Kinetic Energy (foot-pounds)
17 HMR[a]	17	2550	1902
22 CB Short	30	725	34
22 Short, Standard Velocity	29	1045	70
22 Short, High Velocity	29	1095	77
22 Short, High Velocity HP[b]	27	1120	75
22 CB Long	30	725	34
22 Long Rifle, Standard Velocity	40	1138	116
22 Long Rifle, High Velocity	40	1255	140
22 Long Rifle, High Velocity HP	36/38	1280	131
22 Winchester Magnum	30	2200	322
22 Winchester Magnum	40	1910	324
22 Winchester Magnum	50	1650	300

[a] Hornady Magnum Rimfire.

[b] Hollow Point.

TABLE 8.3   Velocity and Kinetic Energy of Centerfire Rifle Ammunition

Cartridge	Type of Bullet[a]	Bullet Weight (grains)	Muzzle Velocity (ft/sec)	Kinetic Energy (foot-pounds)
223 Remington	FMJ	55	3240	1282
243 Winchester	SP	80	3350	1993
243 Winchester	SP	100	2960	1945
270 Winchester	SP	150	2850	2705
7.62 x 39 mm Russian	FMJ	123	2365	1527
30 Carbine	FMJ	110	1990	967
30-30 Winchester	SP	150	2390	1902
30-30 Winchester	SP	170	2200	1827
30-06 Springfield	Silvertip	150	2910	2820
30-06 Springfield	SP	180	2700	2913
303 British	SP	180	2460	2418
308 Winchester	FMJ	150	2820	2648
308 Winchester	SP	180	2620	2743

[a] FMJ — full metal jacket; SP — soft point.

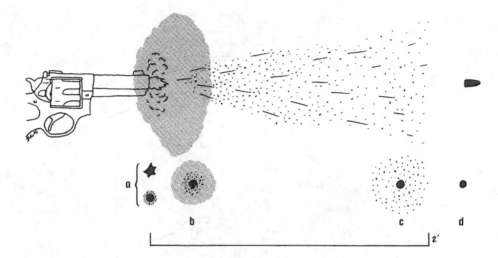

Figure 8.12   The appearance of wounds depends on the muzzle to target distance. (a) Contact of the skin with the muzzle may result in a stellate wound or a wound with a seared muzzle imprint. (b) Wound with soot and dense powder tattooing, but no searing. (c) Intermediate range wound with less dense powder tattooing. (d) Distant wound.

2. In hard contact wounds of the chest and abdomen, whether the weapon is a rifle, handgun or shotgun, one tends to get a circular perforation surrounded by seared and blackened margins. Not infrequently, the gas entering the thoracic and abdominal cavities causes the chest and abdominal wall to bulge outward impacting the muzzle end of the gun, producing a detailed imprint of the muzzle on the skin.

3. The picture is completely different in contact wounds of the head where a thin layer of scalp is stretched over bone.

   a. In contact wounds of the head from handguns, one can have:

      1. A round entrance with blackened and seared margins;
      2. An entrance wound with a muzzle imprint around it; or
      3. A stellate entrance.
      4. The latter two pictures are due to the gas coming out the muzzle of the weapon and collecting between the scalp and bone. This may cause ballooning outward of the scalp with the scalp impacting the muzzle producing a muzzle imprint, or the ballooned-out skin tearing

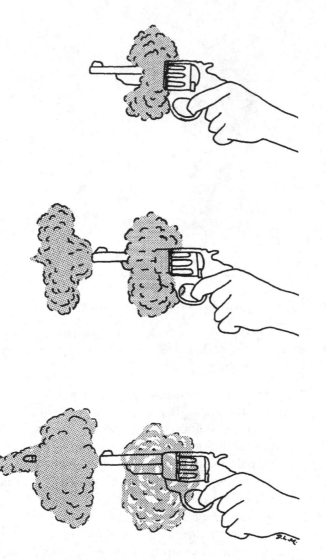

Figure 8.13   As a revolver is fired, gas, soot, vaporized metal and occasionally metal fragments, and gunpowder particles emerge from the cylinder gap prior to emerging from the barrel with the bullet.

at the entrance producing a stellate entrance (**Figure 8.15**).

5. Careful examination of the edges of the stellate entrance will reveal the original circular defect, with blackened and seared margins, from which the tears radiate.

6. The appearance and extent of the injury depend to a degree on the caliber of the weapon.

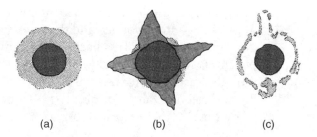

Figure 8.14   Types of hard contact wounds. (a) wound with seared abrasion;
(b) split-open stellate wound; (c) muzzle imprint.

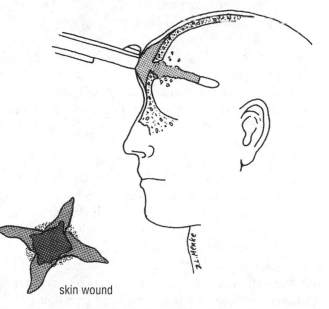

skin wound

Figure 8.15   Contact wound of forehead. Skin balloons out due to gases
trapped between skin and bone. The overstretched skin may split, leading to a
stellate entrance wound.

> a.   With .22 rimfire bullets, the entrance wound tends
>   to be round with blackened and seared margins.
> b.   With a .357 Magnum, one gets the typical stellate
>   wound with ejection of brain tissue.

b.   In contact wounds of the head with centerfire rifles or
      shotguns, there are devastating injuries with large gaping
      tears of the scalp and ejection of brain tissue. This is due
      to the effects of the temporary cavity plus the effects of gas
      under high pressure expanding within the cranial cavity.

c.   In contact wounds of the head, there may be **back splatter**
      onto the weapon or the firer.

1. The back splatter is due to the subcutaneous expansion of gases in contact wounds and the cavitation effect in noncontact wounds. This back splatter emerges from the entrance at every possible angle. For droplets <0.5 mm, the vast majority travel 0 to 40 cm with a maximum travel of 69 cm. For droplets >0.5 mm, the majority travel 0 to 50 cm with a maximum distance of 119 cm.

2. It must be realized that in not all cases will tissue or blood be present on the weapon or firer. This is dependent to a degree upon the type and caliber of weapon as well as the position of the shooter.

3. Back splatter is more common with a weapon such as a shotgun or .357 Magnum than a .22 handgun.

4. In **loose contact** wounds, the muzzle is against the skin, but for a short time following discharge of the weapon, a gap opens up between the muzzle and skin so that a ring of soot is deposited around the entrance hole. This soot can be washed away (**Figure 8.16a**).

5. In some contact wounds, powder will be found not only at the entrance, but also at the exit.

   a. This typically occurs with ball powder and is associated with hard contact wounds of the body.

   b. The powder accompanies the bullet in its travel through the body and is deposited at the exit.

B. In **near contact** wounds, the muzzle is held at a short distance from the skin such that there is a bullet hole surrounded by a band of blackened and seared skin. This band is significantly wider than one sees in a contact wound. With handguns, near contact wounds occur at ranges of less than 10 mm (**Figure 8.16b**).

C. **Intermediate range** gunshot wounds are characterized by the presence of **powder tattooing** around the wound of entrance (**Figure 8.16c**).

   1. Powder tattooing occurs when the muzzle of the weapon is held away from the body at the time of firing, yet is sufficiently close so that the powder grains emerging from the muzzle with the bullet strike the skin, producing punctate abrasions on the skin. These are called powder tattoo marks.

   2. Powder tattooing consists of multiple reddish brown to orange red punctate lesions of the skin surrounding the entrance wound.

   3. Powder tattoo marks are punctate abrasions.

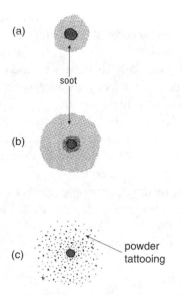

Figure 8.16   (a) Loose contact wound with ring of soot that can be washed away; (b) near contact wound with wide band of soot around the bullet hole; (c) intermediate wound with powder tattooing.

    a.   They cannot be wiped away.

    b.   They are not burns. Unfortunately, they are commonly referred to as powder burns.

        1. The term *powder burn* is very nebulous and incorrect in describing the etiology of the marks.

        2. The term *powder burns* should **never** be used when describing powder tattooing or the searing or blackening of the skin by the flame and/or soot.

  4. In the case of handguns, powder tattooing begins when the muzzle-to-target distance exceeds 10 mm.

  5. The maximum range to which powder tattooing extends depends on the type of powder and the weapon.

  6. Most centerfire handgun cartridges in the United States are loaded with either ball powder or flake (disc) powder (so called because of the shape of the powder grains).

    a.   Flake (disc) powder, the traditional form of powder used in handguns, consists of circular discs of powder. Powder tattooing from cartridges loaded with **flake powder** extends out to **2 feet**.

    b.   In centerfire handguns, powder tattooing with **ball powder** extends out to a maximum of **3 to 4 feet**.

  7. Shotguns use either flake or ball powder.

a. The only shotgun ammunition loaded with ball powder is that produced by Winchester. All other manufacturers use flake powder.

b. Tattooing with shotguns extends out to 2 feet for flake powder and 3 feet for ball powder.

8. In the case of centerfire rifles, two types of powder are used, ball powder and cylindrical powder. In cylindrical powder, the gunpowder has the shape of small cylinders.

a. Powder tattooing from **cylindrical powder** extends out to approximately **2 feet.**

b. **Ball powder** tattooing extends out to **3 feet.**

9. Rimfire ammunition (.22 Short; .22 Long Rifle) is loaded with either ball or disc powder.

a. The only manufacturer who uses ball powder is Winchester.

b. The ball powder used in the rimfire ammunition is extremely fine and does not travel a great distance. Therefore, powder tattooing in the rimfire cartridges generally does not travel beyond **1 $\frac{1}{2}$ feet for ball powder.**

c. **Disc powder** will produce tattooing out to **2 feet.**

10. The palms of the hands and the soles of the feet are very resistant to powder tattooing. Instead of tattoo marks on the surface of these areas, one sees embedded in the skin unburnt or partially burnt grains of gunpowder.

D. If a weapon is held close to the body, soot emerging from the muzzle of the gun will be deposited on either the skin or clothing. For handguns, deposition of powder soot generally does not extend beyond 12 inches, and in many cases, disappears well before 12 inches.

E. Once one exceeds the range at which powder tattooing occurs, one has a **distant gunshot wound.**

1. Distant gunshot wounds have entrances that tend to be round to oval with sharp punched out margins. Typically, the edges are surrounded by an abrasion ring (**Figure 8.17a**).

2. The abrasion ring is caused by the bullet scraping and compressing the edges of the skin as it indents and perforates it. It is not due to the heat of the bullet or its rotary movement.

3. Irregular abrasion rings can be due to:

a. The bullet impacting the skin at an angle (**Figure 8.17b**)

b. Irregularities of the skin at the point of entrance

c. A deformed bullet

d. Destabilization of the bullet in flight

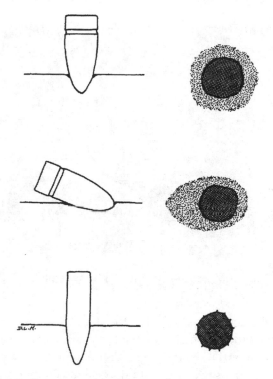

Figure 8.17   (a) Bullet enters the skin at right angle producing a regular, round abrasion collar; (b) bullet enters at an oblique angle resulting in an eccentric or crescent-shaped abrasion collar; (c) entrance wound of centerfire rifle bullet with micro tears around the edge of the entry defect.

4. In certain cases, an entrance wound will not have an abrasion ring around it. This occurs most commonly in centerfire rifle wounds but is also seen in handgun wounds from semi-jacketed and full-metal-jacketed bullets traveling at high velocity, e.g., the .357 Magnum and less commonly the 9 mm.

5. Entrance wounds from centerfire rifles may have small **micro tears** around the entrance defect (**Figure 8.17c**).

    a. These are tears, 1 to 2 mm in length, radiating outward from the circumference of the entrance.

    b. They may or may not be accompanied by an abrasion ring.

    c. They are occasionally seen with very high-velocity pistol ammunition such as a .357 Magnum.

6. Distant entrance wounds of the palms and soles are irregular, often having a stellate appearance, and lack an abrasion ring. They look exactly like exit wounds.

F. A **graze wound** is one in which the bullet travels across the skin at a very shallow angle, producing an elongated area of abrasion,

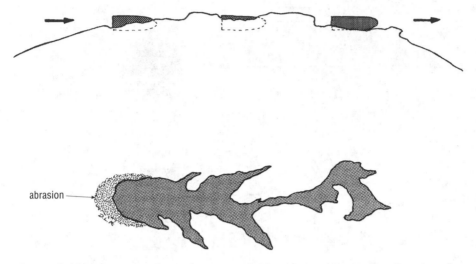

Figure 8.18   Tangential gunshot wound. Skin tears point in the direction the bullet traveled through the skin.

without actually perforating the skin. Often, it is difficult in graze wounds to tell which way the bullet was traveling.

G. In a **tangential wound**, the bullet parallels the surface of the skin producing a shallow wound that extends down to the subcutaneous tissue. There are tears along the margins that point in the direction the bullet was traveling (**Figure 8.18**).

H. **Exit wounds** tend to be larger and more irregular than entrance wounds. This is because by the time the bullet has reached the point of exit, it is destabilized and is not traveling point forward. In addition, it may be deformed.

   1. Exit wounds can vary anywhere from slit-like to stellate shaped, from small to very large.

   2. Typically, they do not have an abrasion ring around them since the exiting bullet does not contact the outer surface of the skin.

   3. Rarely, an exit wound will show an irregular zone of abraded skin around the exit defect. These are so-called **shored exit wounds**. They indicate that at the time the bullet exited, the skin at the point of exit was pushed outward against a firm surface such as the ground or a wall. This surface rubbed raw the everted margin of skin around the exit. Shored exits may also be caused by bra straps, belts or multiple layers of tight clothing.

VIII. **CENTERFIRE RIFLE WOUNDS**

A. Two types of ammunition are used in centerfire rifles:

   1. Full-metal-jacketed military

      2. Semi-jacketed hunting ammunition

B. Wounds produced by the full-metal-jacketed bullet are significantly less severe when compared to wounds produced by cartridges of the same caliber fired from the same weapon but with these cartridges loaded with hunting bullets.

C. Full-metal-jacketed bullets tend to go through the body undeformed. In most cases, no bullet fragments are seen on x-ray.

D. This is not the case for semi-jacketed hunting ammunition.

      1. As the bullet goes through the body, the jacket peels back, exposing the lead core which mushrooms, losing scores, if not hundreds, of small lead fragments. Strips of jacketing may also be lost.

      2. This phenomenon creates the characteristic radiological picture of wounds caused by hunting ammunition — the "**lead snowstorm**" (**Figure 8.19**).

IX. **MICROSCOPIC EXAMINATION OF GUNSHOT WOUNDS**

Microscopic examination of entrance wounds for determination of range is generally of no help. If soot or powder cannot be seen with either the naked eye or by use of a dissecting microscope, microscopic sections tend only to confuse the issue. This is because:

A. When bullets emerge from the barrel, they may be covered with soot, grease and other particulate matter deposited on the interior of the barrel by the discharge or from prior discharges.

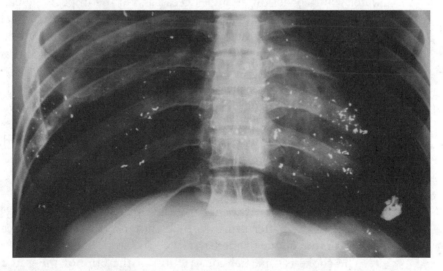

Figure 8.19 (See color insert following page 146) Postmortem chest x-ray demonstrating "lead snowstorm" produced by 6 mm hunting round. The main bullet mass is present in the left lower chest.

   B. When the bullet enters the body and travels through the tissue,
       this material may be wiped off along the sides of the wound track.
   C. When one examines the wound grossly, this material is not readily
       apparent, but microscopic sections will show small clumps of
       black material.
   D. The assumption is then made that this is powder and indicates a
       close-range wound. In fact, it is just debris carried by the bullet
       into the tissue and its presence cannot be used in determining
       range.

 X.   **THE EFFECTS OF INTERMEDIARY TARGETS**
   If an entrance wound is unusually large, with irregular margins and an
eccentric irregular abrasion ring, one must suspect that the bullet was either
a **ricochet** or had passed through an **intermediary target**.
   A. In both circumstances, the bullet is destabilized and/or deformed.
   B. In the case of a semi-jacketed bullet passing through an interme-
       diary target, the jacket may be stripped from the core and, thus,
       two missiles will be coming at the target, the jacket and the core.
       Both may penetrate.

 XI. **RICOCHET BULLETS**
   Ricochet bullets are relatively rare. Most bullets on striking a hard surface
break up or penetrate the surface. There is, however, a **critical angle of impact**
below which a bullet striking a surface will ricochet.
   A. For water, this angle ranges from 3 to 8°. Bullets ricocheting off
       water will ricochet off at angles greater than the impact angle.
   B. The critical angle of impact for ricochet for hard surfaces is much
       more variable. It may vary from 10 to 30°. When the bullet does
       ricochet off the surface, it ricochets off at an angle smaller than
       the impact angle.
   C. The entrance wounds produced by ricochet bullets tend to be
       larger and more irregular in shape with very large irregular areas
       of abrasion around the entrance wound.
   D. Bullets that do ricochet off a hard surface typically have one side
       flattened with a mirrorlike surface. This is true for both jacketed
       and lead bullets.

 XII. **SHOTGUNS**
   A. Shotguns are designed to fire multiple pellets down the barrel.
       The size of the pattern thrown by a shotgun depends to a great
       degree on the **choke** of the barrel.
       1. The choke is a partial constriction of the bore of the gun at
           the muzzle end that controls the size of the shot pattern.
       2. There are four levels of choke:
           a. Full

        b. Modified

        c. Improved

        d. Cylinder

   3. Different degrees of choke give different spreads.

   4. Excluding the .410, shotguns of 12, 16 and 20 gauges of the same choke should throw the same size pattern at the same range. The only difference is that there will be more pellet holes in the pattern produced by the 12 than the 16 and 20.

B. Wounds due to shotguns

   1. Contact wounds of the head from shotguns tend to be explosive, resembling centerfire rifle wounds. X-rays will usually reveal at least a few pellets.

   2. Contact wounds of the chest and abdomen are circular in configuration with blackened and seared margins. A muzzle imprint may be present.

        a. From contact to 2 feet, birdshot fired from a shotgun produces a single round entrance anywhere from 3/4 inch to 1 inch in diameter (**Figure 8.20**).

        b. By 3 feet, the wound has widened and will have scalloped margins due to the separating pellets (**Figure 8.20**).

        c. By 4 feet, one will have an entrance hole approximately 1 inch in diameter surrounded by scattered satellite pellet holes (**Figure 8.20**).

        d. As the range increases, the number of surrounding pellet holes increases.

        e. By approximately 10 feet, there tends to be a ragged central hole surrounded by numerous pellet holes.

        f. Beyond 10 feet, the pattern changes dramatically depending upon the choke, so that one will often get just a pattern of multiple pellet holes.

   3. The size of the shotgun pattern should always be measured and recorded for subsequent range determinations. At that time, the shotgun and identical ammunition are fired at known ranges in an attempt to reproduce the same sized pattern found on the body.

   4. The shotgun wadding tends to go into the entrance wound for the first 5 to 6 feet of range. After that, it tends to drift to the side and may make a separate impact abrasion on the adjacent skin.

   5. Winchester birdshot wadding consists of cylindrical discs of cardboard. If they impact the skin adjacent to the entrance,

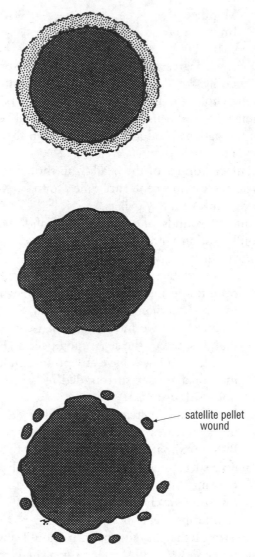

Figure 8.20   Representative shotgun wounds. Upper figure: Wound produced from contact to 2 feet. Middle figure: Wound with scalloped margins produced at about 3 feet. Lower figure: Wound with satellite pellet defects produced at 4 feet.

there will be a circular mark produced. They will mark the skin generally out to 15 feet.

6. In Remington and Federal ammunition, birdshot pellets are enclosed in a cup with a number of slits down the side. When the cup containing the pellets exits the barrel, air resistance

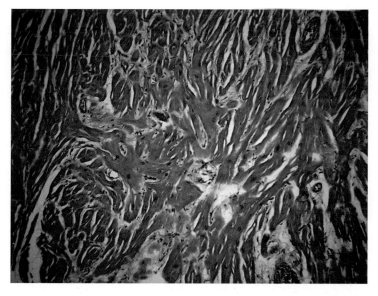

Figure 5.1 Section of interventricular septum in 19-year-old white male with idiopathic hypertrophic subaortic stenosis (IHSS) demonstrating myofiber hypertrophy and disarray.

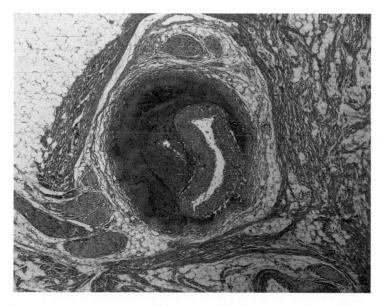

Figure 5.3 Spontaneous acute dissection of left anterior descending coronary artery in 38-year-old white female. No other significant autopsy findings. No documented history of hypertension.

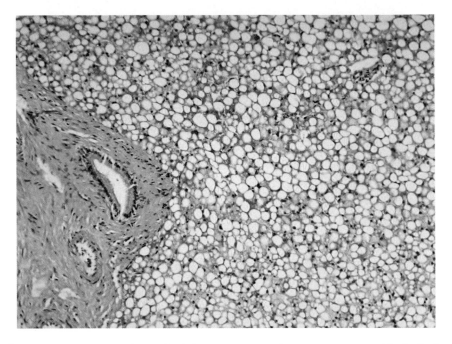

Figure 5.5 Liver with marked fatty metamorphosis in 40-year-old alcoholic, found dead in bed, without any other significant autopsy findings.

Figure 6.1 Motor vehicle passenger, ejected during collision with fixed object. Large brush burn abrasions from sliding across pavement.

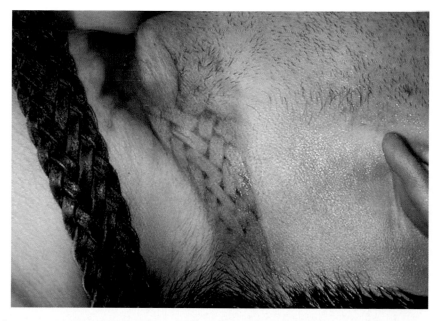

Figure 6.2 Patterned abrasion of neck produced by braided belt used as ligature.

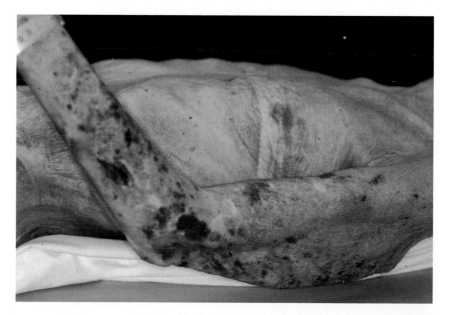

Figure 6.3 Multiple senile ecchymoses on upper extremity of elderly individual, associated with multiple hypopigmented scars.

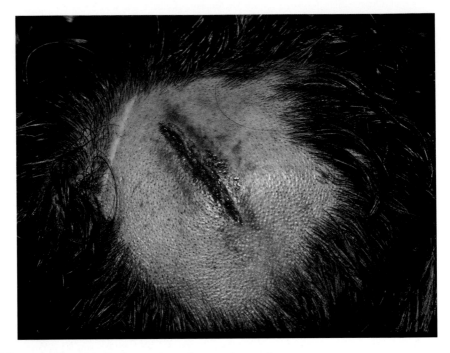

Figure 6.4 Simple laceration of posterior scalp.

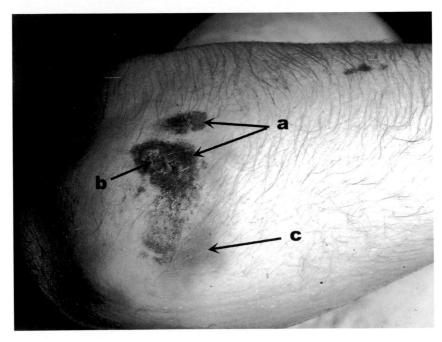

Figure 6.6 Abrasions, lacerations, and contusions may occur together in some cases. **a** — abrasions; **b** — laceration at center of an abrasion; **c** — contusion.

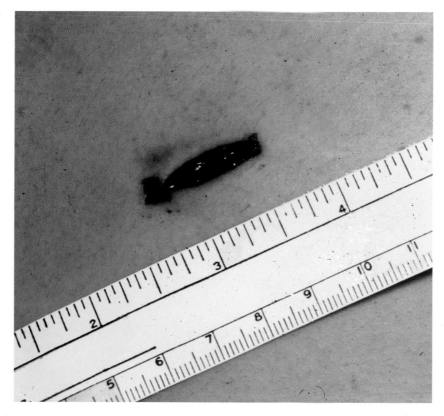

Figure 7.2 Stab wound with abrasion and contusion due to guard, photographed with ruler for documentation of size.

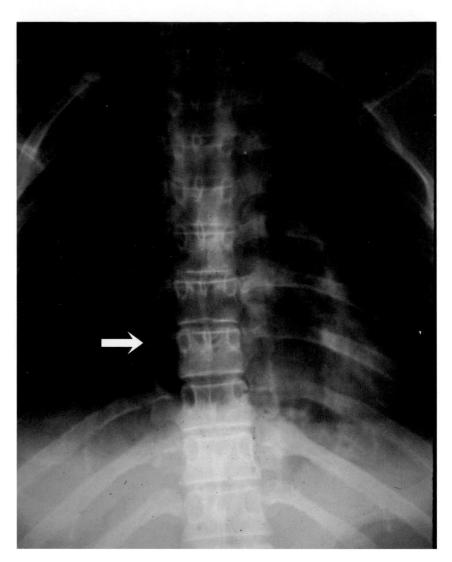

Figure 7.5 Postmortem chest radiograph demonstrating air in right side of heart in victim with incised wound of neck. Air within the right-sided heart chambers allows clear delineation of the wall of right atrium (arrow).

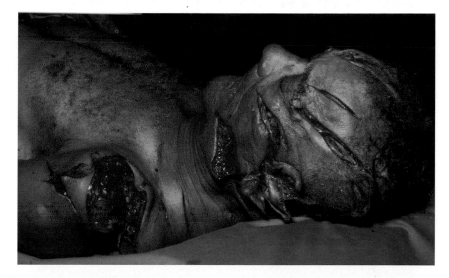

Figure 7.7   Multiple chop wounds produced by attack with machete.

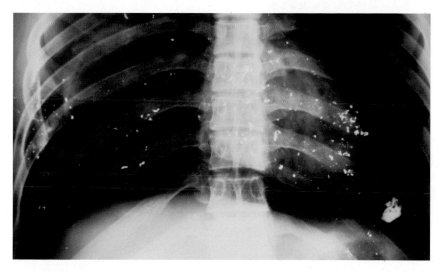

Figure 8.19   Postmortem chest x-ray demonstrating "lead snowstorm" produced by 6 mm hunting round. The main bullet mass is present in the left lower chest.

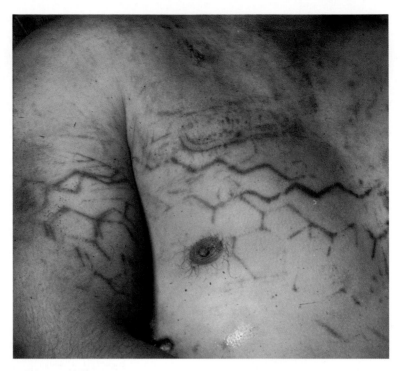

Figure 14.1 Patterned contusion from tire tread.

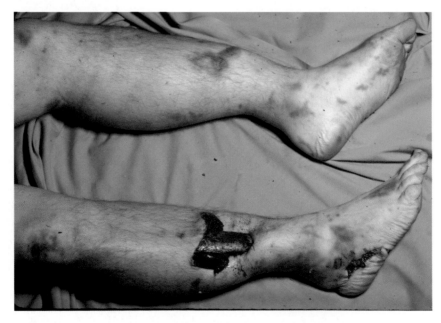

Figure 14.2 "Bumper fractures" in pedestrian struck by motor vehicle.

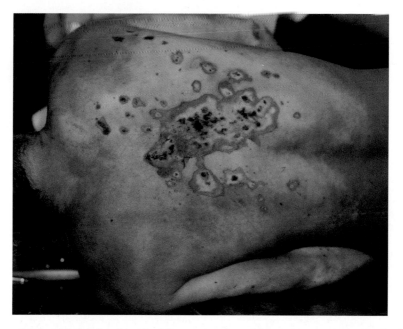

Figure 16.1 Multiple electrical burns produced by current arc across body in high-voltage electrocution.

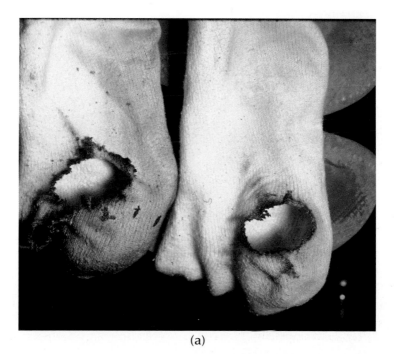

(a)

Figure 16.2 Typical electrical "exit" burns of feet with corresponding burn defects in socks (a) and soles of feet (b). Close-up appearance of electrical burn (c).

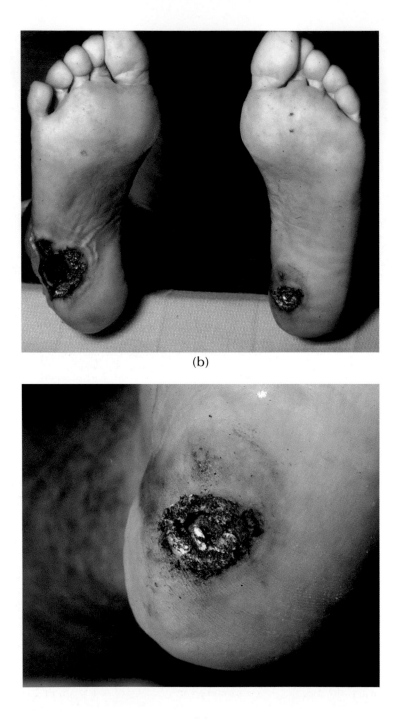

(b)

(c)

Figure 16.2 (continued)

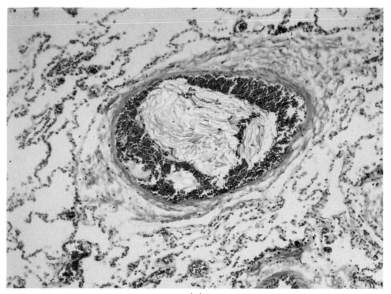

(a)

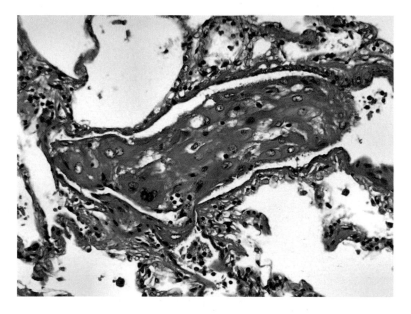

(b)

Figure 19.1 Various pulmonary emboli which may result in maternal death. (a) amniotic fluid embolus in pulmonary vasculature, H & E stain of lung tissue; (b) placental embolus, H & E stain; (c) placental embolus, HCG immunostain of lung tissue.

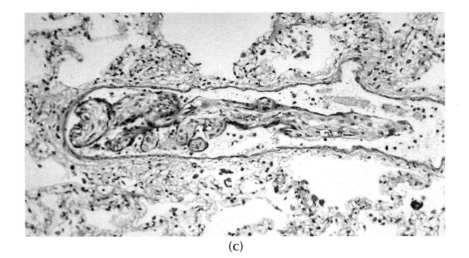

(c)

Figure 19.1 (continued)

causes the petals to open up producing, in the case of the 12-,
16-, and 20-gauge shotgun shells, an open cup with four petals.

    a.   With plastic wadding in 12, 16, and 20 gauge, it takes at least 1 foot of travel for the cup to open up.

    b.   At less than 1 foot of range, one tends to get a circular hole.

    c.   Between one and two feet, the wadding has opened up so that the four petals stick out. One then gets a circular entrance wound with a **Maltese cross pattern** of abrasions encircling it (**Figure 8.21**).

    d.   As the wadding goes through the air, air resistance folds back the petals so that by 3 feet, one will again have a single hole of entrance and not the open petal pattern.

    e.   .410 shotgun ammunition, no matter the manufacturer, uses plastic cups with three petals. The petal marks appear at about 6 inches and are gone by about 3 feet.

7. Buckshot and Magnum birdshot shotgun shells are usually loaded with the lead pellets embedded in finely granulated white plastic material.

    a.   This material emerges with the pellets on firing and accompanies them to the target, at least for the first 5 to 10 feet.

    b.   This material can produce very fine punctate abrasions on the skin around the pellet holes up to 6 to 9 feet from the muzzle. These marks cannot be differentiated from powder tattooing by their appearance.

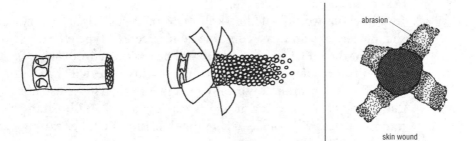

Figure 8.21   Depiction of shotgun wad with enclosed lead shot in plastic cup as it travels through the air after being fired. Left — Less than 1 foot of range. The cup has not opened; if the body is impacted at this stage, the resulting entry wound tends to be round. Middle — 1 to 2 feet of range. The sleeves of the plastic cup have opened and are in the process of being forced backward; if the body is impacted at this stage, a cross-like pattern of abrasion may be found around the entry defect (right).

(a)   (b)

Figure 8.22   The passage of a bullet through bone (middle figure) leaves a distinctive entry wound (a) and exit wound (b). The entry wound usually has a sharp, punched out appearance, while the exit wound is generally beveled in a cone-like fashion.

        c.   Differentiation is usually made by the presence of the white material adherent to the skin and clothing.

XIII. **WOUNDS OF BONE**
    A. Differentiation of an entrance from an exit in bone is usually easy (**Figure 8.22**).
       1. The entrance is round to oval with sharp punched out margins.
       2. Fragments of bone are broken off the edges of the exiting surface and propelled forward, accompanying the bullet on its path. Thus, the exit is beveled out in a cone-like fashion.
       3. When one is dealing with very thin bone, such as the orbital plates or in some instances temporal bone, this beveling appearance may not be present.
    B. If the bullet strikes the skull at a very shallow angle, a **gutter wound** may occur. The most superficial such wound involves only the outer table while the most severe involves the complete thickness of the bone.
    C. In a **keyhole wound** of the skull, the bullet striking at a very shallow angle produces a combined entrance/exit type effect. At the point the bullet impacts, there will be a punched-out sharp-edge entrance defect. The distal end of this hole will have a beveled out appearance, typically seen in an exit. This is usually due to the bullet striking at a very shallow angle and breaking into two pieces with one entering the skull and the other exiting (**Figure 8.23**).
    D. In passing through the skull, bullets produce secondary fractures of the skull due to the temporary cavity effect. The only caliber that tends not to do this is the .22 Short.

XIV. **CALIBER DETERMINATION BY SIZE OF ENTRANCE WOUNDS**
    A. One cannot determine the caliber of a bullet that made a particular entrance wound in the skin by measuring the diameter of the wound. Thus, while most 9 mm bullets tend to produce 9 mm

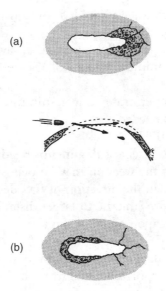

Figure 8.23 A bullet striking bone at a tangential angle may produce a "keyhole" defect which is actually a combined entry and exit defect. (a) Appearance of the outer bone table for wound depicted in middle figure; entry on the left is punched out while the exit on the right is beveled. The inner bone table for the same wound is shown in (b).

holes, the authors have seen cases in which they produce 5.5 mm holes. The reverse may also occur.

B. In regard to bone, full-metal-jacketed bullets tend to produce entrance wounds in the bone the same diameter as the bullet. Thus, a .25 FMJ bullet tends to produce a 6 to 7 mm hole. Semijacketed and lead bullets, however, may produce entrances significantly larger than the bullet diameter. For example, .22 caliber lead bullets generally produce entrance holes 5 to 6 mm in diameter but defects up to 11 to 12 mm in diameter can also occur.

XV. **PERFORATION OF SKIN AND BONE**

A. Skin is second to bone in its resistance to the entrance of missiles.
1. The two major determining factors as to whether a bullet will enter are the **weight** of the missile and the **velocity.** The heavier the bullet, the less velocity it needs to perforate skin.
2. In tests using human skin, it was found that a 113-grain lead round-nose .38 caliber bullet required a minimum velocity of 191 feet per second (58 meters per second) to perforate skin.

3. For a .22 caliber Diabolo-style airgun pellet, weighing an average of 16.5 grains, a velocity of 245 feet/second (75 meters/second) was needed for consistent perforation of the skin.

4. A 0.177 airgun pellet weighing an average of 8.25 grains required a minimum velocity of 331 feet/second (101 meters/second).

B. For bullets to perforate bone, a minimum velocity of 200 to 275 feet/second is needed.

XVI. **GUNSHOT RESIDUE**

A. When a gun is discharged, **gunshot residue (GSR)** escaping from the muzzle of the weapon may be deposited on skin or clothing adjacent to or in the direction of fire, depending on:
1. Range of fire (muzzle to target distance)
2. Type of weapon and ammunition
3. Presence of intervening objects

B. Gunshot residue is composed of sooty smoke, gunpowder, primer components, vaporized metal from the bullet and cartridge case.

C. Gunshot residue originates from the firearm, the cartridge case, and the bullet with most of the residue from the primer.
1. The classic spheroid particle containing lead (Pb), barium (Ba), and antimony (Sb) is characteristic of GSR.
2. Other particles from the primer containing Pb, Ba, or Sb are just consistent with GSR.
3. Special handgun loads intended for use on firearm ranges may have primers that do not contain any of these three elements.

D. Two types of analysis are used for routine detection and identification of GSR on hands:
1. Scanning Electron Microscope with Energy Dispersive X-ray (SEM-EDX) can positively identify GSR by identifying spheroid particles of PbBaSb.
   a. This method of analysis is qualitative, not quantitative.
   b. Positive results mean that the individual either:
     • Fired a gun
     • Was in proximity to a discharging weapon
     • Handled an object on which there was GSR
2. Flameless Atomic Absorption/Inductively Coupled Plasma Spectrometer
   a. Are devices for analysis of Pb, Ba, Sb
   b. Do not specifically identify GSR
   c. Give quantitative results

d. Can be used to determine distribution and quantity of material on hands
e. Can conclude whether distribution and quantity of material assumed to be GSR is consistent with firing a weapon
f. Of more use to a forensic pathologist than SEM alone in suicide cases

3. A negative test for GSR is meaningless, as:
a. Tests are only positive in about half of the cases when an individual is known to have fired a gun.
b. Tests are usually negative in relationship to rifles and shotguns.

E. Clothing may be tested for presence of GSR:
1. **Modified Greiss** test
a. Use of photographic paper and chemical processing to produce visual display of GSR pattern and density of particles.
b. Test is specific for **nitrites** (by-product of combustion of smokeless gunpowder).
c. Performance of test does not interfere with other subsequent tests.
d. Developed pattern of GSR deposits allows for determination of muzzle to target distance.

2. **Sodium rhodizonate** reaction
a. Detects lead from primer or bullet wipe.
b. Does not allow for determination of range of fire.
c. Test may be performed after the modified Greiss test.

3. **Energy dispersive x-ray** (EDX)
a. Detects distribution of barium, antimony, lead, copper particles around entrance hole in target, clothing.
b. Can be used to arrive at range of fire approximation.
c. Nondestructive technique as no chemicals are used.
d. Can be performed relatively rapidly.

XVII. MISCELLANEOUS
A. Regarding the **ability to move** after being shot, one has to be very cautious in expressing an opinion. As a general rule, gunshot wounds of the head or spinal cord are immediately immobilizing. Other wounds may not be. This includes wounds of the heart or aorta. Even if the heart is totally destroyed by a gunshot wound, the individual can still function for 10 to 15 seconds based on the residual oxygen supply of the brain. There are numerous instances of individuals incurring fatal gunshot wounds yet being able to function for a significant amount of time after receiving the injury.

B. **X-raying** of all cases involving gunshot wounds is strongly urged. X-rays will aid the physician in the location of the bullet or pellets as well as giving him an idea of what type of weapon was used.

C. Part of the examination of the body is **examination of the clothing**. If the bullet has gone through clothing, the clothing should always be examined for the presence of soot or gunpowder. The clothing may actually filter this material out, and if the clothing is not examined, one will be presented with a gunshot wound that has the appearance of a distant wound even though it is close range.

XVIII. SUICIDE

A. The most common method of suicide in the United States is by shooting.

1. This is true for both men and women.
2. The particular type of weapon used, a handgun, rifle or shotgun, depends to a certain degree on the region of the country as well as the gender of the individual.
3. A handgun is the most commonly employed firearm by both men and women, though a greater percentage of women use handguns.

B. Most suicidal gunshot wounds are contact and involve the head.

1. For handguns, the temple is the favorite site, followed by the mouth, under the chin or between the eyes.
2. Approximately 5% of right-handed individuals will shoot themselves in the left temple.
3. With long arms, the favorite sites in the head are the temple and the mouth.

C. In approximately 25% of the cases in which suicide is committed with a handgun, the handgun will be found in the hand. For long arms, this is approximately 20%.

D. In approximately 25% of the cases a suicide note is found.

XIX. GENERAL FIREARM TERMINOLOGY

Barrel	Metal tube through which the bullet passes when fired from the cartridge.
Bore	The interior of a barrel, in front of the chamber. Rifles and most handguns have a "rifled" barrel, while shotguns are smooth bored.
Bullet	The projectile that is actually fired by a handgun or rifle.
Caliber	(1) For firearms: the approximate distance between the lands of a rifled barrel.
	(2) For ammunition: numerical term, minus the decimal point, which indicates a rough approximation of the bullet diameter.
Cartridge	The basic "unit" of ammunition, also called a "round," made up of the case, primer, powder, and a bullet.
Chamber	Receptacle for a cartridge, from which the projectile is fired down the barrel.
Cylinder	Rotating part of a revolver which contains several chambers for cartridges.
Double action	Handgun mechanism in which a single pull of the trigger cocks and releases the hammer, firing the round in the chamber (performs two actions).
Ejection port	Slot in slide of semiautomatic pistol through which the empty casing of a fired round is ejected. In most pistols, the casing will eject to the right.
Firing actions	(1) Fully automatic; fires a succession of cartridges so long as the trigger is depressed or until the ammunition supply is exhausted.
	(2) Semiautomatic — autoloading action that will fire only a single shot for each pull of the trigger.
Firing pin	A device that, when struck by the hammer, hits the primer in the cartridge, igniting the powder and firing the bullet.
Gauge	For shotguns, the number of spherical balls of pure lead, each of which exactly fits the bore of the shotgun, that equals 1 pound. This is the "caliber" of a shotgun.
Grain	Measure used to designate the weight of a bullet or the amount of gunpowder in a cartridge. 7,000 grains = 1 pound.
Hammer	Device tripped by movement of the trigger, which impacts the firing pin.
Magazine	Device that holds cartridges in a repeating firearm; fits into the butt of the pistol. Also referred to as a "clip."
Muzzle	End of the gun barrel where the bullet emerges when the gun is fired.
Pistol	(may have two definitions, depending on your viewpoint)
	(1) any firearm designed to be held and fired with one hand. This definition would include revolvers.
	(2) any handgun that does not hold its ammunition (cartridges) in a revolving cylinder.
Primer	Volatile compound that detonates when impacted by the firing pin, causing ignition of the gunpowder.
Rifling	Twisting grooves cut in the barrel of a gun which put a spin on the bullet, making it more stable in flight.
Single action	Handgun mechanism where the hammer must be manually cocked before the gun can be fired by pulling the trigger.
Slide	Top part of a semiautomatic that contains the barrel.
Trigger	The device (lever) that fires the gun when pulled, usually by the index finger.
Wadcutter	Cylindrical bullet designed to cut clean holes in a paper target.

General References

1. Di Maio, V.J.M., *Gunshot Wounds*, 2nd ed., CRC Press, Boca Raton, FL, 1999.

2. Karger, B. et al., Backsplatter from experimental close-range shots to the head, I. Macrobacksplatter, *Int. J. Legal Med.*, 109, 66, 1996.

3. Karger, B., et al., Backsplatter from experimental close-range shots to the head, II. Microbacksplatter and morphology, *Int. J. Legal Med.*, 110, 27, 1997.

Asphyxia

9

Asphyxia is characterized by inadequate oxygenation of tissue. Asphyxial deaths fall into three general categories:
- Suffocation
- Strangulation
- Chemical asphyxia

I. SUFFOCATION

In **suffocation**, asphyxia results from failure of oxygen to reach the blood. There are four types of suffocation:
- Environmental suffocation
- Smothering
- Choking
- Mechanical

A. In **environmental suffocation**, there is inadequate oxygen in the atmosphere due to environmental conditions.
   1. There may be an actual reduction of the oxygen, such as might occur in a closed chamber where fungus has depleted the atmosphere of oxygen.
   2. In other instances, there is displacement of oxygen by carbon dioxide, such as in a silo, or by nitrogen such as occurs in the holds of ships.
   3. A child who becomes locked in a refrigerator suffocates due to environmental deprivation of oxygen.
   4. In these types of death, **there are no specific autopsy findings**. Petechiae are not present.

B. **Smothering** occurs by mechanical obstruction of the nose and mouth.
   1. Such deaths may be accidental, homicidal or suicidal.

2. Examples of accidental deaths are: an infant who becomes wedged between the frame of a crib and the mattress with the face pushed into the mattress; burial in a cave-in.
3. The most common form of suicidal smothering involves using a plastic bag secured about the head, a method more common among the elderly.
4. An example of homicide by smothering is gagging accomplished by occluding the nose and mouth with duct tape. This may occur in robberies, burglaries, or kidnappings where the victim is "gagged" to keep them quiet.
5. More deliberate homicides involve smothering with a pillow or bed clothing; pinching off the nose with fingers and clamping the hand over the mouth. In both instances, the victim is usually a young child.
6. In infants who are smothered:
   a. The child will develop bradycardia in approximately 30 seconds and a flat EEG and cessation of respiration in 90 seconds.
   b. Respiration will not return spontaneously if the smothering is stopped. The child has to be resuscitated.
7. In deaths due to smothering, typically, there are no findings at autopsy. This includes petechiae.
   a. In the case of a suicide with a plastic bag, if it is removed by a relative prior to notification of the police and/or the medical examiner, the diagnosis cannot be made.
   b. In homicides with pillows and young children, again, there are no findings.
   c. If the victim is an adult, and they are conscious and can resist, there may be some bruising of the lips and nose and some scratches. This is especially true if the hands are used to occlude the airway.
C. **Choking.** In choking, there is blockage of the internal airways.
   1. Homicides are rare. Usually they involve cases in which a gag is rammed in the mouth of a burglary or robbery victim in order to keep them quiet. The assailant does not realize that the victim is going to choke to death. The authors have seen deliberate cases of homicide by choking. In one, a pacifier was rammed into the throat of a young child.
   2. Most choking deaths are accidental and involve blockage of the posterior pharynx and larynx by food or foreign objects.
      a. In children, the typical object is a small toy, ball, or a piece of hot dog.

b. Accidental choking deaths in adults are usually associated with acute alcohol intoxication, senility or mental retardation.

3. Occasionally death is ascribed to massive aspiration of food. In actuality, this is rarely a cause of death.

a. The finding of food in the airway does not mean the individual choked to death.

b. Agonal aspiration of food occurs in approximately 25% of all deaths irrespective of the cause.

c. Death from massive aspiration of food with obstruction of the airway occurs only when there is severe central nervous system depression such as in an individual who has had a stroke and in whom there is virtual absence of the gag reflex.

4. A natural cause for obstruction of the airway is acute epiglottitis. While common in children, this is being seen increasingly in adults. It is secondary to a bacterial infection of the epiglottis.

5. In choking victims, the only findings at autopsy are obstruction of the airway. There are no typical findings and no petechiae of the conjunctivae or sclerae.

D. **Mechanical (traumatic) asphyxia** occurs when pressure on the chest and abdomen restricts respiratory movements and thus inspiration.

1. Most such deaths are accidental. Examples are an individual repairing a car when it falls off the jack onto their chest; burial and cave-ins in sand. Such deaths also occur in panics where people are "crushed" to death.

2. In cases of mechanical asphyxia, there may be no internal injuries, even when a car has fallen on an individual.

3. **Overlay** is a variation of mechanical asphyxia which involves not only compression of the chest but probably a component of smothering. It is seen when parents take an infant to bed with them and roll over them during the night. At autopsy, these children show no diagnostic findings and cannot be separated from SIDS deaths.

4. In **positional asphyxia**, a form of mechanical asphyxia, a person is trapped in a position such that they cannot breathe or the respiration becomes inadequate. Examples of this would be an individual suspended upside down for a prolonged period of time.

5. Excepting overlay, in mechanical asphyxia, the face and neck are a deep red to purple color secondary to congestion. There are numerous petechiae of the conjunctivae and sclerae. Confluent scleral hemorrhage may be present.

II. STRANGULATION

In **strangulation**, there is occlusion of the blood vessels in the neck secondary to external pressure. There are three types of strangulation:

- Hanging
- Ligature
- Manual

A. **Mechanism of death** in strangulation cases

In strangulation deaths, occlusion of the airway usually does not occur, and is not the mechanism of death. The **mechanism of death** is cerebral hypoxia secondary to obstruction of the vessels bringing oxygenated blood to the brain.

1. Two thirds to three quarters of the blood supply of the brain is provided by the carotid arteries with the remainder supplied by the vertebral arteries.

2. An individual cannot survive on the vertebral artery blood supply alone, if there is acute occlusion of both carotid arteries.

3. The amount of force necessary to compress the carotid arteries is approximately 11 lb. Complete occlusion of these two vessels will produce **loss of consciousness in 10 to 15 seconds**.

4. Since only 4.4 lb of pressure is necessary to occlude the jugular veins, and they lie adjacent to the carotids, in virtually every case that the carotids are occluded, the jugular veins are also occluded.

   a. The jugular veins are the principal vessels through which blood drains from the head.

   b. Because of this, when the carotid arteries and jugular veins are occluded, while blood will continue to enter the head from the vertebral arteries, drainage is inadequate.

   c. Thus, the face will appear cyanotic with numerous petechiae of the conjunctivae, sclerae and periorbital skin.

5. In hanging, there is often occlusion of the vertebral arteries as well as the carotids, thus, no significant amount of blood reaches the head. The secondary vertebral venous system, however, still drains blood. Because of this, in hangings, the face often appears pale and petechiae are often not present. The picture presented depends on the degree of suspension.

6. Knight feels that another possible explanation for death in strangulation cases is cardiac arrest secondary to stimulation

of the carotid body and sinuses.[1] There is no proof of this and most of the accounts of such deaths are anecdotal.

B. **Hanging.** In hanging, the weight of the body tightens a noose around the neck compressing the vessels of the neck.

1. Hanging does not have to involve complete suspension of the body. Individuals have hanged themselves standing, sitting and even lying down. The weight of the head (10 to 12 pounds) is in fact sufficient to occlude the carotid arteries.

2. Almost all hangings are suicides. There are occasional accidental hangings with homicides extremely rare.

3. Nooses are constructed of whatever material is available. Rope, electrical cords, ties, sheets, belts, dog chains are examples.

4. The noose is typically constructed with a simple slip knot which on hanging is positioned on the side of the neck.

5. The noose imparts a **furrow** to the skin of the neck that has an **inverted V-shaped configuration**, with the apex of the V indicating the point of suspension. A gap in the furrow is often present at the knot site (**Figure 9.1**).

   a. This furrow typically lies above the larynx.

   b. The appearance of the furrow depends upon the noose. A rope will produce a prominent furrow with the weave pattern imparted to the skin; a strip of soft cloth usually produces a discontinuous pattern of irregular areas of abrasion.

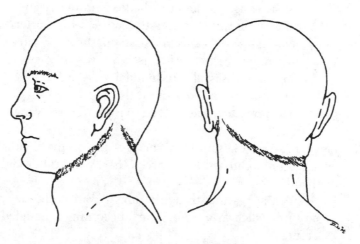

Figure 9.1 Configuration of abraded furrow produced by ligature in hanging death. Point of suspension is just posterior to the left ear, with the furrow crossing the anterior neck **above** the larynx.

    c.   Typically, the furrow is pale yellow initially and becomes brown on drying. The edges are often congested.

6. On viewing the body, the face is usually pale; the tongue protruding and dried out. Mucous drips from the nose.

    a.   Only one quarter of the cases show any evidence of scleral or conjunctival hemorrhage.

    b.   Fractures of the hyoid bone or thyroid cartilage are uncommon, being present in only 12% of the cases.[2]

    c.   Hemorrhage is present in the strap muscles in about 20% of the cases.

    d.   Fracture of the cervical spine is extremely rare and is usually associated with a hanging involving a drop, in an individual who has underlying disease of the vertebral column such as osteoporosis.

    e.   If the individual is completely suspended, there is pooling of the blood in the lower extremities and forearms with the development of petechiae due to hydrostatic rupture of the vessels. These punctate hemorrhages are called **Tardieu spots.**

7. **Autoerotic hangings** are accidental in manner.

    a.   The victim is usually a male, rarely a female.

    b.   In these cases, the individual induces transient cerebral hypoxia, by "hanging" himself or herself for a short period of time, in order to increase the pleasure associated with masturbation.

    c.   Since consciousness can be lost in only 10 to 15 seconds after application of pressure to the carotid arteries, a mistake of only 1 to 2 seconds can put the person in a situation where he or she loses consciousness and dies.

    d.   In many cases, the individual will be found with erotic literature scattered around the body.

    e.   The noose may be padded to prevent furrow marks on the neck.

C. **Ligature strangulation.** Here the pressure on the neck is applied by a ligature tightened by a force other than body weight, often the hands.

1. Accidental ligature strangulations are rare and usually involve clothing, such as a tie or scarf, becoming entangled in machinery.

2. Suicides occur but are very uncommon. An individual is capable of tying a ligature around their neck tight enough to cause death before losing consciousness.

3. Most ligature strangulations are homicide. Women are more often the victims than men with the most common motive rape.

4. In ligature strangulation, **death is due to occlusion of the carotid arteries with cerebral hypoxia.**

5. The ligature occludes both the carotid arteries and jugular veins but does not involve the vertebral arteries. Because of this:

   a. Blood still gets to the head but has great difficulty draining out.

   b. Thus, **the face is markedly congested with numerous petechiae of the sclerae and conjunctivae** and often the periorbital skin and skin of the face.

6. Depending upon the nature of the ligature, the force used, as well as the ability of the victim to resist, there will be great variability in the ligature marks produced on the neck.

   a. The marks are usually yellow parchment in color, turning to brown as they dry.

   b. A soft ligature will leave a poorly defined mark while a thin wire usually leaves a very deep prominent furrow.

   c. **The ligature mark tends to be horizontal and either overlies or lies below the larynx (Figure 9.2).**

7. In ligature strangulation, internal injuries are present in approximately one third of the cases:

   a. Hemorrhage in 20%

   b. Fractures of the hyoid bone and thyroid cartilages in 12.5% of cases[2]

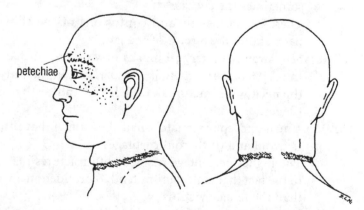

Figure 9.2 Horizontal ligature abrasion in homicidal strangulation. The face is usually markedly congested, with numerous fine facial petechiae, especially periorbital.

8. In elderly individuals and infants, pale crease marks between overlapping rolls of neck skin are often mistaken for ligature marks.

D. **Manual strangulation**. In this entity, pressure by a hand, forearm, or another limb on the neck occludes the blood vessels.

1. Suicide is not possible as loss of consciousness would result in release of the pressure on the neck.

2. **Virtually all cases are homicides**. A higher percentage of victims are women.

3. Occasionally an individual will claim that the death was an accident due to a vasovagal reflex triggered when they just grabbed the deceased around the neck without applying continuous pressure.

   a. Death is alleged to be due to stimulation of the carotid sinuses with resultant bradycardia, vasodilatation, hypotension and cardiac arrest.

   b. Such a story is suspect. In a normal individual, stimulation of the carotid bodies and sinuses will produce only a small drop in blood pressure and mild bradycardia.

   c. In deaths allegedly from this entity in which autopsies have been performed, there is usually severe underlying disease capable of having caused sudden death and the death is probably not due to vasovagal stimulation.

4. In manual strangulation, at autopsy:

   a. The face appears congested.

   b. In 89% of cases, there are **petechiae of the sclerae and conjunctivae** as well as of the skin around the eyes and sometimes the cheeks.[2]

   c. There are **abrasions and contusions of the skin of the neck** and undersurface of the jaw.

   d. Semicircular **fingernail marks** may be present.

   e. In 68.1% of cases, there is **hemorrhage in the muscles of the neck with fractures of the hyoid and/or thyroid cartilages.**[2]

5. Most men and approximately half the women have fractures of the hyoid and/or thyroid cartilages.

   a. The higher percentage of men with fractures may be due to the fact that male victims tend to be older on an average than the female victims.

   b. Usually, fractures of the hyoid and/or thyroid cartilages are not present in young individuals due to the elastic nature of these structures.

6. [Diagnosis of a fracture of the hyoid and/or thyroid cartilage is only valid when there is visible hemorrhage around the fracture site] If there is no visible hemorrhage, or the hemorrhage can only be demonstrated microscopically, then this fracture cannot be designated as being antemortem.

7. Rarely, one will have a manual strangulation in which there is neither external nor internal evidence of trauma. This occurs when the victim was unconscious at the time they were assaulted and the amount of pressure to the neck was so minimal as not to produce either external or internal injury.

8. One should be very cautious in cases of suspected strangulation where the "trauma" is limited to retroesophageal, retrolaryngeal, and/or paracervical vertebral hemorrhages in the absence of other injuries. The presence of these hemorrhages is not diagnostic of manual strangulation. These hemorrhages can be artifactual due to overdistension and rupture of venous sinuses in these areas.

III. CHEMICAL ASPHYXIANTS

These gases prevent the utilization of oxygen at the cellular level. The three most common chemical asphyxiants are carbon monoxide, hydrogen cyanide and hydrogen sulfide. Carbon monoxide deaths are usually accidental, though there are a significant number of suicides involving this gas. Hydrogen cyanide cases are usually suicidal. Hydrogen sulfide cases are virtually all accidental. They involve individuals working in sewer plants and cesspools.

IV. NECK HOLDS

Neck holds are used by police agencies to subdue violent individuals. There are two types of holds: the **bar arm (choke) hold** and the **carotid sleeper**.[3]

A. The **bar arm (choke) hold** acts to occlude the airway by compression of the airway by the forearm.

1. The forearm is placed across the neck. The free hand then grips the wrist of the arm around the neck, pulling it (the arm) rearward, collapsing the airway and displacing the tongue rearwards occluding the hypopharynx.

2. The pressure on the thyroid and cricoid cartilage can cause fractures, especially if they are ossified. Because of this, use of the bar arm hold is not recommended.

B. In the carotid sleeper hold:

1. An arm is placed around the front of the neck cradling the midline of the neck in the crook of the arm. The free hand

then grips the wrist of the arm around the neck pulling it (the arm) rearward, creating a pincer effect by the forearm and arm.

2. This results in compression of the carotid arteries with preservation of the airway (larynx and trachea).

3. The resultant cerebral ischemia results in loss of consciousness in 10 to 15 seconds. On release of the hold, the individual should begin to regain consciousness in 20 to 30 seconds.

C. Deaths associated with these holds are usually due to underlying cardiac disease and/or drugs combined with stress on the heart due to the effects of catecholamines. (See Chapter 10.)

References

1. Knight, B., Fatal pressure on the neck, in *Forensic Pathology*, 2nd ed., Arnold, London, 1996, p. 361.

2. Di Maio, V.J.M., Homicidal asphyxia, *Am. J. For. Med. Path.*, 21(1), 1, 2000.

3. Reay, D.T. and Eisele, J.W., Death from law enforcement neck holds, *Am. J. For. Med. Path.*, 3(3), 253, 1982.

General References

1. Di Maio, V.J.M. and Di Maio, D.J., *Forensic Pathology*, 2nd ed., CRC Press, Boca Raton, Fl, 2001.

2. Spitz, W.U., Ed., *Medicolegal Investigation of Death*, 4th ed., Charles C. Thomas, Springfield, IL, 2006.

Deaths during Arrest and in Police Custody: Excited Delirium Syndrome

10

Some of the most controversial medicolegal cases involve deaths occurring during arrest or while in police custody. These cases have led to riots, federal investigations, and extensive civil litigation. Because of this, in these cases:

- Autopsies should only be performed by or under the supervision of an experienced forensic pathologist.
- All findings should be well documented.
- Complete toxicological testing should be performed.
- Photographs of the body are strongly recommended even if there are no observable injuries.
- No ruling as to cause of death should be made until all testing is complete, unless the autopsy reveals gross evidence of injury incompatible with life, e.g., a gunshot wound.

This chapter will be concerned only with **nontraumatic deaths** where the cause of death is obscure, controversial, or subject to misinterpretation.

I. **DEATHS OCCURRING DURING ARREST — THE EXCITED DELIRIUM SYNDROME (EDS)**
   A. Delirium is characterized by an acute — minutes to hours — temporary disturbance in consciousness and thought. There is:
      1. Disorientation
      2. Disorganized thought processes
      3. Inability to distinguish reality from hallucinations

165

    4. Disturbances in speech

    5. Disorientation to time and place

    6. Misidentification of individuals

B. When delirium is accompanied by violent behavior, it becomes **excited delirium**.

    Nursing protocols recommend a *minimum* of six personnel to physically restrain an individual in the throes of excited delirium.

C. **Excited delirium syndrome (EDS)** involves the sudden death of an individual, during or following an episode of excited delirium, in which an autopsy fails to reveal evidence of sufficient trauma or natural disease to explain the death. In virtually all such cases, the episode of excited delirium is terminated by a struggle with police or medical personnel, and the use of physical restraint. Typically, within a few to several minutes following cessation of the struggle, the individual is noted to be in cardiopulmonary arrest. Attempts at resuscitation are usually unsuccessful.

D. Excited delirium syndrome is characterized by:

    1. Acute onset of symptoms (minutes to hours)

    2. Delirium

    3. Combative and/or violent behavior

    4. Use of physical restraint

    5. Sudden cardiac death

    6. Lack of response to CPR

    7. History of either stimulant abuse or endogenous mental disease

E. The typical story is of an individual acting irrationally and bizarrely. The police are summoned and decide to restrain the individual as he is a danger to either himself or others. A violent struggle ensues; the individual is brought to the ground, handcuffed, and appears to quiet. Subsequently, he is noted to not be breathing. Death may also occur during transport.

F. The scene of death is:

    1. At the scene of the struggle in 48% of cases

    2. During transport in 29% of cases

    3. On arrival at a hospital or jail in 16% of cases

G. Original hypotheses as to the cause of these deaths:

    1. Positional asphyxia due to hogtying

    2. Use of choke holds

II. MECHANISMS OF DEATH IN EDS

A. The **sympathetic nervous system** is the controller of the "fight or flight" response. Excited delirium, the struggle, and stimulant drugs such as cocaine and methamphetamine activate the system.

1. Stimulation of the sympathetic nervous system causes release of two neurotransmitters: epinephrine (E) from the adrenal glands into the blood, and norepinephrine (NE) from the nerve endings into the synapses between the nerves and the end organs, e.g., the heart.
2. These two neurotransmitters bind to receptors on the organs.
3. The neurotransmitters are then removed from the synapse by reuptake mechanisms or diffusion out of the synapse. This rapidly inactivates the action of the neurotransmitters.
4. The receptor sites of most significance are those on the heart muscle and the coronary arteries.
5. The receptors are divided into two broad types: α and β adrenoceptors.
6. Alpha (α) receptors are divided into α1 and α2.
7. Beta (β) receptors are β1, β2, and β3, with β1 being the most important.
8. NE released at the synapses and E released into the bloodstream from the adrenals work on the β1 receptors of heart muscle causing the heart to beat harder and faster. This in turn results in a greater demand for oxygen by the heart muscle.
9. NE and E act on α1 receptors of normal coronary arteries to produce dilatation. In the presence of atherosclerosis or endothelial dysfunction, there is constriction of the arteries reducing the flow of blood to the myocardium predisposing to cardiac arrhythmias.
10. Accelerated development of atherosclerosis and endothelial injury are produced by chronic use of cocaine and methamphetamine.
11. If the coronary arteries contract from chronic use of cocaine and methamphetamine, there will be decreased supply of oxygenated blood to the myocardium at a time when increased amounts are needed. This predisposes to development of cardiac arrhythmias.

B. **"Post-exercise peril"**
   1. In excited delirium syndrome (EDS), death often occurs immediately after the individual is restrained and struggling ceases.
   2. This post-struggle period corresponds to the time of "post-exercise peril" described by Dimsdale et al.[1] as a time where an individual is unusually susceptible to developing a fatal cardiac arrhythmia.
   3. Dimsdale et al. found that during exercise an individual's blood NE and E increased, with NE increasing more sharply. Peak

levels of these catecholamines did not occur during the struggle but in the 3 minutes immediately following cessation of the exercise. Thus, the individual is in a hyperadrenergic state due to very high levels of NE and E.

4. Young et al.[2] found that following cessation of exercise, the potassium level fell rapidly, returning to approximately normal levels in 5 minutes. The maximum rate of fall occurred within the **first or second minute post-exercise**.

5. Low blood potassium predisposes to prolongation of the QT interval, development of *torsade de pointes* (uncommon variant of ventricular tachycardia), and sudden cardiac death.

6. Thus, the physiological effects of strenuous exercise are increasing levels of NE and E peaking in the minutes after cessation of a struggle and rapidly dropping levels of potassium in the minutes after cessation of a struggle with both effects predisposing to sudden death.

C. Other factors:

1. Cocaine stimulates the heart indirectly by activating the sympathetic nervous system and directly at the synapses. Cocaine blocks the reuptake of NE at the synapses causing its accumulation. This results in hyperstimulation of the heart and coronary arteries.

2. There is evidence of polymorphism of α and β heart receptors that results in increased quantities of NE in the synapses and increased sensitivity to the NE by the heart receptors.

3. Individuals with intrinsic mental disease such as schizophrenia and bipolar disease are predisposed to develop excited delirium. Their medications may be cardiotoxic.

4. Other drugs such as diphenhydramine may cause excited delirium.

D. Death due to EDS is due to a cardiac arrhythmia secondary to a hyperadrenergic state and a decrease in potassium due to the synergistic, physiological effects of:

1. Excited delirium
2. The struggle
3. Drugs, illegal and therapeutic
4. Mental disease
5. Possibly a genetic predisposition

III. **HOGTYING — POSITIONAL/RESTRAINT ASPHYXIA**

A. In hogtying, an individual is placed in a prone position, their hands are tied or cuffed together behind their back, and their ankles are bound and tied to their wrists. Based on experiments in the 1980s, it was concluded that if you hogtie an individual, you interfere with their ability to breathe and, thus, can cause death. These deaths were then said to be due to positional/restraint asphyxia.

B. Police stopped use of the hogtie, but individuals kept dying.

C. By this time, the idea of these deaths being due to positional asphyxia was embedded in society and the concept was retained, though not the mechanism. It was claimed these deaths were due to the officers or medical personnel lying on the individual or applying pressure on the thorax with knees.

D. Research by Chan et al.[3] determined that the original experiments were in error. He found that while placing an individual facedown in the hogtie position following strenuous exercise, e.g., a struggle, did produce restrictive pulmonary functioning, as measured by pulmonary function test, these results were not clinically relevant. There was no evidence of hypoxia.

E. Subsequent tests in which weights were applied to the thorax also did not produce clinically relevant decreases in pulmonary functioning. Thus, there is no proof that ordinary force placed on an individual by kneeling on them or lying across their body compromises respiration.

IV. CHOKE HOLD–RELATED DEATHS

Deaths have been reported as being due to the use of **choke holds**.[4] In such deaths, there are two possible mechanisms for death:

A. First is compression of the carotid arteries with resulting cerebral hypoxia. But in such cases:

   1. Compression of the neck would have to be for at least 2 to 3 minutes to cause cessation of respiration.

   2. Such an individual would be expected to respond to cardiopulmonary resuscitation (CPR) but this is not the situation in the cases reported.

   3. One would expect petechiae of at least the conjunctivae and sclerae since such a case is essentially a strangulation. Again, this is not usually seen.

   4. Thus, there is no evidence that such deaths are due to strangulation.

B. The other proposed mechanism of death is cardiac arrest due to severe bradycardia secondary to stimulation of the vagus nerve or carotid receptors. The problem with this explanation is twofold:

   1. A search of the literature for well-documented deaths due to vasovagal stimulation reveals them to occur almost exclusively in elderly individuals with underlying severe vascular disease.[5]

In all probability the underlying disease was the cause of death in these cases.

2. The second problem with the vasovagal hypothesis is that after a struggle, an individual would have tachycardia. Stimulation of the vagus nerve would tend to induce a normal heart rate.

3. At this time, there is no objective evidence that vasovagal stimulation causes death in these cases.

C. Why does death then occur in association with choke holds? Review of these cases almost invariably reveals that death followed a violent struggle and the deceased was on cocaine or a similar stimulant and/or had intrinsic mental disease. These deaths are due to EDS.

V. TASERS

A. Tasers are handheld devices that fire two fishhook-like barbed darts attached to wires, simultaneously, up to a distance of 21 feet.

1. The darts are propelled by a cartridge of compressed nitrogen.

2. The wires are copper-clad steel wires with an insulated coating.

3. At the end of each wire is a barb similar to a fishhook.

4. The darts are designed to penetrate skin or lodge in clothing.

5. On lodging in an individual or their clothing, a circuit is achieved and the Taser provides a series of electrical pulses for up to five seconds.

6. When the dart strikes bare skin, it penetrates until the full flange on the dart stops it.

7. Penetration of skin is not necessary as the electric pulse it delivers can penetrate up to two inches of clothing.

8. A high-voltage (50,000 volt), low-amperage (162 mA) current is delivered down the wires to the target.

9. Each time the trigger is pulled a 5-second pulse is delivered.

B. The Taser is designed to produce electromuscular disruption (EMD), i.e., muscular contractions, via externally applied electric fields, with uncontrollable contraction of the muscles and immediate collapse. The shocks can be repeated.

C. A number of deaths have occurred following use of a Taser. In virtually all cases, the death was associated with excited delirium due to use of stimulants such as cocaine, methamphetamine and/or violent psychosis due to mental disease. These cases appear to be deaths due to excited delirium syndrome in individuals who coincidentally received Taser shocks.

VI. OLEORESIN CAPSICUM (PEPPER SPRAY)
  A. Oleoresin capsicum (OC) is the active ingredient in pepper (OC) spray. It is an extract of the pepper plant of the genus *Capsicum*, consisting of a complex mixture of capsaicinoids.
    1. Inhalation results in coughing, gagging, involuntary closure of the eyes, bronchoconstriction, mucous secretion, shortness of breath, and inability to speak.
    2. The effects of OC spray result in an inability to fight or resist in most individuals, thus the employment of OC spray by police.
    3. The effects disappear in 20 to 30 minutes.
    4. Some individuals experiencing excited delirium are completely resistant to repeated spraying with OC.
  B. Following its widespread use by police, a number of deaths associated with its use began to be reported.
    1. Review of these cases failed to reveal any evidence conclusively linking OC spray with a role in the deaths.
    2. Virtually all of these individuals were in the throes of excited delirium due to drugs or psychosis.
    3. Experiments on volunteers exposed to OC or placebo spray did not result in any significant differences in respiratory function between the OC and placebo groups. There was no evidence of hypoxemia or hypoventilation.[6]

VII. DEATHS OCCURRING IN JAILS
  Deaths in jail (not prison) are usually either accidents or suicides.
  A. Accidental deaths are often due to unrecognized trauma that occurred immediately prior to jailing in individuals who are acutely intoxicated.
    1. Head trauma is probably the most common cause of death in such cases.
    2. Any symptoms observed on admission to the jail are ascribed to the acute alcohol intoxication.
  B. The most popular method of suicide in jail is by hanging.
    1. The individual uses a shirt, trousers or a sheet to fashion a noose.
    2. Suspension may not be and often is not complete.
    3. Incomplete suspension causes the relatives of the deceased to challenge the ruling of suicide in that they assume complete suspension is necessary for such deaths.
  C. Some methods of suicide are bizarre, e.g., wedging a T-shirt in the pharynx, charging headfirst into a concrete wall.

D. Many suicides seem to occur within the first 48 hours of incarceration and involve individuals arrested for relatively minor offenses, e.g., DWI (driving while intoxicated).

References

1. Dimsdale, J.E. et al., Post-exercise peril: Plasma catecholamines and exercise, *JAMA*, 251, 630, 1984.

2. Young, D.B. et al., Potassium and catecholamine concentrations in the immediate post exercise period, *Am. J. Med. Sci.*, 304(3), 150, 1992.

3. Chan, T.C. et al., Restraint position and positional asphyxia, *Ann. Emerg. Med.*, 30, 578, 1997.

4. Reay, D.T. and Eisele, J.W., Death from law enforcement neck holds, *Am. J. For. Med. Path.*, 3(3), 253, 1982.

5. Weiss, S. and Baker, J.P., The carotid sinus reflex in health and disease, *Medicine*, 12, 297, 1933.

6. Chan, T.C. et al., The effect of oleoresin capsicum "pepper spray" inhalation on respiratory function, *J. For. Sci.*, 47(2), 299, 2002.

General Reference on EDS:

1. Di Maio, T.C. and Di Maio, V.J.M., *Excited Delirium Syndrome*, CRC Press, Boca Raton, FL, 2006.

Murder of Infants and Children

11

I. STATISTICS

The murder of infants and young children is relatively uncommon. In the United States in 2004, 176 infants (children under the age of 1); 328 children ages 1 to 4 years; and 73 children between the ages of 5 and 8 years were murdered. These deaths were divided approximately equally between males and females.[1]

II. NEONATICIDE

A. Neonaticide is the deliberate killing of a newborn. The perpetrator is typically the mother with the cause of death usually either **asphyxia** or the effects of **abandonment,** e.g., exposure.

B. In asphyxial deaths, the child is often placed in a plastic bag. Paper or cloth may be stuffed down the mouth. The mother often claims that she did not know that she was pregnant and the child was stillborn. By virtue of the last claim, one of the most important facts to be determined by the pathologist is **whether the child was stillborn or born alive.**

   1. If the child on external examination shows obvious evidence of intrauterine maceration, then the question is settled. One must, however, be able to differentiate between decomposition and maceration due to intrauterine death.

      a. The first sign of maceration is skin slippage. This occurs 6 to 12 hours after intrauterine death.[2]

      b. Fluid-filled bullae appear at 24 hours. Rupture of the bullae will often leave large raw-appearing areas of skin that have been mistaken for scalding burns. Hemolysis gives the tissue a reddish violet color.

      c. Bloody fluids collect in the thoracic and abdominal cavities.

173

      d.   After several days the skull will collapse.

2. For simplicity's sake, one can consider a birth live when the infant breathes after being born. Since most murders of neonates occur immediately after birth, before ingesting food or showing evidence of healing of the umbilical stump, the only method of determining whether a child was born alive is by examination of the lungs.

3. **Microscopic sections** of the lung are of no help in determining if a child breathed. One can see diffuse atelectasis in the lungs of a child who is known to have been alive and breathed, and open apparently aerated alveoli in a child who is known to have been stillborn.

4. The pathologist is essentially left with only the hydrostatic test of the lungs. This test consists of removing the lungs, placing them in a container of water, and seeing whether they sink or float. If they sink, it is presumed that the child was stillborn; if they float, the child was born alive and breathed. There are problems with the test:

      a.   A child may be born alive, take only a few breaths, and have insufficient aeration of the lung for it to float.

      b.   If the body is decomposed and the lungs float, then the child was either born alive or postmortem decomposition has resulted in gas formation in the pulmonary parenchyma causing the lungs to float. Thus, in a decomposed body, tests on the lungs are only significant when they sink.

      c.   Another problem is attempted resuscitation. Here, air may be forced into the lungs of a stillborn, causing them to float when placed in water. Thus, in cases where resuscitation has occurred, floatation of the lungs does not necessarily signify that the child was born alive.

III. DEATHS IN THE FIRST 2 YEARS OF LIFE

A. If a child survives the immediate neonatal period, the next 2 years are the most dangerous as the highest rate of homicides for children occurs in the first 2 years of life. The causes of death are different between the first and second years.

1. In the first year, 85 to 90% of the deaths will be due to craniocerebral injuries.

2. In the second year, this drops down to around 55% with most of the other children dying of blunt force abdominal injuries.

B. Deaths in the first 2 years of life usually fall into three categories based on how the victims are killed. These are:

1. The battered child (including the neglected child)

2. The impulse homicide (including the punished child)
3. The gentle homicide (including Munchausen syndrome by proxy)

IV. **BATTERED CHILD SYNDROME**
  A. Typically, this child is brought in with multiple bruises and abrasions of the body of various ages.
     1. Some of the injuries may be patterned. Thus, one may see the outline of a belt, a belt buckle, or a metal wire hanger.
     2. X-rays often reveal fractures of the ribs and extremities, often of varying ages.
        a. Any fracture of a rib in a child 2 years of age or less is considered to be evidence of child abuse unless there is a history of severe trauma, such as a motor vehicle accident.
        b. The fractures of the ribs are produced either from a direct blow, such as a kick, or due to squeezing. In this latter case, fractures are typically located on the posterior aspect of the rib cage.
        c. Cardiopulmonary resuscitation will not fracture the ribs of infants and young children.
     3. The explanation given by the parents for the fatal injuries is often preposterous, e.g., "He rolled off the bed; he fell out of the highchair; he slipped out my arms; I was throwing him up in the air and I missed him."
     4. There is often a delay between the time the fatal injuries were incurred and the time the child is brought to the emergency room.
  B. In the first year of life, most of these children have head injuries: subarachnoid and/or subdural hemorrhage with and without skull fractures.
     1. One can have a fracture of a skull with no brain injury and severe brain injury without a fracture.
     2. Most forensic pathologists believe a fall from a height of 36 inches or less, even on a concrete floor, will not cause any injury to a child's brain.[3]
     3. Occasionally, one will see a case of a fatal head injury without any **external** evidence of trauma. This again illustrates the necessity of doing autopsies in young children who die suddenly and unexpectedly.
  C. In children with abdominal injury:
     1. In approximately 43% of the cases, there is no evidence of external injury.

2. Approximately 80% have lacerations of the liver. The liver may be essentially transected secondary to a punch or kick to the abdomen. This results when the abdominal wall is driven backward almost to the vertebral column.

D. Included in the Battered Child category are children suffering from severe malnutrition due to neglect.

1. The parents claim that the child was a "poor eater" or just stopped eating a day or two before.

2. The child presents with severe malnutrition often appearing skeletal. Dehydration and electrolyte abnormalities are typically present.

3. A complete autopsy has to be performed in such cases to rule out any natural disease that can be claimed to explain why the child is malnourished.

4. There should be a background investigation to see if the child has ever been in the hospital or under the care of another individual during which time the child thrived.

V. IMPULSE HOMICIDES

A. In these cases, the child presents with an acute injury and no or minimal evidence of chronic abuse.

1. There may be a few scattered bruises but there are not the multiple old fractures and the extensive injuries seen in the Battered Child Syndrome.

2. What usually has happened in these cases is that the child annoys an adult who either kicks, punches, or throws the child.

B. Included in this category is the punished child. This is the child who comes in with scalding burns of the body due to immersion in hot water.

1. The explanation the parent gives is that the child was taking a bath when the hot water was accidentally turned on by the child and they incurred the burns.

2. The true history, when finally obtained, is often that the child has soiled himself and as punishment he is immersed in hot water.

3. The distribution of the burns usually indicates that the child was dipped in hot water. As the child is lowered into the water, his feet hit the hot water, and he involuntarily flexes his legs. The knees are brought up against the abdomen; the lower legs fold back against the thighs. The child is then lowered into the water up to his waist. Because of the flexed position, there is sparing of the skin in the inguinal region and the popliteal

TABLE 11.1 Water Temperature Necessary to Develop Scalding Burns

Temperature (°F)	Time (seconds)	
	Threshold for Epidermal Injury	Full-Thickness Burns
120	290	600 (10 min)
125	50	120
130	15	30
140	2.6	≈7
150	<1	2.3

Note: Based on data from Moritz, A.R. and Henriques, F.D., Studies of thermal injury. II. The relative importance of time and surface temperature in the causation of cutaneous burns, *Am. J. Path.*, 23, 695, 1947.

fossae. There is often a sharp line of demarcation around the waist. (See **Figure 13.4.**)

4. **Table 11.1** gives the amount of time necessary to incur third-degree burns based on water temperature. Many of the new heating units have their water temperature adjusted to 120°F to prevent accidental burns.

VI. **GENTLE HOMICIDE**

A. The method used to kill children in this group is asphyxia, specifically smothering.

1. The children are smothered with a pillow or bedclothes; have their face pressed hard against the perpetrator's chest, or hands are used to clamp their nose and mouth shut.

2. In these instances, there will not be any physical findings, either externally or internally. Typically, petechiae are absent.

3. There is no way that a diagnosis of smothering can be made solely on autopsy findings. It is only by taking into account the circumstances leading up to and surrounding the death that a diagnosis can be made.

4. In all such cases, a complete autopsy must be performed with microscopic examination of tissue and a complete toxicologic examination to rule out other causes of death.

5. There is no way to differentiate a case of smothering from a case of SIDS. Because of this, all forensic pathologists know that a small (5 to 10%) but significant percent of SIDS cases are actually homicidal asphyxias.

B. Often, the diagnosis of homicidal asphyxia is only made in retrospect when the perpetrator continues to kill children.

1. The perpetrator in such cases is usually the mother.

2. The original cause(s) of death is ascribed to SIDS.

   3. It is not until the second or third child dies that someone realizes what is happening.
   4. Typically, these children are not killed outright, but rather brought repeatedly to emergency rooms with a history of apneic episodes and cyanosis.[4]
      a. If hospitalized, they have no problems unless left alone with the mother.
      b. Secret videotapes may show the mother smothering the child in the hospital.[5]
   5. The pattern of repeated admissions continues until the child is finally brought in dead.
   6. For many years such deaths were felt to represent aborted cases of SIDS.
C. The general policy in cases of sudden unexpected death of a child between the ages of 1 month and 1 year is:
   1. The first death is certified as SIDS, if there is no evidence of any trauma or disease to explain death.
   2. A second child from the same mother is certified as undetermined.
   3. The third child homicide. While it is theoretically possible, though highly improbable, for a woman to have two SIDS deaths, three is impossible.
   4. Occasionally, the second death is ruled homicide because the story presented by the parent is so bizarre.
   5. Metabolic tests should be performed, as one defense tactic is to claim the multiple deaths were due to an inherited metabolic disorder.

VII. SHAKEN BABY SYNDROME

The "shaken baby syndrome" is an alleged condition in infants characterized by intracranial bleeding (subdural and/or subarachnoid hemorrhage) and retinal hemorrhage in the absence of impact trauma to the head.

   A. The injuries are said to be due to violent shaking of a young child with resultant whiplash movement of the relatively heavy head causing tearing of the bridging veins.
   B. In essentially all such cases coming to autopsy, however, injuries to the scalp and skull (contusions and fractures), explainable only by impact trauma, are found.
   C. Thus, the brain injuries are more easily and more logically explained by direct trauma to the head, a proven etiology for such findings.

D. Attempts by Duhaime et al. to experimentally reproduce the biomechanical forces necessary to injure the brain by shaking resulted in the conclusion that the injuries cannot be caused by shaking.[6]

E. Because of this, many forensic pathologists doubt that the shaken baby syndrome exists, and if it does, feel that it is extremely rare.

F. Some individuals contend that retinal hemorrhages are pathognomonic of the shaken baby syndrome and make the diagnosis of this entity based on their presence alone. Since one cannot prove that the syndrome exists, one cannot describe a pathognomonic finding. In addition, retinal hemorrhages can be due solely to blunt trauma to the head.

References

1. U.S. Department of Justice, Uniform Crime Reports for the United States 2004, U.S. Govt. Printing Off., Washington, D.C., 2005.

2. Wigglesworth, J.S., *Perinatal Pathology*, 2nd ed., W.B. Saunders, Philadelphia, 1996.

3. Helfer, R.E., Slovis, T.L., and Black, M., Injuries resulting when small children fall out of bed, *Pediatrics*, 60, 533, 1977.

4. Di Maio, V.J.M. and Bernstein, C.G., A case of infanticide, *J. Forensic Sci.*, 19(4), 744, 1974.

5. Southall, D.P. et al., Covert video recordings of life-threatening child abuse: Lessons for child protection, *Pediatrics*, 100(5), 735, 1997.

6. Duhaime, A. et al., The shaken baby syndrome: A clinical, pathological, and biomechanical study, *J. Neurosurg.*, 66, 409, 1987.

General References

1. Firstman, R. and Talan, J., *The Death of Innocents*, Bantam Books, New York, 1997.

2. Di Maio, V.J.M. and Di Maio, D.J., *Forensic Pathology*, 2nd ed., CRC Press, Boca Raton, FL, 2001.

Sexually Related Homicides

12

Sexually related homicides fall into two categories: rape homicides and homosexually related homicides.

I. RAPE HOMICIDES

A. The victim is typically female.
   1. She is found on her back, naked, with her legs spread apart. If not completely nude, she will be naked from the waist down with her bra often pushed up above her breasts.
   2. There may be bite marks and/or bruises of the breasts as well as bruising of the inner thighs.
   3. Trauma to the vagina and anus is common, though not invariable. When present, it is usually relatively minor.
      a. Abrasions, contusions, and/or small superficial lacerations may be present at the introitus of the vagina. They are most common at the six-o'clock position.
      b. In the anus, minor injuries are present at the anal verge, scattered around the circumference in a random fashion.
      c. Examination of the perineum, perianal area, and thighs using ultraviolet light may reveal seminal deposits. This light will cause semen to fluoresce though this is not specific. The suspected semen should be recovered for analysis.
   4. Rape homicides rarely involve shooting. Usually there is evidence of strangulation, not uncommonly associated with blunt trauma to the head and/or stabbing. Often, two of these three elements are present; occasionally, all three.

B. In **children**, rape may be very violent, with severe vaginal/rectal tears, due to the small size of the vagina and rectum.

   C. In all rape and suspected rape cases, swabs of the mouth, rectum, and vagina should be taken.

     1. Semen is not always found in rape cases. This may be due to failure of ejaculation, aspermia, or even use of a condom.

     2. Laboratory examination of these specimens consists initially of the examination of slides made from the swabs for sperm. If these are present, then one can perform DNA analysis. If no sperm are seen, chemical tests such as acid phosphatase should be performed. DNA tests may still be positive in the absence of sperm.

     3. Sperm can be recovered from a dead body for days after death, or at least until advanced decomposition sets in.

     4. In individuals who after being raped were able to get up, dress, and move about prior to being killed, their panties should be examined for drainage of seminal fluid.

     5. It is important to remember that in taking swabs of the rectum, the body should always be turned facedown, the buttocks spread, and the swabs inserted directly into the anus without contacting the perianal skin. This is because drainage from the vagina can run posteriorly, between the buttocks, contaminating the perianal skin. If the swabs are allowed to contact the perianal skin, they may pick up some of this material, thus indicating anal intercourse occurred when it may not have.

     6. Human bite marks should be documented photographically and if possible with impressions. Prior to taking any impressions, one should always swab the area for saliva that could be used for DNA examination. The classical method of swabbing was using a wet swab. There is a newer method called the double swab technique in which a wet cotton swab of the bite is made and then followed by a dry cotton swab.[1] The material then can be analyzed by DNA analysis.

II. HOMOSEXUALLY RELATED HOMICIDES

Homosexually related homicides are relatively uncommon. Most deaths are not "rapes" but due to personal conflicts. There is rarely evidence of sexual assault.

   A. They tend to be more violent than heterosexual homicides, with a greater number of injuries (sharp, blunt, and total) per case with the injuries more extensive.[2]

   B. The deaths are characterized by numerous stab marks, blunt trauma and asphyxia. There is significantly less use of firearms compared to heterosexual homicides.

   C. Some cases are very bizarre in their presentation.

III. EVIDENCE OF CHRONIC ANAL INTERCOURSE[3]

Objective evidence of chronic anal intercourse is important in suspected cases of sexual abuse of a child.

    A. The traditional description, in both children and adults, was of a gaping patulous anus and/or a funnel anus. These findings, however, are usually not diagnostic of chronic anal intercourse.

    B. The patulous anus can be routinely seen postmortem in both children and adults who have not engaged in anal intercourse.

    C. The funnel anus is an anatomical variant.

    D. Only extremely marked dilatation of the anus is now considered significant.

    E. There is, of course, no tone in an anus after death.

    F. Chronic irritation of the skin around the anus may be totally unrelated to sexual intercourse but rather due to inflammatory problems.

References

1. Sweet, D. et al., An improved method to recover saliva from human skin: The double swab technique, *J. Forensic Sci.*, 42(2), 320, 1997.

2. Bell, M.D. and Vila, R.I., Homicide in homosexual victims, *Amer. J. Forensic Med. Path.*, 17(1), 65, 1996.

3. McCann, J. et al., Postmortem perianal findings in children, *Am. J. For. Med. Path.*, 17(4), 289, 1996.

Fire and Thermal Injuries

13

Burns continue to be a major cause of injury and death in the United States. Fires account for 34% of fatal injuries in children less than 16 years of age.[1] The very young and the very old are at greatest risk from burn accidents. In all fire deaths, the forensic pathologist should attempt to determine:

- The positive identity of the deceased, especially if the body is charred beyond visual recognition (the procedures used for identification have already been discussed in Chapter 4)
- Whether or not the deceased was alive prior to ignition of the fire, or whether the fire was set and the body burned in an attempt to conceal a homicide
- The cause and manner of death
- Whether or not contributing factors are present, such as alcohol/drug intoxication

I. CLASSIFICATION OF BURNS ACCORDING TO DEPTH OF INJURY

Burns are generally classified according to their depth of injury (tissue destruction).

A. **First-degree** burns are described as those limited to the *superficial* epidermis.
1. There may be associated erythema and edema. Blistering is usually not present; however, the skin may peel.
2. Usually painful.
3. No scarring upon healing.
4. Example: mild sunburn.

   B. **Second-degree** burns are described as *partial thickness* burns that involve all of the epidermis and some of the dermis, with sparing of skin appendages. Second-degree burns may be superficial or deep.
1. Blisters are usually present.
2. The senses are intact, with some associated pain.
3. Usually heal without scarring, except in deep burns which may scar.
   C. **Third-degree** burns are described as *full-thickness* burns, with necrosis of all skin layers, including the skin appendages.
1. The burned area appears white.
2. All sensation is lost.
3. Severe scarring almost always results.
   D. **Fourth-degree** burns are described as *charring* injury, due to incineration of the tissues. There is complete destruction of the skin and subcutaneous tissue, as well as complete or partial charring of the bone.

II. **BURN SEVERITY FACTORS**

The severity of the burn depends on:
   A. The **intensity** of the heat. In ordinary house fires, temperatures are usually less than 1200 to 1600°F, while in some industrial fuel fires, the temperatures may be greater (1900 to 2100°F).[2]
   B. The **duration** of exposure. For example, human skin heated to 45°C (113°F) for 2 hours will become hyperemic without loss of the epidermis, but if the duration of exposure is increased to 3 hours, complete epidermal necrosis occurs.[3]
   C. In order to cremate a human body (adult, average build) in a gas-fired chamber, the remains must be heated to 1500°F for 1 to 1$\frac{1}{2}$ hours.[4]

III. **DOCUMENTATION OF EXTENT AND PATTERN OF BURN**

In all burn cases, the extent and pattern of the burn should be documented, preferably on a body diagram.
   A. The burned area is usually expressed as a percentage of the total body surface area (TBSA). The percent of TBSA that a specific body part comprises is dependent on the age of the individual. Several means are available for the estimation of percent of TBSA involved:
1. An age-adjusted surface area chart may be used, such as those depicted in **Figure 13.1.**
2. In adults, the "rule of nines" may be used, while in infants and young children, the "rule of fives" may be used (**Table 13.1**).

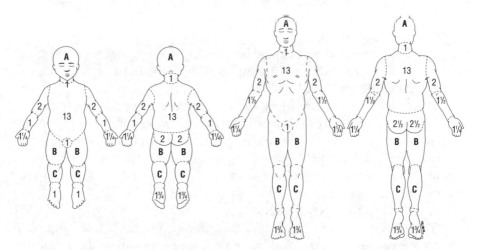

Percentage (%) of TBSA

A = half of head	0	1	5
A = half of head	9 ½	8 ½	6 ½
B = half of one thigh	2 ¾	3 ¼	4
C = half of one lower leg	2 ½	2 ½	2 ¾

Percentage (%) of TBSA

	10	15	Adult
A = half of head	5 ½	4 ½	3 ½
B = half of one thigh	4 ¼	4 ½	4 ¾
C = half of one lower leg	3	3 ¼	3 ½

Figure 13.1 Body surface area diagrams that allow calculation of percentage of total body surface area (TBSA) for various body parts in child (left) and adult (right). (Adapted from Demling, R.H. and Way, L.W., Burns and other thermal injuries, in *Current Surgical Diagnosis and Treatment*, 9th ed., Way, L.W., Ed., Appleton & Lange, Norwalk, CT, 1991, pp. 235–249.

TABLE 13.1 Estimation of Percentage of Body Surface Area Burned in Adults and Children

Area of Body	Percentage (%)		
	Infant	Child	Adult
Head and neck	20	15	9
Anterior chest	20	20	18
Back	20	20	18
Upper extremity — right/left	10/10	10/10	9/9
Lower extremity — right/left	10/10	15/15	18/18
Genitalia & perineum	0	0–1	1
Total	100	≈100	100

Source: Adapted from Meyer, A.A. and Salber, P.R., Burns and smoke inhalation, in *Current Emergency Diagnosis and Treatment*, 2nd ed., Mills, J. et al., Eds., Lange Medical Publications, Los Altos, CA, 1958, pp. 417–428.

    3. Military burn centers use a chart similar to that shown in **Figure 13.2.**

B. The burn pattern should be carefully documented, as many times it will provide a crucial clue as to how the burn occurred.

IV. BURN SURVIVABILITY

Whether or not a burn injury will result in death depends on the age of the individual, the degree of the burn, and the percentage of total body surface area involved. A simplified "probability" chart is shown in **Figure 13.3,** where the percentage of full-thickness burn is plotted against the age of the patient. **Table 13.2** gives percent survival rate in combined second- and third-degree burns, depending on the age of the patient.

V. CLOTHING AND BURNS

The presence of clothing can alter the outcome of a burn injury. If clothing is present, and the clothing ignites, the morbidity and mortality of the injury is greatly increased. Three factors are involved, when considering the fire hazard of clothing.[5]

A. The type of fabric involved and its ability to ignite.

B. The type or design of the garment. Close-fitting garments tend to be safer than long, loose garments, such as nightgowns.

C. The environment in which the garment is used.

VI. SIX CATEGORIES OF BURNS

Depending on the agent, burns may be arbitrarily divided into six categories:

A. **Flame burns** occur when the skin is in direct contact with a flame.
    1. The severity depends on the length of time the flame is applied to the skin.
    2. Variant of flame burn is the **flash burn**.
        a. Caused by the sudden ignition or explosion of fine particulate matter or gases
        b. Produces a uniform burn (first or second degree) of all of the exposed areas of skin; singes the hair

B. **Contact burns** occur when the skin is in direct contact with a hot object, such as a hot iron. These burns may have the configuration or shape of the hot object that was applied to the skin.

C. **Radiant burns** occur when the skin is exposed to heat waves.
    1. Contact with the source emitting the heat waves is not necessary for a burn to occur.
    2. May produce skin blisters and erythema.
    3. If there is prolonged exposure, charring may result.

D. **Scalding burns** occur when the skin is contacted by a hot liquid (usually water).

AGE

BODY AREA	Birth– 1 year	1–4 years	5–9 years	10–14 years	15 years	ADULT	2nd Degree	3rd Degree	TOTAL
Head	19	17	13	11	9	7			
Neck	2	2	2	2	2	2			
Ant. Trunk	13	13	13	13	13	13			
Post. Trunk	13	13	13	13	13	13			
R. Buttock	2 ½	2 ½	2 ½	2 ½	2 ½	2 ½			
L. Buttock	2 ½	2 ½	2 ½	2 ½	2 ½	2 ½			
Genitalia	1	1	1	1	1	1			
R. U. Arm	4	4	4	4	4	4			
L. U. Arm	4	4	4	4	4	4			
R. L. Arm	3	3	3	3	3	3			
L. L. Arm	3	3	3	3	3	3			
R. Hand	2 ½	2 ½	2 ½	2 ½	2 ½	2 ½			
L. Hand	2 ½	2 ½	2 ½	2 ½	2 ½	2 ½			
R. Thigh	5 ½	6 ½	8	8 ½	9	9 ½			
L. Thigh	5 ½	6 ½	8	8 ½	9	9 ½			
R. Leg	5	5	5 ½	6	6 ½	7			
L. Leg	5	5	5 ½	6	6 ½	7			
R. Foot	3 ½	3 ½	3 ½	3 ½	3 ½	3 ½			
L. Foot	3 ½	3 ½	3 ½	3 ½	3 ½	3 ½			

TOTAL | | | |

AGE _____

SEX _____

WEIGHT _____

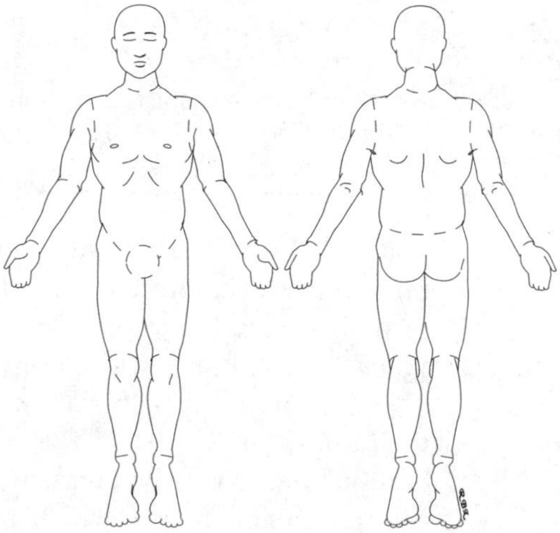

Figure 13.2 Burn chart that allows more precise calculation of total body surface area burned.

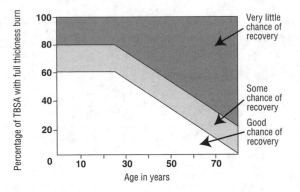

Figure 13.3 Simplified "probability" chart showing how chance of recovery varies with patient age and amount of total body surface area (TBSA) burned. (Adapted from Muir, I.F.K., Barclay, T.L., and Settle, J.A.D., Treatment of burns shock, in *Burns and Their Treatment*, Butterworths, London, 1987, p. 50.)

TABLE 13.2   Percent (%) Mean Survival Rate

| | Patient's Age (years) | | | | | | |
% TBSA Burn[a]	0–1	2–4	5–34	35–49	50–59	60–74	>75
0–10	>95	>95	>95	>95	>95	95	90
10–20	95	>90	>95	>90	>85	80	50
20–30	90	90	95	90	75	50	25
30–40	75	80	90	80	60	30	<10
40–50	50	65	80	60	40	10	<5
50–60	40	50	60	45	30	<10	<5
60–70	20	30	40	20	15	<5	0
70–80	5	20	25	10	5	0	0
80–90	0	<10	<10	<10	<5	0	0
90–100	0	<5	<5	<5	0	0	0

Source: Adapted from Demling, R.H. and LaLonde, C., Management of the burn wound, in *Burn Trauma*, Thieme Medical Publishers, Inc., New York, 1989, p. 48.

[a] TBSA — Total body surface area; combined second- and third-degree burns.

1. Water at 158°F (70°C) will produce a third-degree burn of normal adult skin in 1 second of contact; at 131°F (55°C), 25 seconds is required to produce the same burn.[3]
2. Water heaters in most U.S. homes arrive from the factory set at about 130 to 140°F; however, newer units are now adjusted to around 120°F.
3. Scalding burns may be divided into three types:
   a. **Immersion burns,** which may accidental or homicidal. Homicidal immersion burns occur most commonly when a small child is placed into a basin or tub partially filled with scalding hot water, in an attempt to discipline or

punish the child. A characteristic pattern of burn is produced as the child reflexively withdraws from the water. A
circumferential area of skin encircling each knee region
will be spared as the child is forced to squat in the water
(**Figure 13.4**).

b.   **Splash,** or **spill burns** are usually accidental, caused by the
splashing or spilling of a hot liquid over the body. Spill
burns can occur when a small child pulls a pot of boiling
water down from the stove, and the liquid spills downward

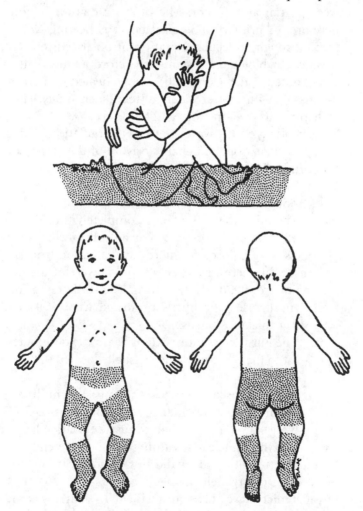

Figure 13.4   Child abuse by scalding. The child is usually grasped beneath the
arms, and lowered into the scalding water (upper figure). The resulting burns will
have a characteristic pattern with sparing of the knees, popliteal fossae, and
inguinal regions (lower figure).

over the body. In such cases, the pattern of the burn should correspond to the story, with the more severe burns to the scalp or head.

   c. **Steam burns** are usually accidental. Superheated vapor can cause severe injury to the mucosa of the airway. In some cases, massive laryngeal edema has occurred, leading to asphyxia and death.

E. **Microwave burns.** Microwaves are electromagnetic waves which span 30 to 300,000 MHz in frequency and have wavelengths between 1 mm and 30 cm. Microwave radiation is nonionizing; therefore, its primary biological effect is heating, which is produced through molecular agitation of polarized molecules, such as water. In biological systems, therefore, tissues with a higher water content (such as muscle) will be heated to a greater extent than tissues with a lower water content (such as fat). The standard kitchen microwave operates at 2450 MHz.

  1. Depending on the wavelength of the radiation, and the thickness, orientation, and characteristics of the target, any one or a combination of three things may occur:

    a. The microwaves may be reflected.

    b. The microwaves may be absorbed.

    c. The microwaves may pass completely through the target.

  2. Surrell et al.[6] in 1987 reported on a study in which anesthetized piglets were exposed to microwave radiation from a 750-watt household microwave oven, on full power, for periods of time ranging from 90 to 120 seconds. The study revealed:

    a. In all cases, the burns produced were well-demarcated, full-thickness burns.

    b. The burns were more extensive on the body surfaces closest to the emitting device (usually located in the top of the oven).

    c. Light microscopy revealed the consistent finding of relative sparing of the subcutaneous fat, but burning of the overlying skin and underlying muscle (**relative layered tissue sparing**); nuclear streaming was not present.

    d. Electron microscopy did not demonstrate any unique cellular or organelle damage.

  3. Most microwave burns are accidental, occurring as an individual reaches into a microwave that has not turned off completely or by ingestion of a scalding hot liquid heated in a microwave. In one report,[7] a man wearing a transdermal nitro patch received a second-degree burn beneath the patch when he sat

next to a leaking microwave oven. Presumably, the aluminized plastic in the adhesive strip of the patch may have been a factor in the burn.

4. An unusual form of child abuse was reported in 1987 by Alexander et al.[8] which involved two separate cases in which a 5-week-old female infant, and a 14-month-old male received burns consistent with placement in microwave ovens which had been turned on.

F. **Chemical burns** are produced by chemical agents such as strong acids and alkalis, as well as other agents such as phosphorus and phenol. The burns produced develop slower than those produced by thermal agents.

  1. The extent of injury is dependent on:
    a. The chemical agent
    b. The strength or concentration of the agent
    c. The duration of contact with the agent

  2. Alkaline agents:
    a. Tend to cause more severe injury than acid agents
    b. That produce burns generally have a pH greater than 11.5
    c. Frequently produce full-thickness injury
    d. Produce burns that appear pale, and feel leathery and slippery

  3. Acid agents usually produce only partial thickness burns, which may be accompanied by erythema and superficial erosion.

VII. DEATH DUE TO BURN INJURY (IMMEDIATE OR DELAYED)

A. **Immediate death** is considered death within minutes to hours of the injury. This may result from:

  1. **Neurogenic shock** due to overwhelming pain.

  2. Direct **thermal injury.** Burned skin exudes/loses large amounts of fluid, which can lead to hypovolemia, shock, and acute renal failure.

  3. **Inhalation of toxic gases.** This should be suspected in any case where soot is readily visible in the nares or mouth.
    a. There may be extensive thermal injury of the airway mucosa, which may lead to mucosal necrosis and edema, bronchospasm, or upper airway obstruction due to laryngeal edema.
    b. The primary toxic gas is **carbon monoxide** (CO). Carbon monoxide is an odorless, colorless gas produced when any carbon fuel (gasoline, propane, natural gas, oil, wood, coal or charcoal briquettes, tobacco) is incompletely burned.

Carbon monoxide binds to hemoglobin with an affinity more than 200 times as great as oxygen, and in so doing displaces oxygen from the hemoglobin molecule, leading to profound tissue hypoxia and death if untreated. The postmortem blood carboxyhemoglobin (COHb) level should be determined in all cases involving fires.

1. In some cases, a lethal level of CO may be present in the absence of gross soot in the airway.

2. In cases of conflagration or flash fires where the victim is rapidly consumed by flame, the postmortem CO level may be low, but some level of CO is almost invariably present.

3. The range of CO levels (30 to 60%) in fire deaths tends to be lower than in suicides resulting from the inhalation of vehicle exhaust fumes, where the range varies from 60 to 80% in healthy adults.

4. Chain-smokers may have elevated baseline carboxyhemoglobin concentrations of 8 to 10%.

5. In cases where carbon monoxide poisoning has occurred, but death is delayed, there may be bilateral necrosis of the globus pallidus or anoxic changes in the cerebral cortex, hippocampus, cerebellum, or substantia nigra. These changes are nonspecific and may be seen in any death where hypoxia has occurred.

6. If the victim survives, there may be late central nervous system sequelae, including cortical blindness, incontinence, parkinsonism, memory loss, or personality changes.

7. Different atmospheric CO levels will lead to varying blood carboxyhemoglobin concentrations and symptoms, depending on time of inhalation. **Table 13.3** describes possible symptoms that may appear in healthy adults at various COHb concentrations in relation to atmospheric CO levels and time of inhalation.

c. In addition to CO, smoke may contain other **noxious agents:**[9]

1. Cyanide may be present in the smoke of residential fires. Cyanide gas is rapidly absorbed and acts by inhibiting the cytochrome oxidase system for cellular oxygen utilization. The exact role that this form of cyanide plays in the eventual death of the fire victim is still being evaluated.

TABLE 13.3   Possible Symptoms Associated with Various Carboxyhemoglobin Concentrations in Healthy Adults, in Relation to CO Air Concentration and Time of Exposure

Carbon Monoxide (concentration in air in parts per million)	Inhalation Time	Approximate Carboxyhemoglobin Concentration	Possible Symptoms
50 ppm[a]	<8 hours	<10%	None
100 ppm	Several hours	10–20%	Dyspnea on moderate exertion; tightness across head
200 ppm	2–3 hours	20–30%	Headache, fatigue, dizziness, nausea
400 ppm	1–2 hours	30–40%	Severe headache, dim vision, dizziness, nausea, irritability, tachycardia
	3 hours	40–50%	Life-threatening
800 ppm	2 hours	40–50%	Unconsciousness
	2–3 hours	>50%	Coma, seizures, death
1600 ppm	<20 minutes	30%	Headache, dizziness, nausea
	1 hour	60%	Death
3200 ppm	25–30 minutes	>70%	Death
6400 ppm	10–15 minutes	>70%	Death
12,800 ppm	1–3 minutes	>70%	Death

[a] 50 ppm is the maximum allowable CO concentration for continuous exposure for healthy adults in any 8-hour period, according to the Occupational Safety and Health Administration.

2. Acrolein — a reactive aldehyde produced by the burning of wood and petroleum products; causes injury by protein denaturation.

3. Hydrochloric acid — produced by the combustion of some plastics, furnishings, building components; onset of pulmonary edema may be delayed for 2 to 12 hours after exposure; toxic levels of hydrochloric acid may still be present an hour after fire has been put out.

4. Toluene diisocyanate — may be produced by burning of polyurethane (synthetic product widely used in seat cushions, mattresses, carpet backings); may cause severe bronchospasm.

5. Nitrogen dioxide — may be produced in fires involving automobiles, or agricultural waste; even brief exposures to high concentrations can cause broncho/laryngospasm and pulmonary edema; chronic interstitial lung disease may be a late complication.

B. **Delayed death** may occur as a result of numerous possible complications.
   1. Ongoing fluid loss may lead to delayed shock and/or renal failure.
   2. Respiratory failure may occur as a delayed complication of damaged respiratory epithelium and development of adult respiratory distress syndrome (ARDS).
   3. Sepsis may occur primarily due to widespread burns or secondarily due to pneumonia.
   4. Death may be due to pulmonary embolus secondary to prolonged immobilization.

VIII. **CHARRED BODIES**

When dealing with charred bodies, the pathologist should be aware of several unique features that may be present.

A. Charring of the body may produce large splits in the skin and/or muscle. The splits occur parallel to muscle fibers, and are not due to antemortem trauma.
B. The body may assume a **"pugilistic" attitude**, with flexion of the upper extremities, similar to a boxer holding his hands in front of his face. The flexures develop as the body cools, and are not a reflection of the position of the body prior to burning.
C. There may be complete absence of fingers, toes, and portions of the extremities due to charring. Occasionally, portions of the body may become detached as the remains are removed from the fire scene. Heat fractures of the extremities may occur, and should not be confused with antemortem fractures, which usually have associated soft tissue hemorrhage.
D. Postmortem total body radiographs should be done in all cases of severe charring, in order to determine the presence of bullets or other identifying items such as metallic sutures, etc.
E. There may be charred defects in the skull that need to be distinguished from antemortem trauma. Occasionally a **"heat epidural"** may form as the blood boils out of the venous sinuses. The postmortem heat epidural is usually chocolate brown in color, spongy or crumbly, and located over the frontal, temporal, or parietal areas of the brain.
F. The weight and length measurements of a charred body are unreliable and artifactually reduced from the true antemortem weight and height.
G. Although charred outside, internal organs and body fluids are usually well preserved. Internal organs may reveal knife wound paths or gunshot wound tracks not readily apparent externally.

Usually, blood, vitreous, bile, and urine may be obtained for toxicology.

H. The presence of black carbonaceous matter (soot) within the upper and lower airway, easily seen on gross exam, is considered to be a reliable indication that the deceased was alive prior to the fire. However, carbon monoxide intoxication can occur without visible soot in the airway. When death occurs from conflagration or flash fires, there may be no visible soot in the airway, despite the victim being alive at the moment of consumption.

IX.   CLASSIFICATION OF FIRE DEATHS

The majority of fire deaths are accidental, with some classified as homicidal, and some due to suicidal actions.

A. A large number of accidental deaths occur as a result of smoking, or due to children playing with matches, or from faulty electrical wiring.

B. If a fire is determined to have been deliberately set or started, and an individual dies as a result of the fire or due to complications from injuries received in the fire, then the death is classified as a homicide. In order to make such a ruling, the pathologist should wait for, and obtain, the official fire marshal's report/ruling as to the source of the fire.

C. Suicidal fire deaths occur occasionally when an individual douses himself or herself with gasoline or some other highly flammable substance and then causes the substance to ignite. Remnants of clothing should be retained and analyzed for the presence of accelerants or volatile substances. If no clothing is present, it may be possible to perform a similar analysis on fragments of body tissue. The clothing or body tissue recovered should be placed in an airtight container, such as a metal or glass jar with an airtight lid.

X.   ANTEMORTEM VERSUS POSTMORTEM BURNS

It is usually impossible to distinguish antemortem burns from postmortem burns.

A. In cases where the victim survives for some period of time following the burn, microscopic examination of the burn may not reveal a vital reaction, such as inflammatory infiltrate. This may be due to heat thrombosis of the dermal vessels, preventing the influx of neutrophils into the injured tissue, or perhaps due to accumulation of large numbers of inflammatory cells in other areas of the body, such as the lungs, due to developing pneumonia.

B. It is possible to produce a postmortem burn of the skin which has identical gross features as an antemortem burn. If a flame is applied to the skin after death, a blister may be produced which may or may not have an associated rim of red tissue, giving it a hyperemic appearance.

References

1. Walker, A.R., Emergency department management of house fire burns and carbon monoxide poisoning in children, *Curr. Opin. Pediatr.*, 8(3), 239, 1996.

2. Ripple, G.R., Torrington, K.G., and Phillips, Y.Y., Predictive criteria for burns from brief thermal exposures, *J. Occ. Med.*, 32(3), 215, 1990.

3. Moritz, A.R. and Henriques, F.C., Studies of thermal injury. II. The relative importance of time and surface temperature in the causation of cutaneous burns, *Am. J. Path.*, 23, 695, 1947.

4. Spitz, W.U., Thermal injuries, in *Medicolegal Investigation of Death*, 3rd ed., Spitz, W.U., Ed., Charles C. Thomas, Springfield, IL, 1993, p. 413.

5. Gordon, P.G. and Pressley, T.A., The fire hazard of children's nightwear: The Australian experience in developing clothing fire hazard standards, *Burns*, 5, 12, 1978.

6. Surrell, J.A. et al., Effects of microwave radiation on living tissue, *J. Trauma*, 27(8), 935, 1987.

7. Murray, K.B., Hazard of microwave ovens to transdermal delivery system (letter), *NEJM*, 310(11), 721, 1984.

8. Alexander, R.C., Surrell, J.A., and Cohle, S.D., Microwave oven burns to children: An unusual manifestation of child abuse, *Pediatrics*, 79(2), 255, 1987.

9. Meyer, A.A. and Salber, P.R., Burns and smoke inhalation, in *Current Emergency Diagnosis and Treatment*, 2nd ed., Mills, J. et al., Eds., Lange Medical Publications, Los Altos, CA, 1985, pp. 417–428.

Transportation Deaths

14

Death may occur as the result of a vehicular collision or crash. Virtually all modes of transportation are capable of causing death or injury. However, in this chapter, the discussion will be limited to findings associated with motor vehicle accidents, pedestrian deaths, motorcycle and bicycle mishaps, and aircraft crashes.

In transportation-related deaths, the postmortem examination is performed for a number of reasons:

- To positively establish the identity of the deceased, especially if the body has been burned, charred, or mutilated
- To determine the actual cause of death and whether or not death was due to the vehicular mishap
- To determine the extent of injury
- To identify any contributing or precipitating factor(s) which may have been present, such as myocardial infarct or drug intoxication
- To document findings for possible use in criminal or civil proceedings which may follow

I. MOTOR VEHICLE DEATHS

A. The **causes** of motor vehicle accidents include:

1. Impairment of the driver by alcohol and/or drug intoxication. Many drivers at fault are intoxicated with alcohol at the time of the collision. Drugs which may be found associated with these accidents include marijuana, cocaine, and some prescription drugs such as diazepam (*Valium*).

2. Human factors — such as speed, recklessness, falling asleep at the wheel.

   3. Environmental hazards/factors — slick, wet pavement; icy
      roads; road construction or repair; fog, etc.
   4. Natural disease, such as myocardial infarct or stroke.
B. Motor vehicle deaths may be divided into four broad categories,
   depending upon the direction of impact to the vehicle — frontal,
   side, rear, or rollover. However, during a collision or accident, a
   combination of the four basic types may also occur.
   1. **Frontal** collision. This is the most common of the four types,
      making up approximately 80% of all vehicular crashes. The
      frontal crash occurs when two vehicles collide head-on, or the
      front portion of a vehicle strikes a fixed object, such as a wall
      or telephone pole. As a result of kinetic motion, the occupants
      of the motor vehicle will continue forward (if unrestrained)
      and impact the steering wheel or dashboard, windshield, or A-
      beam of the vehicle (deceleration injury). Different patterns of
      injury will result depending on the position of the occupants
      within the vehicle.
      a. **Driver** injuries
         1. The **head** may impact the windshield, visor area, re-
            sulting in vertical cuts and abrasions of the forehead,
            nose, and chin. If the rearview mirror is contacted,
            distinctive cuts may be produced. Internal injuries in-
            clude basilar skull fractures, closed head injuries with
            diffuse axonal injury, and neck fractures (both hyper-
            flexion and hyperextension). Hyperflexion injury of
            the neck may lead to posterior atlantooccipital frac-
            ture/dislocation and may be the sole cause of death in
            some cases. The best way to demonstrate this injury is
            by dissection of the posterior neck. **Therefore, in all
            accidental deaths where the routine autopsy fails to
            reveal an obvious cause of death, the posterior neck
            should be examined and explored.**
         2. The **chest** may impact the steering wheel with great
            force, resulting in a patterned abrasion or contusion or
            no visible injury at all. This occurs less frequently due
            to the introduction of compressible steering columns.
            The internal injuries may include:
            a. Transverse fractures of the sternum, and bilateral
               rib fractures, anterior or extensive (flail chest)
            b. Puncture wounds of the lung due to displaced rib
               fractures

      c. Cardiac injuries, including contusion, laceration, rupture, rarely dissection of a major coronary artery

      d. Aortic transection, just distal to the origin of the left subclavian artery

      e. Lacerations of the liver and less commonly the spleen; occasional formation of a subcapsular hematoma, with delayed rupture hours or days later, and death from intraperitoneal hemorrhage

3. **Upper extremity** injuries include wrist or forearm fractures, closed or open, consistent with hands-on-wheel attitude at impact.

4. **Lower extremity** injuries include:

      a. Fractures of the patella(e), or femur as the knees impact the dashboard

      b. Ankle fractures may occur if the foot/feet are braced against the floorboard, or pressed firmly against the accelerator or brake pedal (look for impressions), or if the floor buckles at impact

5. **"Dicing injuries"** of the left face and left arm may occur. In American-made automobiles, the side windows and rear window are composed of *tempered* glass, which is made to shatter into small cubical fragments upon impact. When these cubical fragments impact the skin, characteristic cuts or abrasions are produced, which tend to be superficial, L-shaped, right-angle, or linear.

  b. **Front seat passenger** injuries tend to be the same as those of the driver, except the unrestrained passenger will strike the dashboard and not the steering column, so there should not be a steering wheel imprint under ordinary circumstances. "Dicing injuries" should be to the right face and/or arm.

  c. **Rear seat passengers** (unrestrained) may be thrown forward, impacting the back of the front seat, the front seat passengers, the sun visor area, or even the windshield.

  d. Restraining devices have dramatically reduced the number of injuries that occur in motor vehicle accidents, especially in low-speed collisions.

    1. Restraining devices (shoulder and lap belts), if worn at the time of the collision, may or may not leave characteristic abrasions/contusions on the body. Their loca-

tion on the body will depend on the position of the victim within the vehicle.

   a.   Driver — rectangular or linear abrasion/contusion will angle downward from the left neck or shoulder toward the anterior midline of the chest.

   b.   Passenger — the abrasion/contusion will angle downward from the right neck or shoulder area.

   c.   The lap belt may produce a horizontal linear contusion or abrasion of the abdomen.

2. Restraining devices have been reported to cause injuries.

   a.   Lap belts may cause mesenteric tears, omental lacerations, or bowel contusions.

   b.   Driver and passenger air bags have become mandatory in all newly manufactured cars in the U.S. Several cases of death related to deployment of the supplemental restraint system (SRS) in low-speed, minor-impact collisions that were otherwise survivable have been reported. The majority of these involve children or short adults.

2. **Side (or lateral)** impact collisions usually occur at intersections when one vehicle impacts another or may also occur when a car skids sideways into a fixed object, impacting on its side.

   a.   May see the same injuries as those in frontal impact collisions, including aortic transection and basilar skull fractures.

   b.   If the impact is to the left side of the vehicle, the driver tends to have left-sided injuries, and the front seat passenger will have fewer injuries due to cushioning by the driver.

   c.   If the impact is to the right side of the vehicle, the passenger will tend to have right-sided injuries, as will the driver if no passenger is present.

3. **Rollover** collisions tend to be more lethal than side impact collisions, especially if no restraints are worn, and the occupant is ejected from the vehicle or is thrown about the passenger compartment.

   a.   If full ejection occurs, numerous injuries may result when the victim lands on a firm surface, or in some cases, the ejected victim will be found crushed or trapped beneath the vehicle. The sole cause of death in these cases may be **traumatic asphyxia.**

      b. If partial, transient ejection occurs, the body part involved may be crushed or amputated.

   4. **Rear impact** collisions may cause "acceleration" injuries and are the least likely to result in death. The most common injury resulting from this form of collision is the "whiplash" injury of the neck. In rear-impact collisions, the impact is reduced or absorbed to some degree by the trunk and rear seat compartment, thereby protecting the front seat passengers from severe, life-threatening injury.

C. Trace evidence may be found in motor vehicle accidents and in selected cases should be collected and retained as evidence. The evidence may become important at a later date if the exact position of the occupant within the vehicle at the time of the collision comes under question. The trace evidence may be found inside the vehicle or on the victim's body.

   1. **Inside the vehicle** — look for hair, blood, or clothing fibers or strands from the occupant left on broken glass, knobs, or impact surfaces.

   2. **On the victim's body** — check for paint chips, glass fragments, or broken pieces of the vehicle embedded in wounds.

D. Toxicology should ideally be performed on both the driver and the passenger(s) in motor vehicle accidents. The analyses should include tests for alcohol; carbon monoxide; acid, basic, and alkaline drugs (prescription and nonprescription drugs); marijuana; and other drugs of abuse such as cocaine and opiates.

E. Some motor vehicle accidents are caused by the **suicidal** actions of the driver. Several features may be common to these cases.

   1. The vehicle is noted to have left the roadway and driven directly into a fixed object, or rarely into another oncoming vehicle.

   2. Scene investigation reveals no evidence of braking.

   3. The victim usually has a prior history of suicide attempt or mental illness.

   4. Corroborating evidence may be found on the victim's body, such as recent or old incised wounds of the wrists, or ingestion of a lethal amount of drug prior to getting into the car. Occasionally, an individual will shoot themselves in the chest or head while operating a motor vehicle.

   5. Other evidence may be found within the vehicle, such as a rock or large object placed beneath the brake pedal in an attempt to thwart last-minute indecision.

F. If the vehicle crash results in fire, and the body is burned or charred, every attempt should be made to positively identify the

remains. The techniques used have already been discussed in
Chapter 13.

II. PEDESTRIAN DEATHS

When individuals traveling on foot (pedestrians) are struck by a moving
motor vehicle, a well-recognized pattern of injury will result. The injuries
received may be primary (due to impact with the vehicle) or secondary (due
to impact with the ground or other object after being thrown off the vehicle).

A. Four factors influence the type and appearance of the injuries
received — the speed of the vehicle involved; the type of vehicle
involved; whether or not braking occurred; the size/age of the
victim (adult or child).

1. The **speed of the vehicle** at the time of impact.
   a. In high-speed impacts, with late or no braking, the adult
      pedestrian is picked up and thrown over the top of the car.
   b. In low-speed impacts with minimal braking, the adult
      pedestrian is picked up. As the vehicle continues forward,
      the victim may land on the hood, or continue backward
      to strike the windshield, before sliding off on the right or
      left of the vehicle.
   c. With hard braking,
      1. The adult victim may be thrown forward, knocked
         down, or picked up slightly and then propelled for-
         ward.
      2. The child victim may be thrown forward, or knocked
         down and run over.

2. The **type of vehicle** involved. Vehicles with higher bumpers
   (i.e., trucks) tend to impact the adult pedestrian at or above
   their center of gravity, knocking them down instead of picking
   them up.

3. Braking will cause the front end of a vehicle to dip or lower
   and thus change the level of impact on the pedestrian.
   a. If the impact is above the center of gravity (adult or child),
      the victim tends to be knocked down and run over.
   b. If the impact is below the center of gravity, the adult victim
      is picked up, while the child victim is usually knocked
      forward.

B. Tire tread marks may or may not be present on skin or clothing
in cases where the tire of a vehicle has passed over the deceased.
If present, tire tread marks should be carefully documented by
photography with a scale in the picture for size comparison
(**Figure 14.1**).

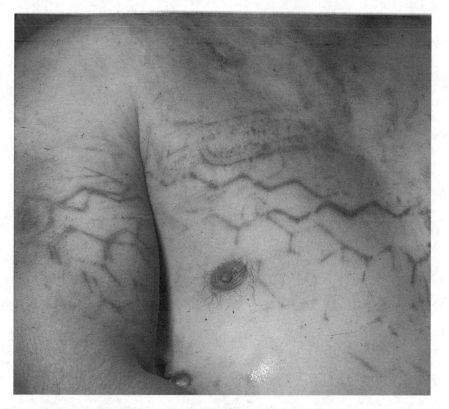

Figure 14.1 (See color insert following page 146) Patterned contusion from tire tread.

C. Patterned imprints or injuries corresponding to parts of the vehicle (bumper, headlights) that impacted the pedestrian may be present. When present, these should also be carefully documented and photographed (with scale), and the location of the wound on the body in reference to the heel or ground should be measured and documented.

D. When a pedestrian is struck by a moving motor vehicle, a chain of events is thrown into motion.

1. As the bumper strikes the lower extremities of the pedestrian, **"bumper fractures"** may be produced (**Figure 14.2**). These may be open or closed and involve one or both bones of the lower leg. They may or may not be associated with external injuries at the level of fracture. When present, the height above the heel or ground at which the fracture occurs should be measured and documented.

   a. If both legs are fractured at the same level, this implies the victim was standing still at the time of impact.

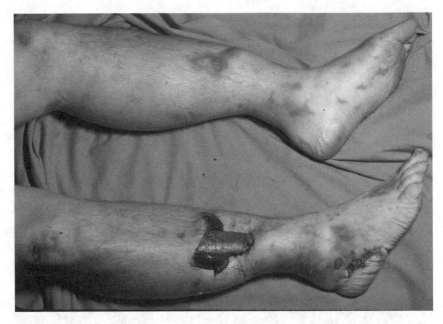

Figure 14.2 (See color insert following page 146) "Bumper fractures" in pedestrian struck by motor vehicle.

      b. If the legs are fractured at different levels, this implies the victim was walking or running when struck.

      c. A side impact generally causes fractures of only one leg, on the side of the impact.

2. The buttocks or thigh area of the pedestrian may then impact the front of the vehicle or hood. This may lead to large subcutaneous, blood-filled pockets of hemorrhage within the buttocks and thighs, or pelvic fractures.

3. As the body flexes, the skin within the inguinal folds may become overstretched, leading to the formation of superficial "stretch" lacerations within these areas, which appear dry, yellow, and bloodless.

4. The head and neck may impact the windshield of the vehicle, resulting in large scalp lacerations with or without avulsion, skull fractures, and neck fractures or injuries. The neck injuries may be severe and include internal decapitation with massive fracture separation of the atlantooccipital joint and severing of the spinal cord or brain stem.

5. As a result of the impact, clothing may be stripped from the body. This is largely dependent on the speed of the impact. In most high-speed impacts, the victim is literally knocked out

of his/her shoes, and the body will often arrive at the morgue
without the shoes.

E. Occasionally, a pedestrian may step or run in front of an oncoming
vehicle in a **suicide attempt.** Eyewitness reports are important in
the investigation. The postmortem examination should include
procedures already discussed in section I.E of this chapter. (suicide
by motor vehicle).

F. Trace evidence may by present in these cases. The evidence may
be left on the impacting vehicle or the impacted pedestrian. If
present, it should be documented, photographed in situ before
removal, and retained with a clear chain of evidence procedure.
The trace evidence may become a critical factor in linking a victim
with a vehicle, as in a hit-and-run death.

   1. On the vehicle, look for hair, skin, and blood from the victim
   deposited on the vehicle at the time of impact. Broken windshield glass may retain a strand of hair or fabric. There may
   be clothing imprints on the hood of the vehicle.

   2. The victim should be carefully examined for paint chips, tire
   tread marks, or grease from the undercarriage. In all cases,
   retain a sample of the victim's head hair for later comparison.
   In hit-and-run cases, the clothing should be retained for more
   extensive examination.

G. Depending on the jurisdiction, "hit-and-run" deaths may be classified as homicides or accidents. The latter classification is justified
only if there was no clear intent to injure. However, in most cases,
since the driver of the motor vehicle fled the scene of the incident,
this may never be known. There is no question that a motor vehicle
may be used to deliberately run down or injure a pedestrian, or
occasionally a passenger is pushed out of a moving vehicle, incurring lethal injures from the fall. In such cases, the correct desig-
nation as to the manner of death should be homicide.

III. MOTORCYCLE DEATHS

In most motorcycle accidents, the operator and/or passenger are readily
thrown from the vehicle, incurring severe impact injuries to the head, torso,
and extremities. Head impact may cause severe angulation of the neck, with
resultant neck injury, such as atlantooccipital fracture separation.

A. The **most common lethal injury** is to the **head.** Head injuries may
occur with or without the use of protective head gear, such as a
helmet, especially in moderate or high-speed collisions. The most
common head injury is a basilar skull fracture. In low-speed incidents, helmets appear to provide some protection from significant head injury.

    B. When passengers fall off of motorcycles, they tend to fall backward, incurring posterior scalp lacerations, fractures of the posterior skull (basilar fossae), and contrecoup brain contusions.

    C. When the motorcycle riders are thrown from the vehicle, they may receive large brush abrasions of the exposed body surface areas.

    D. The causes of motorcycle accidents, in general, are similar to those of motor vehicle accidents:
1. Alcohol or drug intoxication
2. Reckless, careless driving
3. Road conditions or environmental factors
4. Failure of motor vehicle operators to see the motorcycle prior to the collision, possibly due to the low profile of the motorcycle, or concealment of the cycle in the "blind space" of the motor vehicle

    E. **Traumatic asphyxia** may occur in cases where heavy, large motorcycles are involved. When thrown, the victim may hurtle forward at a faster rate than the heavier motorcycle. Since both the operator and the motorcycle will tend to proceed in the same direction, the motorcycle may come to rest on top of the victim, causing crush injury or traumatic asphyxia.

IV. BICYCLE (PEDAL-CYCLE) INJURIES

Most accidents involving bicycles are caused by carelessness or inexperience. Considering the number of bicycles in use, the incidence of death related to their use is extremely low.

    A. When injuries occur, they are usually mild and non-life-threatening, having been produced at low speeds usually.

    B. If the bicyclist is struck by a motor vehicle, the injuries may be primary (from the impact), or secondary (impact with ground).

    C. The degree of the injury is mostly dependent on the speed at which the impact takes place.

    D. **"Bicycle spoke injury"** is a specific injury that may occur when a rider or passenger on a bicycle slips from the seat or handlebars, causing the foot or leg to pass through the spokes of the wheel.[1]
1. Usually involves a child.
2. Soft tissue of the lower leg is crushed, with internal avulsion or damage.
3. The extent of the injury may not be evident for 24 to 48 hours.
4. The necrosis may be severe enough to require a full-thickness skin graft.

V. AVIATION-RELATED INJURIES AND DEATH

Airplane crashes involve all sizes and types of aircraft, including light/private aircraft used in general aviation, commercial airliners, and military aircraft. This section will provide only basic information about private and commercial aircraft crashes, as a more detailed discussion is beyond the scope of this handbook.

A. **Light/private airplane crashes.** Most of these crashes are due to pilot error, followed by mechanical defect, weather conditions, or some combination of all three.

1. If the crash is a low-speed one, the injuries produced may be similar to those in high-speed motor vehicle impacts.

2. High-speed crashes usually result in massive blunt force injury, with mutilation of the body, and even disintegration into multiple small body parts and pieces.

3. When presented with the duty of performing a postmortem examination on victims involved in a light plane crash, the forensic pathologist should be concerned with accomplishing the following goals:

a. Positive identification of the remains. In many cases, the remains may be severely mangled or lacerated, or burned beyond visual recognition.

b. If multiple victims, the pathologist should attempt to determine which victim was the pilot in command at the time of the crash. This may or may not be readily apparent at the scene. The pattern of injury may aid in this determination.

1. DNA analysis of swabs of the yoke may help in identifying the pilot.

2. Postmortem radiographs of the body may aid in the demonstration and documentation of fractures. If the body is charred or burned, total body x-rays should be taken.

c. Complete toxicology should be performed, ideally on all victims, but especially on the pilot, if it is known for sure which victim was in control of the airplane at the time of the crash.

4. Occasionally, death may result from an individual walking into a spinning airplane propeller. The injuries received may be massive and are usually chopping injuries.

B. **Commercial aircraft crashes.** The main role of the pathologist in such crashes is identification of the bodies, which may be frustrating and drawn out, hampered by the sheer magnitude of the task and complicated by logistics, media attention, and lack of qualified personnel.

1. If the casualty count is great, only selected victims receive a complete autopsy. This would include all members of the flight crew, especially the pilot and copilot, where the pattern of injury is documented much the same as in a private airplane crash, and possible contributing factors are looked for, such as heart disease or the presence of drugs, alcohol, or carbon monoxide.
2. Some passengers may also be autopsied, in an attempt to document injury patterns, which may aid in the search for the actual cause of the crash. Toxicology may reveal the presence of toxic gases or substances previously unrecognized.
3. A temporary morgue may have to be set up at the crash site, using tents or refrigerated trucks.
4. If the bodies can be transported to a morgue, refrigerated trucks may be used. Advantages of examination at a forensic facility would include access to x-ray equipment, although portable x-ray equipment may also be used at the site. If there is suspicion of explosive (bomb) injury, the bodies should be radiographed prior to significant manipulation.

C. Airplane crashes tend to occur in **six general patterns**:[2]
   1. *Hole-in-the-ground* pattern is consistent with a nose-down, high-speed dive into the ground at an angle between 45 and 90°. The crater formed is usually deep and relatively small compared to other crashes.
   2. *Spin-impact* crashes occur as the plane dives into the ground while spinning, usually in a nose-down attitude, but occasionally in a flat spin. These impacts tend to produce more shallow craters than those described above.
   3. *Spiral-impact* crashes. The wreckage is spread over a large, fan-shaped area.
   4. *Small- (or shallow-) angle-of-impact* crashes may be low or high speed.
      a. Low-speed shallow-angle impacts occur usually when the pilot has been forced to land suddenly.
      b. High-speed shallow-angle impacts occur when the pilot is flying too low, usually in adverse weather conditions with decreased visibility.
   5. *In-flight disintegration*. In these crashes, parts of the aircraft and occupants are spread over a large area without a logical pattern. This type of crash is typical with in-flight explosions or midair collisions.

6. *Wire strikes* may cause a crash, usually when the plane is flying too low or there is reduced visibility.

References

1. Strauch, B., Bicycle spoke injuries in children, *J. Trauma*, 6(1), 61, 1966.
2. Di Maio, V.J.M. and Di Maio, D.J., Airplane crashes, in *Forensic Pathology*, 2nd ed., CRC Press, Boca Raton, FL, 2001, p. 321.

Environmental Deaths

15

Individuals, by their nature, must interact with the environment and, in so doing, encounter varying environmental conditions that may on occasion lead to death. Environmental deaths are usually accidental. The causes of environmental death to be discussed in this chapter include those due to drowning, temperature extremes (hyperthermia and hypothermia), and deaths by lightning.

I. DROWNING

Drowning accounts for approximately 8000 deaths per year in the United States, with a large number of those deaths involving children less than 4 years of age. As a cause of death, drowning must be considered whenever:

- A deceased individual is recovered from a body of water.
- A body is found on the bank or shore of a body of water or near a water-filled container.
- A body is found with its head submerged in water or some fluid medium.

A. Questions to be considered or addressed in such cases include:
1. Was the individual alive or dead prior to submersion?
2. Are wounds present on the body artifacts or evidence of primary injury which occurred prior to submersion?
3. If drowning is determined to be the cause of death, is the manner of death accident, suicide, or homicide?

B. In acute drownings, the mechanism of death is irreversible cerebral anoxia. Several stages are involved when a conscious person becomes submerged:
1. Initial stage — Characterized by voluntary breath holding, until involuntary urge to breathe becomes overwhelming.

2. If the individual's head is still below the water when the involuntary urge to breathe happens, fluid will be aspirated into the upper airway. Large volumes of fluid/water may be inhaled and/or swallowed.

3. The involuntary aspiration of water may continue for some time, until respirations stop due to anoxic cerebral insult.

4. The resulting cerebral hypoxia progresses to anoxia and irreversible brain death.

5. Consciousness is usually lost within 3 minutes of submersion.

6. Vomiting (with or without aspiration of vomitus), defecation, urination, and seminal emission may or may not occur during the agonal period.

C. Whether or not saltwater drowning tends to be more lethal or severe than freshwater is not clear.

1. In **freshwater** (hypotonic) drownings, large volumes of water can quickly pass through the alveoli and increase the blood volume, as well as cause hemolysis. Freshwater also denatures pulmonary surfactant.

2. In **saltwater** (hypertonic) drownings, plasma is osmotically drawn into pulmonary alveoli resulting in a decrease in blood volume, hemoconcentration, and an increase in blood electrolyte levels. Saltwater dilutes and/or washes away pulmonary surfactant.

D. The loss or denaturing of pulmonary surfactant leads to alveolar collapse, with a decrease in lung compliance, leading to severe, often profound, ventilation-perfusion mismatches and worsening hypoxia.

E. **"Near drowning"** is a term used when a previously submerged victim "survives" for at least 24 hours after being rescued. The individual may or may not be conscious. These individuals may develop pulmonary edema, hemoglobinuria, cardiac arrhythmias, pneumonitis, fever, sepsis, as well as symptoms related to cerebral hypoxia (convulsions, amnesia, confusion, coma). A major cause of death within the first 24 hours is the sudden development of cerebral edema.

F. Survival without neurological deficit is possible after prolonged underwater submersion in very cold, icy water. Many such cases have been reported in the literature, with a large number involving children or infants. One report describes a case in which a child was submerged for 66 minutes.[1] Protection from cerebral hypoxia may occur in these cases due to an active **diving reflex**, where cold-water immersion leads to bradycardia and intense vasocon-

striction of all blood vessels, except for those supplying blood to
the brain and heart.

G. In **warm water,** irreversible cerebral anoxia may occur in as little
as 3 to 10 minutes after submersion.

H. The autopsy findings in cases of drowning are highly variable and
dependent to a large degree upon the condition of the body when
recovered. The diagnosis of drowning is basically *one of exclusion*;
therefore, a complete autopsy must be done in these cases in order
to rule out any other cause of death. The autopsy should include
complete toxicology and, ideally, complete microscopic examination of the body organs. However, adequate microscopic examination is not always possible, as many drowning victims, when
found, are in the early or advanced stages of decomposition.

   1. If a body is recovered within a short period of time, abundant
   bloody edema froth may be present throughout the airway,
   and water may be present in the stomach. There may also be
   a suggestion of cerebral edema.

   2. Historically, **petrous** or **mastoid hemorrhage** was described
   as a finding common to, and perhaps diagnostic of, drowning.[2]
   However, this is now regarded as a nonspecific sign, having
   also been described in many other cases in which the cause of
   death was not drowning.

   3. The skin of the hands and feet will appear shriveled and pale
   ("washerwoman hands") after being submerged in water for
   greater than 1 to 2 hours. This change occurs regardless of
   whether the individual was alive or dead prior to submersion.
   Shriveling of the skin can also occur if the hands or feet are
   kept moist by wet clothing or surrounding environmental matter (such as wet dirt or mud), and is, therefore, not specific
   for drowning.

I. Over the years, attempts have been made to develop a laboratory
test that would scientifically confirm the diagnosis of drowning.
Most of these tests are now considered to be nonspecific and/or
unreliable for making that determination. Some of the more historical tests include:

   1. 1902 — Carrara, in the German literature, reported on the
   analysis of whole blood, taken from the right and left sides of
   the heart in cases of drowning; he examined the specific gravity, freezing point, and electrical conductivity of the blood.

   2. 1921 — Gettler chloride test. When analyzing the chloride
   concentration of blood from the right and left heart chambers,
   he reportedly found a difference of more than 25% to be

indicative of drowning. If the death occurred in saltwater, the blood chloride concentration was greater in the left heart chambers when compared to the right, due to hemoconcentration. If the death occurred in freshwater, the blood chloride concentration was greater in the right heart chambers when compared to the left, due to hemodilution.[3]

3. **Diatom** identification/analysis. Theoretically, if an individual drowns and aspirates fluid which contains diatoms (microscopic algae), the diatoms may be found in the lungs, as well as in other body organs, if blood circulation is still present at the time of aspiration.

    a. Diatoms are microscopic, unicellular algae, reportedly present in all types of water, in moist soil, and in the atmosphere.

    b. Diatom analysis should be done on a **closed organ system** (such as the femoral bone marrow), in a nondecomposed body, taking care to avoid contamination by environmental factors which may contain diatoms. The analysis is best performed in a research or reference laboratory accustomed to such analyses. The tissue collected is digested with acid, or more recently with detergents or enzymes, and the resultant centrifuged pellet is examined microscopically. A sample of water taken from the suspected site of the drowning is used for comparison. A negative result **does not** rule out drowning as the cause of death.

    c. The validity and/or reliability of the diatom test is still a much debated topic among investigators in the field and forensic pathologists.

J. After drowning has occurred, the body usually sinks and will not move far from the area in which the drowning has occurred, unless strong currents are present.

    1. Postmortem artifacts may occur to the face or extremities as the body "hangs" in the water and scrapes along rough surfaces.

    2. Postmortem artifacts may also occur due to animal (fish, turtles, crabs) activity or feeding on the body.

    3. As decomposition sets in, the body will gradually rise to the surface. The amount of time necessary for this to occur is dependent mostly upon the temperature of the water. In average temperatures, a submerged body will decompose in approximately half the time as one in air. Obese individuals may sink for shorter periods of time and rise to the surface sooner, as a result of the increased buoyancy of fat.

K. According to a recent survey, men are much more likely to drown than are women.[4] This article reports that in 1990, out of 4685 U.S. drowning deaths, 3854 (82%) were men, while only 831 were females. The article cites several factors which may account for the difference. These include:
   1. Men are more likely to be exposed to aquatic environments and to high-exposure activities than are women.
   2. Young men are usually more likely to take risks in the water, possibly by overestimating their swimming abilities.
   3. Men tend to consume more alcohol on or near the water than women do.

L. **Bathtub** drownings usually involve infants or young children who have been left unattended in a tub which may be only partially filled with water. These deaths may be accidental or homicidal and can occur in relatively sparse amounts of water, sometimes only a few inches.[5]
   1. Adults who drown in bathtubs are usually found to have contributing factors such as natural disease (cardiac, seizure disorders) or toxicological abnormalities (alcohol/drug intoxication).
   2. Adult bathtub deaths may be homicidal.[6] If an individual is stuporous, or drugged, he/she may be placed in a tub or body of water, leaving no evidence of the act. Rarely, the victim may be pulled suddenly, by the feet, beneath the surface of the water, causing the head to submerge suddenly and the victim to involuntarily aspirate water. Such deaths are probably, however, very uncommon.

M. In more recent years, a number of deaths have been reported in association with the use of **hot tubs, spas,** or **heated whirlpools.**
   1. Most of the cases reported in the literature involve children. In these deaths, it is important to remember that **anoxic brain injury occurs more rapidly in elevated water** temperatures.[7-9]
   2. Accidental adult deaths in hot tubs are known to occur but are rarely reported in the literature. Many of these deaths are unwitnessed, and usually associated with alcohol or drug intoxication. In some cases, however, hot tub drownings occur in the absence of significant alcohol or drug intoxication. The mechanism of such deaths is postulated to be transient hypotension produced when the individual stands up to exit the hot tub, after marked vasodilatation has occurred while being seated in the tub, as a consequence of the elevated water temperature.

II. HYPERTHERMIA

Hyperthermia is defined as an elevated core body temperature of **105°F** (40.5°C) or higher. Hyperthermia is the hallmark symptom of the condition known as **heat stroke**. Milder forms of heat illness also exist, and are related to exertion during periods of increased environmental heat.

A. The milder forms of heat illness include **heat cramps** and **heat exhaustion.**

   1. **Heat cramps** occur during vigorous exercise or exertion in an individual not acclimated to the increased environmental heat. The cramps involve the large muscle groups being used, usually the legs, and are thought to be caused by salt depletion. The skin is moist and cool; the body temperature is normal; there is minimal distress. Treatment involves rest in a cooler environment and salt replacement.

   2. **Heat exhaustion** may occur under the same conditions as heat cramps and is usually due to the loss of both salt and water. Symptoms include headache, nausea, vomiting, dizziness, weakness, irritability, or cramps. The core body temperature is normal or only slightly elevated. The treatment is essentially the same as for heat cramps.

B. **Heat stroke** occurs when the normal heat-dissipating mechanisms of the body become incapable of compensating for increased environmental heat. Heat stroke is a life-threatening condition that requires immediate treatment if the individual is to survive. Heat stroke in the United States causes 4000 deaths per year. The marked increase in body core temperature causes direct thermal tissue injury. Even with rapid therapy, the mortality rate may be as high as 76% for body temperatures equal to or greater than 106°F (41.1°C).[10]

   1. Preexisting conditions which may predispose an individual to heat stroke include:

      a. Alcoholism, cerebral or cardiac atherosclerosis, use of certain drugs (major tranquilizers, tricyclic antidepressants, monoamine oxidase inhibitors)

      b. Obesity. Obese people tend to be more susceptible to heat stroke for several reasons:

         1. Body fat acts as insulation, preventing ready dissipation of body heat, even under normal circumstances. With increased environmental temperatures, this problem is compounded.

         2. Obese individuals, even under normal conditions, tend to have difficulty dissipating body heat due to the fact

that increased body mass (fat) generates increased body
heat. But the proportionate increase in the body surface
area is insufficient to effectively dissipate the increased
body heat.

2. Two major settings of heat stroke deaths:

   a. *Classic* heat stroke occurs during prolonged environmental
      heat waves. The elderly are usually affected more than the
      young. Other individuals at increased risk include those
      with chronic illnesses, obese individuals, poor individuals
      lacking air conditioning, and alcoholics.

   b. *Exertional* heat stroke involves relatively young individuals
      undergoing extreme exertion, such as long-distance run-
      ners, football players, military recruits, and laborers.

3. The **symptoms** of heat stroke include hyperthermia; hot, dry
   skin; and central nervous system dysfunction. The symptoms
   may appear suddenly or be preceded by nausea, vomiting,
   muscle cramps, or dyspnea.

   a. As the body temperature rises above 42.4°C, vasodilatation
      occurs, with a resultant decrease in blood volume, which
      leads to circulatory collapse and cardiac failure.

   b. If the individual survives the initial acute insult, compli-
      cating factors may occur, including the development of
      pneumonia, tubular necrosis of the kidneys, adrenal hem-
      orrhage, hepatic necrosis, myocardial fiber necrosis, and
      disseminated intravascular coagulation (DIC).

   c. If the individual survives for some period of time following
      the acute hyperthermic injury, nonspecific degenerative
      changes in cortical neurons may be visible with light mi-
      croscopy. There may also be marked changes in the cere-
      bellum, including necrosis of Purkinje cells (which appear
      dense, red, and eosinophilic) and a marked decrease in the
      number of Purkinje cells present.

4. **Autopsy** findings are nonspecific in cases of heat stroke. The
   diagnosis of heat stroke is best made antemortem, from physical signs and symptoms and determination of the rectal temperature.

5. If a deceased individual is found shortly after death and the
   environmental conditions are such to suggest the possibility of
   heat stroke, a core body temperature (either rectal or liver)
   should be taken at the scene; at the same time, the environmental temperature should be determined. If the postmortem
   core body temperature indicates hyperthermia, and the envi-

ronmental temperature is lower, and the autopsy does not reveal any other cause for the hyperthermia or other obvious cause of death, the diagnosis of probable heat stroke can be made.

III. HYPOTHERMIA

Hypothermia refers to a core body temperature **below 95°F** (35°C), caused usually by exposure to low environmental temperatures. Mild hypothermia occurs at 34 to 35°C, moderate at 30 to 34°C, and severe at less than 30°C. Extended exposure to cold environmental temperatures may occur in association with alcohol or drug abuse, injury or immobilization, or mental impairment.

A. Susceptibility to cold is dependent on various factors:
 1. Age. Infants are much more susceptible to cold than are adults, because their ratio of body surface area to body mass is greater than an adult's ratio. Newborn infants, especially in the first few weeks of life, tend to be more susceptible to hypothermia due to underdeveloped reflex centers.
 2. Obese individuals tolerate cold better than nonobese or thin people.
 3. Women tend to tolerate cold better than men, due to their thicker layer of subcutaneous fat.
 4. Immersion in icy cold water (**immersion hypothermia**) causes a more rapid loss of heat than would occur in dry, cold air of the same temperature. This is due to the fact that water dissipates heat from a body much faster than dry air.
    a. Observations from concentration camps indicate it takes 70 to 90 minutes for a man (malnourished) to die when placed in water at 4 to 9°C.[11]
    b. Observations on shipwreck victims showed survival times in seawater ranging in temperature from about 5 to 12°C to be around 1 to 2 hours.[12]
    c. At water temperatures close to freezing (32°F), fatal cooling can occur very rapidly, within 30 minutes.[13]
B. When an individual is exposed to a cold environment, several things begin to happen:
 1. Vasoconstriction occurs in blood vessels of the skin and muscles.
 2. Shivering begins in an attempt to generate additional body heat. Maximal shivering can produce four times the amount of heat produced by the normal basal metabolic rate.
 3. Cellular metabolism increases, also in an attempt to generate body heat. This occurs mostly in **brown fat.** Adults have rela-

tively small amounts of brown fat and cannot, therefore, generate significant amounts of energy by this process. In contrast, infants have large stores of brown fat and are capable of generating significant amounts of energy by this process.

4. If the compensatory mechanisms fail, and the body temperature drops below 90°F (32°C), there is a relatively linear decrease in the pulse rate, and metabolic processes begin to fail. The effects of hypothermia are summarized below:[14,15]

Body Temperature	Effect
32°C (90°F)	Ability to shiver is lost
	Cerebral function impaired (analgesia, hallucinations, slowed reflexes)
	P-QRS wave is prolonged due to slowing of depolarization
30°C (86°F)	An extra wave (J wave) appears after the P-QRS wave on the electrocardiogram
	Cold narcosis appears
<30°C	Atrial fibrillation may appear
25–28°C (77–82°F)	Ventricular fibrillation occurs
	No pupillary reflex
<20°C	May have occasional, rare heart beat (3–4 per minute); EEG usually flat
10°C	No cardiac activity, but the heart may begin to beat again when the body is rewarmed

C. **Autopsy findings** associated with hypothermia:
   1. A classic postmortem finding in deaths due to hypothermia is the presence of **cherry red lividity**, resulting from the accumulation of oxyhemoglobin in the tissues, presumably due to underutilization. This finding is not always present, as some victims appear extremely pale, almost white. Cherry red or pink lividity is **not specific** for hypothermia. It may also be seen in deaths due to carbon monoxide intoxication, in cyanide poisoning, and in bodies refrigerated for increased periods of time.
   2. If death is not immediate, and the individual survives for a short time, he/she may develop:
      a. Hemorrhagic pancreatitis
      b. Erosions (ulcers) or focal hemorrhages of the gastrointestinal mucosa (stomach, ileum, colon)
      c. Pneumonia
      d. Acute tubular necrosis
      e. Myocardial fiber necrosis/degeneration

    D. **"Paradoxical undressing"** can be seen in cases of hypothermia. This refers to the fact that victims of hypothermia are often found undressed.

       1. The explanation for this paradox involves the terminal hallucinations and subjective feelings of warmth that occurs in the terminal stages of the process.

       2. In 1995, Rothschild and Schneider[16] reported on a series of 69 cases of lethal hypothermia. Paradoxical undressing occurred in 25% of the cases. Additionally, bodies that were completely or partially disrobed were found in a somewhat protected position, such as under a bed, behind a wardrobe, or in a shelf. The authors theorized this behavior was due to activation of a primitive brain stem reflex of burrowing behavior (for protection), as can be seen in hibernating animals. The phenomenon occurred usually with slow decreases in temperature and moderately cold conditions.

IV. LIGHTNING

Lightning may be defined as a momentary, atmospheric, transient, high-current electrical discharge whose path length is measured in kilometers. Most lightning discharges are within clouds (intracloud), with fewer occurring cloud-to-ground. Most human deaths are caused by **cloud-to-ground** lightning strikes. Lightning causes several hundred deaths per year in the United States and is responsible for more fatalities each year than any other type of natural disaster.[17] Most lightning strikes occur during thunderstorms, but lightning strikes can also occur in the absence of rain. Most lightning discharges are negative, while approximately 5% are positive.

    A. Lightning may cause death in several ways:

       1. An individual may be struck **directly** by a lightning bolt. In these cases, the resulting amperage is in the kiloamp range.

       2 An individual may also be struck **indirectly**, either by a side-flash, or by conduction of the charge through an intermediary object.

          a. Side-flash — Lightning strikes an object, such as a tree, and then arcs from that object to the victim, usually standing nearby.

          b. Occasionally, individuals may be injured while indoors during a lightning storm. This may occur while in the shower or bathtub (current travels along water pipes) or while using the telephone (current travels along wire).[18]

    B. Approximately one third of lightning strikes are fatal, with most due to direct strikes. Direct strikes to the head have a high degree of fatality. Death is due to high-voltage, **direct** current. The current may spread over the body surface diffusely, enter or pass through the body, or both.

C. In the majority of cases, the strike will cause:

1. Clothing defects, including large tears, holes, ruptures, singed holes, bursting of the shoes; in many cases, the clothing is actually ripped or torn from the body, leaving the body nude. Such a scene may give the false impression of death due to rape/assault, if the true nature of the death is not immediately recognized.

2. Singing of the body hair, focally or diffusely.

D. In some cases, the lightning strike *may* cause:

1. Skin burns where the skin is in contact with metallic objects, such as jewelry, belt buckles, or zippers.

2. Rupture of the eardrums, with flow of blood from the external ear canals. This may be misinterpreted as evidence of head trauma.

3. Magnetization of iron or steel objects in the pockets of the victim. If such items are present, they can be easily checked for magnetization with a pocket compass.[19]

E. The external burn pattern is highly variable. Arcing burns may be present in direct strikes or side-flashes.

F. In some cases, a pathognomonic sign of lightning strike is present. This patterned injury (also called *Lichtenberg* figure) is described as a **fern-like, arborescent, dendritic red mark** found on the skin of some lightning victims (**Figure 15.1**). Numerous theories exist concerning the actual pathogenesis of the lesion, but the exact cause has yet to be elucidated.[20] The mark reportedly appears within 1 hour after the strike and gradually fades within 24 hours.

G. The mechanism of death in fatal cases is usually immediate, non-reversible cardiopulmonary arrest, and/or electrothermal injuries. In some cases, secondary traumatic injuries, resulting from a fall or being thrown to the ground after the strike, cause the death.

H. Wetli[21] reported on a study of 45 lightning fatalities that occurred in Dade County, Florida, between the years from 1956 to 1994. His findings included:

1. Age of the victims ranged from 13 to 65 years of age (average 32 years), with the majority white males (about 73%).

2. The incidents occurred most frequently in the early afternoon, in the summer months (June to September), in a field, usually while the victim was standing near a tree.

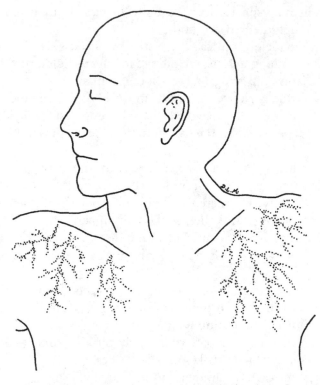

Figure 15.1 Fern-like, arborescent skin mark (**Lichtenberg** figure), which may be present in about one third of individuals dying from lightning strike.

3. 58% of the victims were engaged in recreational activities; 31% were at work; 11% were engaged in miscellaneous activities (at home, walking).

4. Greater than 90% of the victims had some form of cutaneous injury.

5. About one third of the victims had *Lichtenberg* figures present.

6. Greater than 80% had ruptured tympanic membranes, in the cases where the eardrums were examined.

7. Some cases had craniocerebral injury and cardiac contusion as a direct consequence of the lightning strike.

8. Two of the 45 deaths were documented to have occurred during clear weather.

9. In 20 of the 45 cases, the cardiac rhythm present when the victim was found was documented; the most frequently encountered rhythm was ventricular fibrillation, followed by asystole, with EMD and idioventricular rhythm in only a few (2/20).

References

1. Bolte, R.G. et al., The use of extracorporeal rewarming in a child submerged for 66 minutes, *JAMA*, 260, 377, 1988.

2. Niles, N.R., Hemorrhage in the middle-ear and mastoid in drowning, *Am. J. Clin. Path.*, 40(3), 281, 1963.

3. Gettler, A.O., A method for the determination of death by drowning, *JAMA*, 77, 1650, 1921.

4. Howland, J. et al., Why are most drowning victims men? Sex differences in aquatic skills and behaviors, *Am. J. Pub. Health*, 86(1), 93, 1996.

5. Schmidt, P. and Madea, B., Death in the bathtub involving children, *For. Sci. Inter.*, 72, 147, 1995.

6. Schmidt, P. and Madea, B., Homicide in the bathtub, *For. Sci. Inter.*, 72, 135, 1995.

7. Shinaberger, C.S., Anderson, C.L., and Kraus, J.F., Young children who drown in hot tubs, spas, and whirlpools in California: A 26-year survey, *Am. J. Pub. Health*, 80(5), 613, 1990.

8. Monroe, B., Immersion accidents in hot tubs and whirlpool spas, *Pediatrics*, 69(6), 805, 1982.

9. Tron, V.A., Baldwin, V.J., and Pirie, G.E., Hot tub drownings, *Pediatrics*, 75(4), 789, 1985.

10. Knochel, J.P., Heat stroke and related heat stress disorders, *Dis. Month*, 35(5), 301, 1989.

11. Simpson, K., Exposure to cold, starvation, and neglect, in *Modern Trends in Forensic Medicine*, Simpson, K., Ed., Mosby Co., St. Louis, 1953, p. 116.

12. Molnar, G.W., Survival of hypothermia by men immersed in the ocean, *JAMA*, 131, 1046, 1946.

13. Cooper, K.E., Hunter, A.R., and Keatinge, W.R., Accidental hypothermia, *Int. Anes. Clin.*, 2(4), 999, 1964.

14. Trevino, A., Razi, B., and Beller, B.M., The characteristic electrocardiogram of accidental hypothermia, *Arch. Inter. Med.*, 127, 470, 1971.

15. Fay, T. and Smith, G.W., Observations on reflex responses during prolonged periods of human refrigeration, *Arch. Neurol. Psychiatry*, 45, 215, 1941.

16. Rothschild, M.A. and Schneider, V., "Terminal burrowing behavior" — A phenomenon of lethal hypothermia, *Int. J. Legal Med.*, 107(5), 250, 1995.

17. Lifschultz, B.D. and Donoghue, E.R., Deaths caused by lightning, *J. For. Sci.*, 38(2), 353, 1993.

18. Andrews, C.J., Telephone-related lightning injury, *Med. J. Aust.*, 157, 823, 1992.

19. Lifschultz, B.D. and Donoghue, E.R., Electrical and lightning injuries, in *Medicolegal Investigation of Death*, 3rd ed., Spitz, W.U., Ed., Charles C. Thomas, Springfield, IL, 1993, pp. 526–527.

20. Resnik, B.I. and Wetli, C.V., Lichtenberg figures, *Am. J. For. Med. Path.*, 17(2), 99, 1996.

21. Wetli, C.V., Keraunopathology: An analysis of 45 fatalities, *Am. J. For. Med. Path.*, 17(2), 89, 1996.

Electrocution

16

Deaths due to electrocution are infrequent. While most electrocution deaths are accidental, occasional suicidal electrocutions occur. Homicidal electrocutions are rare. For an electrocution to occur, the victim must become part of an electrical circuit.

In the United States, electrical deaths are almost always due to alternating current (AC), with those between 39 and 150 Hz (cycles/second) the most lethal. In the United States, alternating current operates at a rate of 60 Hz, well within the range to cause death. Human beings are four to six times more sensitive to alternating current (AC) than to direct current (DC). Direct current is found in some industries requiring electrolytic activity, such as metal plating operations.

I. OHM'S LAW

A basic understanding of **Ohm's law** is necessary to discuss variables involved in most electrocutions. Ohm's law is expressed as:

$$I = \frac{V}{R}$$

where

I = current in amperes
V = electromotive force in volts
R = resistance in ohms

The amperage (current) is the **most important factor** in most electrocutions. As can be seen from Ohm's law, the current is directly related to the voltage and inversely related to the resistance. Therefore, the greater the voltage, the higher the current, and the greater the resistance, the lower the current.

II. FACTORS DETERMINING SEVERITY OF ELECTRICAL INJURY

Whether or not an electrical source will cause an injury, and how severe or extensive the injury will be, is dependent on several factors:

- The nature of the current (AC, DC, or pulsating DC)
- The voltage involved
- If alternating current, the frequency involved
- The amount of current
- The length of time the victim is in contact with the current
- The condition of the earth (dry or wet), if the earth is part of the circuit
- Resistance of the body
- The path of the current through the body

III. LOW-VOLTAGE VERSUS HIGH-VOLTAGE DEATHS

Deaths due to electrocution may be caused by **low-voltage** or **high-voltage** sources.

A. By convention, a voltage source less than 1000 volts is considered **low voltage**, while sources greater than 1000 volts are considered **high voltage**.

　　1. In U.S. residential households, the voltage supplied to the main circuit breaker box is usually 220 to 240 volts. At the circuit breaker box, the voltage is split, making the voltage at the wall outlets within the house 110 to 120 volts.

　　2. High-voltage sources include:

　　　　a. Primary distribution power lines, with voltages between 2300 and 23,000 volts;

　　　　b. High-tension (transmission) power lines, which carry voltages from approximately 60,000 to 100,000 volts or greater.

B. In **low-voltage** (household current) electrocutions:

　　1. The cause of death may not always be obvious.

　　2. There must be direct contact between the victim and the electrical circuit.

　　3. Death is primarily due to ventricular fibrillation.

　　4. If the current is low, but the contact time is great (minutes), death may still occur, but the mechanism of death is usually by muscle paralysis, with secondary asphyxia.

C. **High-voltage** electrocutions may occur accidentally when a worker operating a cherry picker comes into contact with a high-voltage power line, or an individual on the ground contacts a high-voltage power line with a long pole (antenna mast) or a kite.

1. Direct contact with the electrical source or wire is not necessary, as the current may **arc** to the victim.
    a. An electric arc can generate extremely high temperatures, as high as 4000°C.
    b. The distance an arc of electricity may jump is related to the voltage, as described by Somogyi and Tedeschi.[1]

	Metric	U.S.
1,000 volts	A few millimeters	
5,000 volts	1 cm	3/8 inch
20,000 volts	6 cm	2 3/8 inches
40,000 volts	13 cm	5 1/4 inches
100,000 volts	35 cm	14 inches

2. Death in high-voltage electrocutions is due to respiratory arrest or electrothermal injuries caused by heat generated by the current. The electrothermal injuries are usually irreversible.
3. Death due to lightning strike is a form of high-voltage electrocution (direct current), which has already been discussed in Chapter 15.

IV. RESISTANCE AND CURRENT FLOW

Since voltage is usually fairly constant, changes in resistance become an important factor in determining the amount of current that will flow through the body.

A. Human **skin** provides the greatest degree of resistance to electrocution of all of the body organs, followed by bone, fat, nerves, and muscle, with the least resistant being blood and body fluids.
B. Different types of skin produce different degrees of resistance.[2]

Type of Skin	Resistance (ohms)
Dry, calloused or thickened	1 million
Dry, noncalloused	100,000
Moist	1,000
Moist, thin	100

C. The amount of resistance present is also dependent on the type of clothing present in the contact areas. Rubber boots can insulate the feet from the ground, while rubber gloves can insulate the hand from the conductor.

V. CURRENT FLOW THROUGH THE BODY

When an electrical current flows through the body, it follows the shortest path, and not necessarily the path of least resistance.

A. The current may take different paths through the body, depending on the entry and exit sites. For example, the path may be hand to foot, hand to hand across the chest, head to foot, chest to foot, or chest to hand. When the current follows a path that includes the heart or brain, a fatal outcome is more likely to occur than if the path does not traverse either of these organs, as in a leg-to-ground path.

B. Different amounts of current traveling through the body will have different effects on the body.[1,3] The possible effects on the body of varying amounts of current (AC, 60 cycle), with at least 1 second of contact, are described below:

Current (in mA)	Effect on Body
1	Threshold of perception, with possible tingle
5	Muscle tremor
15	Muscle contraction, which prevents release of the line
40	Possible loss of consciousness
75–100	Ventricular fibrillation
2000 (2 Amps)	Ventricular arrest

C. In cases where an extremely high current (2 amps or greater) has affected the heart and produced ventricular arrest, the heart should begin to beat spontaneously after contact with the current is broken, provided no irreversible electrothermal injuries have also occurred.

VI. ELECTROCUTION AND LOSS OF CONSCIOUSNESS

Unconsciousness may not occur immediately in cases of electrocution. This is especially true of low-voltage incidents, where the electrical shock produces ventricular fibrillation. In these cases, the brain has approximately 10 to 15 seconds of oxygen reserve, which allows cerebral activity to continue despite inefficient cardiac output. The victim may be heard to cry out or speak. In some cases, the victim has been found some distance from the electrical source, or the defective device is found switched off or unplugged. In cases with sustained depolarization, instantaneous rigor mortis may occur.[4]

VII. ELECTRICAL BURNS OF THE SKIN

When electricity contacts the body, the thermal heat produced by the current can cause **electrical burns** of the skin. Whether or not electrical burns occur is dependent on the voltage involved, amount of current flow, the area contacted, and the duration of contact with the electrical source.

A. In **low-voltage** electrocutions:

1. Electrical burns occur in only about 50% of cases.

2. If the current is diffused over a relatively broad area, a discrete burn is usually not seen. An example of such a circumstance would be electrocution of an individual sitting or standing in a tub filled with water, into which an electrical appliance is dropped. In these cases, the appliance need not be turned on, but merely plugged into a wall outlet.

3. If the victim remains in contact with the electrical source, severe burns may be seen.

4. Electrical burns may be hidden inside the mouth or lips, i.e., a small child places a defective electrical cord in his/her mouth or bites into a live cord.

B. In **high-voltage** electrocutions:

1. Electrical burns are seen in virtually all cases.

2. The burns produced may be severe, with charring of the tissue, especially if there is prolonged contact with the source.

3. Multiple small, pitted burns may occur as the current arcs or "dances" across the body (**Figure 16.1**); "flash burns" may involve large areas of skin.

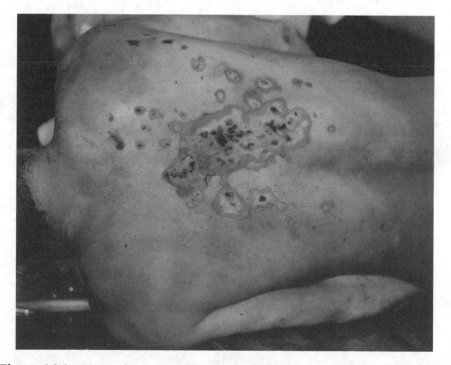

Figure 16.1 (See color insert following page 146) Multiple electrical burns produced by current arc across body in high-voltage electrocution.

    4. The heat generated within the body may cause explosive injuries, including loss of extremities or rupture of organs.

C. If electrical burns are produced by contact, or near contact, with an electrical source:

    1. They tend to occur on the fingertips or palms (usual entry sites), and the soles of the feet (usual exit site), as depicted in **Figure 16.2.**

    2. The typical burns are chalky white, or yellow/tan, with a central crater and raised pale border. Some burns may have focal, small areas of blackening. The burns may be surrounded by a zone of erythema. The burns range in size from punctate (a few millimeters) up to 1 to 2 cm.

    3. Less severe electrical burns may resemble small, punctate second-degree thermal burns.

D. Recent, fresh electrical burns of the skin may have a distinctive odor, described by some as that of burnt cork.

E. **Microscopic examination** of electrical burns:

    1. Can be difficult, as the skin involved is usually firm, making it difficult to obtain good histologic sections

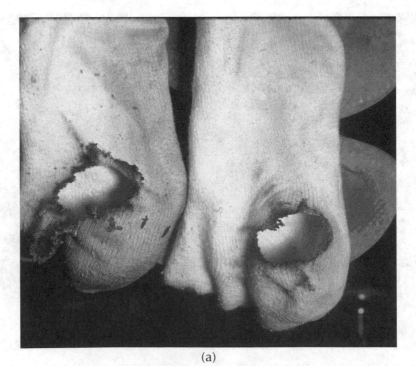

(a)

Figure 16.2 (See color insert following page 146) Typical electrical "exit" burns of feet with corresponding burn defects in socks (a) and soles of feet (b). Close-up appearance of electrical burn (c).

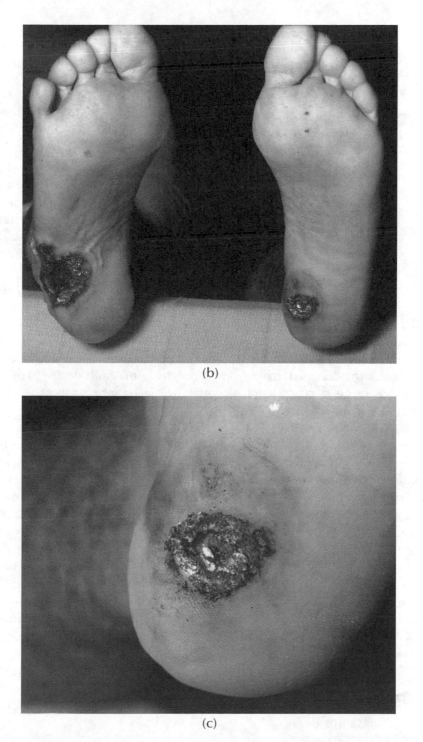

(b)

(c)

Figure 16.2 (continued)

2. May show:
   a. Detachment of the epidermis, or multiple small cystic spaces within the epidermis, giving it a "Swiss cheese" appearance.
   b. **"Streaming"** of the basal epidermal nuclei. The nuclei are thin, elongated, and lie parallel to each other.
3. The microscopic findings described above are not specific for electrical burns but can also be seen in thermal burns.
F. Suspected electrical burns, when possible, should also be examined with a dissecting microscope, or the burn may be excised from the body and examined with scanning electron microscopy, as small, minute pieces of metal or debris from the conducting apparatus (i.e., wire) may be deposited in the wound. Also, the apparatus should be examined for the presence of retained hair or tissue from the body. **DNA analysis can be performed on this material.**
G. As a general rule, antemortem electrical burns cannot be distinguished from postmortem electrical burns.

VIII. SUICIDAL ELECTROCUTION

Suicidal electrocutions occur but are rare. Often, the individual involved has some knowledge of electricity and may be an electrician or engineer. In some cases, the deceased may use an elaborate, home-built device to deliver the shock, or an electrical appliance may be placed into a tub of water in which the victim is sitting.

IX. GROUND-FAULT CIRCUIT INTERRUPTERS (GFCIs)

From 1979 to 1982, about 100 deaths occurred in the United States as a result of electrical appliances (usually hair dryers) coming into contact with bathwater.[5] **Ground-fault circuit interrupters** (GFCIs) are electronic devices that were introduced in an effort to prevent such deaths. This device protects an individual by interrupting the circuit it is monitoring when it detects a difference of 5 mA or greater between the hot side of the circuit and ground. The disconnection occurs within a fraction of a second, but the individual may still feel a shock. A person in normal health should experience no ill effects from the shock, but infants and very small children may still be affected. Depending on where the wiring defect is within the appliance or device, a GFCI will not always protect an individual from electrocution.

X. INVESTIGATION OF SUSPECTED ELECTROCUTIONS

In all cases of suspected or possible electrocution:
A. The clothing should be carefully examined for burn defects that may have been produced by contact with the electrical source, and the corresponding areas on the body should also be carefully examined.

B. The suspect electrical appliance or device should be obtained and carefully examined for evidence of defect or retained skin or hair from the victim. The aid of an electrician, or individual familiar with the evaluation of electrical devices, may be needed in some cases. The evaluation should include complete documentation of the defect, if possible by photography and/or x-rays. In all cases, a chain of custody should be maintained.

XI. THIRD-RAIL ELECTROCUTIONS

Electrocution can occur due to contact with the third rail of rapid-transit tracks. Several cases of death in New York have been reported, in which death was caused by urination on the third rail, which is reportedly charged with 600 volts of direct current (DC).[6]

XII. ELECTRICAL SHOCK AND PREGNANCY

In cases where a pregnant female has received an electrical shock, the severity of the maternal injury **does not** correspond to the degree of fetal injury.

A. The fetus is more sensitive to an electrical shock than the mother, due to its size, thin skin, and the increased conduction capabilities of the amniotic fluid and blood-filled placenta.

B. The electrical shock of a pregnant female can result in several different outcomes:
   1. There may be no effect, and the pregnancy continues without any problems or long-term effects.
   2. The shock may cause the death of both the mother and the fetus.
   3. The mother may not be affected, but the fetus may die and be aborted soon after the shock, or within days or weeks of the shock.

C. Autopsy findings on the fetus are usually nonspecific and may include maceration and hemorrhages in the brain, kidney, lung, and liver.

D. In 1993, Fatovich[7] reported on a literature search of all case reports of electric shock during pregnancy in the English literature. The study revealed:
   1. Fifteen cases of pregnant females who had been exposed to electric shock at various stages of pregnancy (9 to 40 weeks).
   2. Fourteen of the 15 cases involved household AC current.
   3. Although there were no maternal deaths or loss of consciousness, fetal death occurred in 73% of the cases (11/15).
   4. The time interval from injury to delivery varied from hours to 21 weeks.

    5. Oligohydramnios and/or growth retardation was associated with some cases.

    6. Some of the mothers noted the sudden loss of fetal movement at the time of the shock.

    7. In all cases, the current path was hand to foot (which included the uterus). In electrical shocks that do not include the uterus in their path (i.e., electroconvulsive therapy and DC cardioversion), the fetus is usually not affected.

XIII. STUN GUNS

Stun guns are devices designed to deliver short bursts of electrical energy that cause temporary muscle paralysis.

    A. Stun guns are:

        1. Purported to be nonlethal devices, used primarily by law enforcement personnel in subduing violent or agitated offenders

        2. Also promoted as self-defense devices and can be purchased legally in most states through mail-order catalogs or in gun shops

    B. Stun guns have been reported to have been used in some cases of torture, rape, and child abuse.[8]

    C. When a stun gun is activated while in contact with human skin, characteristic, patterned injuries may result. The lesions produced tend to be small, round or slightly linear abrasions or areas of erythema, with or without central paling, which occur in pairs. The distance between the paired skin lesions should correspond to the distance between the stun gun electrodes contacting the skin. These electrodes are usually the **outer** electrodes of the stun gun.

    D. Microscopic sections of the skin lesions may show nonspecific changes, or changes similar to a thermal heat injury of the skin.

    E. Ikeda et al. reported on a case of homicidal manual strangulation in which the victim also had multiple skin lesions caused by the use of a stun gun. In order to evaluate whether or not the stun gun wounds were inflicted prior to or after death, the authors inflicted anesthetized pigs with stun gun shocks prior to and after death. When the stun gun was used prior to death, identical marks to those of the human victim were produced on the pigs, but when the shocks were delivered to the pig skins after death, no lesions were produced.[9]

XIV. JUDICIAL ELECTROCUTIONS

The use of electrocution as a means of capital punishment was first introduced in the mid–19th century, in New York, largely in response to the unpredictable outcome of judicial hanging.

A. The first execution by electric chair occurred in New York in 1890, in which a 1400-volt, 150 Hz AC current was applied to a prisoner for 17 seconds before death was declared. Within a minute of death being declared, the prisoner reportedly groaned, and respiratory movement was noted to occur and deepen. The current was re-applied for an additional $2\frac{1}{4}$ minutes before the prisoner was finally declared dead. Eyewitnesses of the execution reported smoke rising from the burnt corpse.[10]

B. Autopsies performed on electrocuted prisoners have revealed marked, extensive heating and burning of body tissues, as well as severe burns of the skin.

C. The electric chair is the sole method of execution in Nebraska.

D. In Alabama, Florida, South Carolina, and Virginia, the inmate is offered a choice between lethal injection and the electric chair.

E. In Arkansas, Kentucky, and Tennessee, the electric chair is offered as an alternative to lethal injection if the crime was committed prior to certain dates.

F. In Oklahoma and Illinois, the electric chair is authorized as a method of execution if lethal injection is ever found to be unconstitutional.

References

1. Somogyi, E. and Tedeschi, C.G., Injury by electrical force, in *Forensic Medicine*, Tedeschi C.G. et al., Eds., W.B. Saunders Co., Philadelphia, 1977, p. 645.

2. Bruner, J.M.R., Hazards of electrical apparatus, *Anesthesiology*, 28, 396, 1967.

3. Di Maio, V.J.M. and Di Maio, D.J., Electrocution, in *Forensic Pathology*, 2nd ed., CRC Press, Boca Raton, FL, 2001, p. 410.

4. Wright, R.K., Death or injury caused by electrocution, *Clin. Lab. Med.*, 3(2), 343, 1983.

5. Budnick, L.D., Bathtub-related electrocutions in the United States, 1979 to 1982, *JAMA*, 252, 918, 1984.

6. Lifschultz, B.D. and Donoghue, E.R., Electrical and lightning injuries, in *Medicolegal Investigation of Death*, 3rd ed., Spitz, W.U., Ed., Charles C. Thomas, Springfield, IL, 1993, p. 523.

7. Fatovich, D.M., Electric shock in pregnancy, *J. Emer. Med.*, 11, 175, 1993.

8. Frechette, A. and Rimsza, M.E., Stun gun injury: A new presentation of the battered child syndrome, *Pediatrics*, 89, 898, 1992.

9. Ikeda, N., Harada, A., and Suzuki, T., Homicidal manual strangulation and multiple stun-gun injuries, *Am. J. For. Med. Path.*, 13(4), 320, 1992.

10. Jones, G.R.N., Judicial electrocution and the prison doctor, *Lancet*, 335, 713, 1990.

Deaths in Nursing Homes

17

I. DEATHS IN NURSING HOMES

Deaths in nursing homes (NH) are for the most part natural and, as such, do not usually fall under the medical examiner's jurisdiction. Exceptions are:

A. Deaths due to **drug overdoses**, either inadvertent or intentional.

B. **Accidental deaths not involving medications**; these include asphyxial deaths due to bedrails and restraint vests; drinking of cleaning fluids by senile patients; burns due to immersion in hot bath water; falls: etc.

C. **Homicides** by nursing home personnel, visiting family members, or fellow patients.

D. **Suicides.**

E. **Gross neglect** of patients. Nursing homes and/or personnel have been charged with homicide for improper and inadequate care of patients. In one case involving a death resulting from infected decubitus ulcers, the care-home provider was convicted of manslaughter.[1]

II. SIGNS OF NEGLECT

A. **Decubitus ulcers** (pressure sores)

1. Decubitus ulcers (pressure sores) are entirely preventable.
2. Predisposing factors to development of pressure sores are:
   a. Depressed sensory and/or motor function
   b. Altered consciousness
   c. Pressure over bony prominences
   d. Malnutrition
   e. Shearing forces and moisture (fecal and urinary incontinence)

239

   3. Decubitus ulcers are divided into **four stages** based on their
      clinical appearance and extent:
      a. Stage I: The initial lesion seen following compression of
         skin and tissue is reactive hyperemia (reddening of the
         skin).
      b. Stage II: These range in severity from a blister to ulceration
         of the skin; they are partial-thickness ulcers involving epi-
         dermis and/or dermis.
      c. Stage III: These are full-thickness ulcers extending through
         the skin and subcutaneous fat up to the fascia.
      d. Stage IV: The ulcer extends down through the fascia into
         muscle, often to the bone; osteomyelitis may develop.
   4. Stage III and stage IV ulcers indicate poor or lack of nursing
      treatment and thus neglect. Preventative measures involve ba-
      sic nursing techniques and practices.
   B. Other signs of neglect are contractures, malnutrition, and dehy-
      dration.
III. **DEATHS DUE TO HOSPITAL BED SIDE RAILS**
   A. Bed side rails are intended to prevent patients from injuring them-
      selves. They are not suitable for and will not restrain individuals
      who are active or ambulatory, no matter the mental status.
   B. Bedrails cause injury indirectly when patients fall as they attempt
      to climb over the rails.
   C. Bedrails may cause death directly by entrapment of the patient by
      the mattress, the bed frame, or the rails.[2] The mechanism of death
      is asphyxia.
IV. **DEATHS DUE TO MEDICAL RESTRAINTS**
   Restraints are mechanical devices, materials or equipment that restricts
an individual's freedom of movement or normal access to his body. If indi-
viduals attempt to escape from such devices, they run the danger of ligature
strangulation or traumatic/positional asphyxia.[3]

References

1. Di Maio, V.J.M. and Di Maio, T.G., Homicide by decubitus ulcers, *Am. J. For.
   Med. Path.*, 23, 1, 2002.

2. Parker, K. and Miles, S.H., Deaths caused by bedrails, *J. Amer. Geriatrics Soc.*,
   45(7), 797, 1997.

3. Miles, S.H. and Irvine, P., Deaths caused by physical restraints, *Gerontologist*,
   32, 762, 1992.

Deaths Due to Starvation

18

I. MALNUTRITION, STARVATION DEATHS IN GENERAL

Deaths due to or associated with malnutrition and starvation are encountered by the medical examiner in the following situations:

- Abuse of a child, an elderly individual, or a mentally handicapped individual
- In association with chronic debilitating diseases
- Starvation used as a political tool

A. In child abuse deaths due to starvation, there is often a contention by the defense that the child was suffering from some obscure disease that caused failure to thrive. This has to be countered two ways:

1. First by a **complete autopsy** with microscopic examination of all organs and conduction of specialized laboratory tests when appropriate to rule out natural disease.

2. Second, there should be an **investigation** of the child's past medical and social history. Often such an investigation will reveal that at one time they were seen in a hospital or cared for by someone else and under these circumstances gained weight.

B. In the case of abuse of the elderly, a complete autopsy and an investigation of the deceased's medical history should be conducted.

1. In individuals dying in nursing homes, one often finds records indicating that the deceased consumed every meal, every day, the whole time they were in the home, yet consistently lost weight.

2. These patients generally have to be hand-fed — a long tedious process. The person supposed to feed them often has to feed

241

too many patients in the allotted time. What happens is that this individual makes cursory attempts to feed the patient and then writes down that the patient completed the whole meal.

II. NUTRITION AND BODY WEIGHT

The amount of nutrition required by a person to maintain their body weight depends on their:

- Body size
- Activity
- Age
- Sex
- Health
- Environment

A. A weight loss of 35 to 50% in an individual who is not obese is life-threatening. An individual can live without eating for approximately 1 1/2 to 2 months.

B. The **basal metabolic rate** (BMR) is the amount of energy required of an awake individual, at rest, to maintain his or her cellular function at the lowest level. It can be calculated using the Harris-Benedict equation.

1. Males: Calories = 66 + (13.7 x weight in kilograms) + (5 x height in centimeters) − 6.8 x Age.

2. Females: Calories = 655 + (9.6 x weight in kilograms) + (1.85 x height in centimeters) − 4.7 x Age.

3. Using these equations for a 25-year-old male weighing 70 kilograms (154 lb) and 177.8 cm tall (5 feet 10 inches), the calorie requirement is 1744 calories.

4. For a 25-year-old female weighing 60 kilograms (132 lb) and 167.6 cm tall (5 feet 6 inches), the calorie requirement is 1281 calories.

C. These formulas do not take into account **activity** and **stress**. If one does, then:

1. Calories = BMR x AF (Activity Factory) x SF (Stress Factor).

2. The Activity Factor for a moderately active individual is at least 1.5.

3. In the aforementioned 25-year-old male, this would increase the calories needed to 2616 calories.

4. Stress such as skeletal trauma or infection may increase calorie requirements by a Stress Factor of 1.2 to 1.6.

a. Thus, the 25-year-old male with skeletal trauma may require as much as 3139 calories; with severe infection, 4185 calories.

    D. In addition to just calories, an individual needs protein. The normal **daily protein** intake should be:

Daily Protein = 0.8 to 1.0 g/kg ideal body weight/day for a normal individual (1.2 to 1.5 for an individual with infection, pregnancy, or stress).

      1. A decrease in serum **albumin** concentration is an indication of protein calorie malnutrition.

        a. When it falls below 3.5 g/dl, it is significant.

        b. Below 2.5 g/dl, there is severe malnutrition.

      2. A decrease in **transferrin** also occurs in malnutrition and is, in fact, a more sensitive indicator of nutritional status.

        a. In a moderate degree of malnutrition, transferrin is between 100 and 149 mg/dl.

        b. Severe malnutrition produces levels less than 100 mg/dl.

III. **PHYSICAL MANIFESTATIONS OF STARVATION**

    A. Severely malnourished individuals are immediately recognizable by their appearance:

      1. Sunken eyes and features

      2. Brittle hair

      3. A skeletal appearance, with their skin stretched over bone

    B. Some individuals may present with **wet starvation** manifested by:

      1. Edema of the face, torso, and extremities

      2. Ascites and pleural effusions

    C. In cases of starvation, at autopsy there is:

      1. No body fat

      2. A decrease in size of most of the organs

      3. Empty bowel

      4. In some cases, generalized ulceration of the colonic mucosa

IV. **DEHYDRATION DEATHS**

Death due to dehydration is more rapid than that of starvation.

    A. It can occur in a few hours with infants, or a few days, depending on the environment.

    B. Daily fluid requirements, assuming no unusual environment, are:

      1. 125 to 135 ml/kg per day for infants

      2. 100 to 120 ml/kg per day for children

      3. 50 ml/kg for adults 18 years and up

    C. The fluids can be ingested directly as fluids or indirectly in food.

    D. In high-temperature conditions, tremendous loss of fluid can occur due to sweating. An individual can lose 500 ml per hour.

    E. Symptoms of fluid loss are:

      1. Nausea

      2. Vomiting

   3. Apathy
   4. Weakness
   5. Fainting

General References

1. Winick, M., ed., *Hunger Disease: Studies by the Jewish Physicians in the Warsaw Ghetto*, John Wiley & Sons, New York, 1979.
2. Ewald, G.A. and McKenzie, C.R., Eds., *Manual of Medical Therapeutics*, 28th ed., Little, Brown, and Co., Boston, 1995.

Deaths in Association with Pregnancy

19

I. **DEATHS SECONDARY TO COMPLICATIONS OF PREGNANCY ARE RELATIVELY UNCOMMON BECAUSE OF:**
   - Better prenatal care than in the past
   - More sophisticated diagnostic procedures
   - More aggressive medical therapy
   A. Berg et al.[1] found that of 1453 pregnancy-related deaths:
      1. 54.9% followed a live birth.
      2. 7.7% occurred while still pregnant.
      3. 7.1% followed a stillbirth.
      4. 10.7% followed an ectopic pregnancy.
      5. 5.6% followed an abortion.
      6. The status of the rest of the cases could not be determined.
   B. The most common causes of death, in order of frequency, are:
      1. Hemorrhage
      2. Embolism
      3. Pregnancy-induced hypertensive complications
      4. Infection
   C. After this are a variety of other categories involving small numbers of cases, e.g., cardiomyopathy, air emboli, and anesthetic-related deaths. A rare complication of pregnancy is a dissecting aneurysm of the coronary arteries.
   D. In deaths from hemorrhage, the most common etiology is an **ectopic pregnancy.**[1]
   E. In cases of death due to embolism:

1. Pulmonary **thromboemboli** are somewhat more common than amniotic fluid emboli.
2. Of 286 deaths attributed to embolism:
   a. 158 were due to thrombotic emboli.
   b. 111 were due to amniotic fluid emboli.[1]
3. Virtually all **amniotic emboli** deaths occur at the time of birth.
   a. The mortality rate is approximately 50%.
   b. Definitive diagnosis is made by identification of fetal squames and lanugo in pulmonary vessels (**Figure 19.1a**).
   c. In a substantial number of cases where there is no doubt clinically that death was due to amniotic fluid embolism, no fetal elements are identified.[2]
   d. The clinical signs of amniotic fluid emboli are respiratory distress and cardiovascular collapse, characterized by hypotension.
   e. If death does not occur immediately, the patient will often go into disseminated intravascular coagulopathy (DIC).

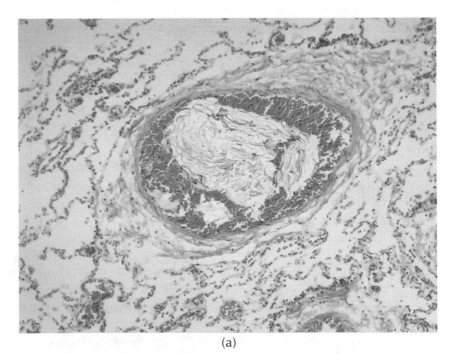

(a)

Figure 19.1 (See color insert following page 146) Various pulmonary emboli which may result in maternal death. (a) amniotic fluid embolus in pulmonary vasculature, H & E stain of lung tissue; (b) placental embolus, H & E stain; (c) placental embolus, HCG immunostain of lung tissue.

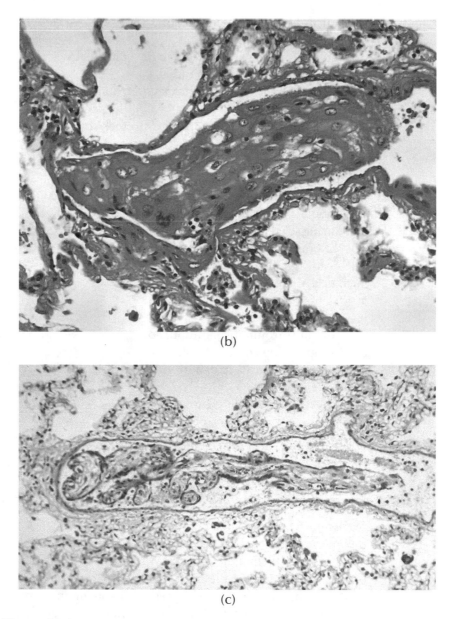

(b)

(c)

Figure 19.1 (continued)

4. In cases of placental abruption resulting from trauma, fragments of placenta may embolize to the lung and result in collapse and death (**Figure 19.1b, c**).

F. Preeclampsia and eclampsia account for the pregnancy-induced hypertensive complications.

G. **Air embolism** is a rare cause of death.
   1. It usually occurs during oral sex.
   2. Air bubbles can be demonstrated in the epicardial vasculature, giving them a beaded appearance.
   3. Air is found in the right ventricle and atrium.

II. **ABORTION-RELATED DEATHS**
   A. Deaths related to illegal abortion are extremely rare nowadays. The mechanisms of death in such cases are:
      1. Hemorrhage and/or sepsis complicating perforation of the uterus
      2. Endometritis progressing to septicemia
      3. Air emboli
   B. Deaths during legal abortions are also relatively rare.[3]
      1. They average approximately ten a year in the United States. The death rate increases with the gestational age.
      2. Such deaths are due to:
         a. Hemorrhage
         b. Infection
         c. Emboli (thrombotic, amniotic, or air)
         d. Complications of anesthesia
      3. Deaths by method of abortion, in decreasing rate of occurrence, are:
         a. Hysterectomy/hysterotomy
         b. Installation methods (including saline)
         c. Evacuation procedures (defined as suction and curettage performed at or greater than 13 weeks of gestation)
         d. Curettage procedures (defined as suction and sharp curettage performed at or less than 12 weeks of gestation)[3]
      4. Curettage is the most common method of abortion used and results in the most deaths because of this, even though it has the lowest rate of death by type of procedure.
      5. Deaths due to hemorrhage and sepsis usually are complications of perforation of the uterus. While perforation is a recognized complication of any procedure involving instrumentation of the uterus, death due to sepsis or hemorrhage should not occur and strongly suggests the possibility of medical malpractice.

References

1. Berg, C.J. et al., Pregnancy related mortality in the United States, 1987–1990, *Obst. Gynec.*, 88(2), 161, 1996.

2. Clark, S.L. et al., Amniotic fluid embolism: Analysis of the national registry, *Am. J. Obst. Gynec.*, 172(4), 1158, 1995.

3. Lawson, H.W. et al., Abortion mortality, United States, 1972 through 1987, *Amer. J. Obstet. Gynec.*, 171(5), 1365, 1994.

Intraoperative Deaths

20

Deaths during diagnostic or operative procedures fall into five categories:

- Deaths due to underlying disease
- Disruption of a vital organ during a procedure
- Air embolism occurring during surgery
- Anesthetic-related deaths
- Cause of death cannot be ascertained

I. DEATHS DUE TO UNDERLYING DISEASE
The first group includes **deaths occurring because of an underlying disease** process that necessitated the operative/diagnostic procedure. *These deaths are not due to the procedures being carried out.* An example is an individual put on a cardiac bypass pump for coronary bypass surgery, whose heart, when removed from the pump, does not come back.

II. DISRUPTION OF A VITAL ORGAN DURING A PROCEDURE
The second group includes deaths due to **inadvertent mechanical disruption of a vital organ during a procedure,** e.g., the surgeon, while going through the sternum, inadvertently punctures the heart.

      A. A number of deaths have occurred when catheters being passed into the right atrium, right ventricle, or pulmonary artery have perforated one of these chambers or the artery.[1]

      B. Perforation of the coronary artery can occur during angiography or an angioplastic procedure.

      C. Some of the mechanical disruptions are not unexpected when one realizes that one is dealing with a diseased and often friable vessel or organ.

III. **AIR EMBOLISM OCCURRING DURING SURGERY**
  A. This occurs most commonly in surgery of the:
      1. Central nervous system
      2. During laminectomy procedures[2,3]
  B. Any time death occurs during procedures such as these, one should immediately suspect air embolism.
  C. Air can be demonstrated in the epicardial vessels of the heart as well as in the right ventricle and atrium.

IV. **ANESTHETIC-RELATED DEATHS**
  A. Examples of such deaths are:
      1. Intubation of the esophagus
      2. Administering the wrong gases
      3. Drug overdoses
      4. Allergic reactions to iodine-based dyes
      5. **Malignant hyperthermia:**[4]
          a. When it occurs, it is usually associated with halogenated anesthetics and succinylcholine.
          b. Characterized by a rapid rise in body temperature and a two- to threefold increase in total body oxygen consumption; other symptoms include arrhythmias, tachycardia, and skeletal muscle rigidity.
          c. Individual involved usually has a genetic predisposition to the syndrome.
          d. May be fulminant or insidious; may or may not occur every time anesthesia is administered.
          e. Complications include rhabdomyolysis, electrolyte abnormalities (especially hyperkalemia), and disseminated intravascular coagulopathy (DIC).
  B. Occasionally death is due to an overdose of a drug or the wrong medication is given. This is more common in emergency rooms.
  C. Deaths complicating local anesthesia are due to either an allergic reaction to the agent or an overdose.
      1. Allergic reactions are very rare.
      2. More common is either a straight overdose or inadvertent intravascular or intrathecal injection of the agent.
      3. Most local anesthetics are cardiotoxic and thus can cause a fatal cardiac arrhythmia.
      4. Epinephrine is usually added to local anesthetics. If the local anesthetic is injected intravascularly, the epinephrine can potentiate the toxic effect of the agent on the myocardium.

V. CAUSE OF DEATH CANNOT BE ASCERTAINED

The fifth category includes cases where, after a careful investigation of the circumstances surrounding the death, a complete autopsy, and toxicology analysis, **no cause of death can be ascertained.** The mechanism in such deaths appears to be cardiac, but what the underlying process(es) is which results in death is unknown.

References

1. Robinson, J.F. et al., Perforation of the great vessels during central venous line placement, *Arch. Intern. Med.*, 155(11), 1225, 1995.

2. Palmon, S.C. et al., Venous air embolism: A review, *J. Clin. Anesth.*, 9(3), 251, 1997.

3. Albin, M.S. et al., Venous air embolism during lumbar laminectomy in the prone position: Report of three cases, *Anesth. Analg.*, 73, 346, 1991.

4. Di Maio, V.J.M. and Di Maio, D.J., The effects of heat and cold: Hyperthermia and hypothermia, in *Forensic Pathology*, 2nd ed., CRC Press, Boca Raton, FL, 2001, p. 426.

Forensic Toxicology 21

I. FORENSIC TOXICOLOGY

Forensic toxicology is the study and practice of the application of toxicology to the purposes of the law. Forensic toxicology involves not just **the identification and quantifying** of a drug, poison, or substance in human tissue but also the **ability to interpret** the results of one's findings.

A. In medical examiners' offices, the results of toxicologic analyses are correlated with:
   1. The medical history of the deceased
   2. The autopsy findings
   3. The circumstances leading up to and/or surrounding the death

B. This is done to determine whether a drug:
   1. Was a cause of death
   2. Was a contributory factor
   3. Played no role in the death

C. In many instances, drug levels cannot be interpreted by themselves.
   1. All physicians and toxicologists have had cases with "fatal drug" levels where the drug had nothing to do with the cause of death.
      a. This is seen typically in drug abusers who may acquire a tolerance to a drug such that levels that would kill an ordinary person will not cause death in the drug tolerant.
      b. This same situation may also be seen by clinical physicians: the patient admitted to the emergency room is conscious and coherent with drug levels associated with unconsciousness or death in normal individuals.

II.   TISSUES TO BE COLLECTED

No matter how good a toxicology lab is, if it does not receive the proper samples of tissue, in sufficient quantity, it cannot perform an adequate analysis.

A. The tissue of most importance for analysis is blood.
  1. It is the blood level of the drug that has the effect on the individual.
  2. A drug detected in the urine or bile had an effect on the individual at one time, but it cannot be said that the drug was having an effect on the individual at the time the patient died if the drug is not detected in the blood.
B. The materials to be collected for a proper toxicologic analysis are:
  1. In the living individual:
    a. Blood
    b. Urine
  2. In deceased individuals, not autopsied:
    a. Blood
    b. Vitreous
    c. Urine
  3. In all autopsy cases:
    a. Blood
    b. Vitreous
    c. Urine
    d. Bile
  4. If death is believed to be due to an oral overdose of a drug, then stomach contents may be retained.
  5. When the body is too decomposed to collect the aforementioned fluids, collect at least **50 g** of each of the following tissues:
    a. Muscle from the thigh
    b. Liver
    c. Kidney
  6. Levels of drugs in muscle more accurately reflect blood levels than the liver or kidney.
  7. In some cases, by virtue of the nature of the case, other body tissue is retained. Thus, in suspected arsenic cases, to determine if there has been chronic poisoning, hair is saved.

III.   COLLECTION OF MATERIALS

A. Fluids should **always** be collected with a clean needle and a new syringe.
  1. Blood must always be collected in glass containers; if it is collected in plastic containers, blood, being slightly acidic, can

leach out plastic polymers from the plastic, creating fallacious peaks in gas chromatograph (GC) analyses.

2. In the case of blood specimens, always label the tube as to the source of the blood, e.g., the femoral vessels or the heart.

B. **Collect:**
   1. All the vitreous and place in a 10 cc test tube
   2. A 10 cc test tube of bile
   3. A 20 cc test tube of urine
   4. Blood:
      a. 20 cc in a red-top tube(s).
      b. 20 cc in two 10 cc gray tops (preservatives potassium oxalate and sodium fluoride).
      c. 10 cc in a purple top (preservative EDTA); this tube is for DNA analysis.
      d. For analysis of **volatile** compounds, the blood must be collected in test tubes with screw-top lids so that these compounds do not diffuse through rubber stoppers.

C. In the case of bodies not autopsied:
   1. Blood is collected from the femoral vessels. If not obtainable from these vessels, use the subclavian vessels.
   2. Collection of blood by blind transthoracic needle stabs is not acceptable as there may be inadvertent contamination of the blood with fluid contents from the esophagus, pericardial sac, stomach, or pleural cavity.
   3. Urine is collected using a long needle inserted through the lower abdominal wall just above the pubic bone.

D. For autopsied bodies:
   1. Collect blood from femoral vessels.
   2. If blood cannot be collected from the femoral vessels, then the other sites in descending order of preference are:
      a. The subclavian vessels
      b. The root of the aorta
      c. The pulmonary artery
      d. The superior vena cava
      e. The heart
   3. The blood should then be labeled as to the site of collection.
   4. In rare instances, usually involving massive trauma, no blood can be collected from the vasculature but there is free blood in the body cavities.
      a. This blood is collected and labeled as to its source.

      b. If it is tested for drugs and found negative, then one is safe in assuming the individual was not under the effects of a drug at the time of death.

      c. A positive test must take into account the possibility of contamination. In such a case, another material such as vitreous or muscle must be analyzed to evaluate the accuracy of the test results on the cavity blood.

IV. ROUTINE TESTING

A. In all cases, whether thought to be drug-related or not:

   1. Routine toxicology screens on blood and urine are recommended.

   2. Vitreous should be analyzed for alcohol when a positive blood alcohol is obtained. Analysis for other drugs is also possible.

B. In some cases, especially infants, analysis of vitreous electrolytes for sodium, chloride, potassium, glucose, urea nitrogen, and creatinine should be performed (**Table 21.1**).

C. With rare exception, virtually all drugs and their major metabolites can now be detected in blood in any modern toxicology lab.

   1. Heroin is at present an exception, but even in this case one can usually prove conclusively that it was taken.

      a. After injection, heroin (diacetylmorphine) is almost immediately metabolized to monoacetylmorphine and then to morphine.

      b. In drug deaths, the detection of morphine in the blood was assumed to indicate that the individual died of an overdose of heroin. In some deaths in an emergency room, it was contended that the individual was inadvertently given morphine thus causing death, i.e., the deceased had not taken heroin. With the recent ability to easily detect monoacetylmorphine, it is now possible to positively prove the individual died of an overdose of heroin. Monoacetyl-

TABLE 21.1 Normal Vitreous Electrolytes

Sodium	135–151 meq/l
Potassium	Internal control[a]
Chloride	105–132 meq/l
Blood Urea Nitrogen	Same as blood
Creatinine	Same as blood

[a] When vitreous potassium is 15 meq/l or greater, the sodium and chloride levels are depressed, making interpretation of these levels valid only when elevated. Vitreous potassium levels are only valid when <3.5 meq/l, when they indicate hypokalemia.

morphine can be detected in the vitreous after it has dis
appeared from the blood.

V. **DRUG SCREENS IN MEDICAL EXAMINERS' OFFICES**
  A. There is no such thing as a complete drug screen.
     1. One can only screen for groups of drugs based on their struc-
        ture and chemical properties.
     2. A complete drug screen may screen for five drugs, 50, or 150.
     3. The ideal drug screen should possess sensitivity, specificity, and
        a capability to detect a wide range of drugs and should be
        relatively easy to employ.
     4. Unfortunately, the various traits we wish for in this ideal drug
        screen are to a degree conflicting.
     5. As a test becomes more and more sensitive, it must usually
        sacrifice specificity.
     6. In turn, as a test becomes more specific, it loses sensitivity. The
        wider the range of drugs a test can detect and the lower the
        detection limit, the less specific the test.
  B. The great majority of drugs of forensic interest may be classified
     as **acidic, neutral, or alkaline** on the basis of their extraction
     characteristics. The majority of drugs of forensic interest are al-
     kaline drugs.
  C. Before a drug can be reported as being present in forensic cases,
     it must be absolutely identified and, if significant, quantified.
     In hospital toxicology, absolute identification of a drug is often
     not necessary and semi-quantification is acceptable.

Methods of Analysis

VI. **THIN-LAYER CHROMATOGRAPHY**
  A. This method of analysis is based on separation of various com-
     pounds dissolved in fluid as they move across a plate (usually a
     piece of glass coated with a compound such as silica) by capillary
     action.
     1. The compounds are gradually distributed along the moving
        liquid phase.
     2. After the liquid front has moved a sufficient distance, the plate
        is removed from the chamber and dried.
     3. A number of chemical sprays are then used to stain the sepa-
        rated compounds.

4. The compounds are identified based on their staining characteristics and distance of migration when compared to known standards.

B. The lack of specificity of this method and sensitivity to certain drugs, e.g., cocaine, combined with the development of immunoassay tests, make this method of analysis of mostly historical interest in the forensic toxicology lab.

C. The immunoassay methods of analysis are more specific and more sensitive.

VII. **IMMUNOASSAY METHODS OF ANALYSIS**

A. These are the most convenient and popular methods of drug screening. If properly used, and if their limitations are understood, they are invaluable in a modern forensic lab.

B. There are three immunological procedures in general use nowadays:
1. Radioimmunoassay (RIA)
2. Enzyme immunoassay
3. Fluorescent immunoassay
4. All three of these methods are based on the same general principle:
   a. A drug is given to an animal in such a way that the animal becomes immunized to it and produces antibodies to the drug.
   b. Detection of the reaction between an antibody for the drug and the drug is the basis for immunoassay tests.

C. Unfortunately, even if one is dealing with monoclonal antibodies, **there is still some cross-reactivity.**
1. The antibody is not absolutely specific for the drug.
2. The antibody will react with a structurally similar compound.
3. A positive reaction can be due to the specific drug or an analog.
4. One can take advantage of this cross-reactivity by using the antibodies to test for a class of drugs, i.e., the benzodiazepines.

D. **Immunoassay tests are excellent for screening** for a specific drug or group of drugs at very low concentrations, much lower than those detected by TLC.
1. Enzyme immunoassay and fluorescent immunoassay tests were developed for screening for drugs in urine, not blood. Generally these methods should not be used on blood.
2. Radioimmunoassay (RIA) has had the advantage over the other two methods in that it could easily be used to screen for drugs in blood. RIA possesses, however, the undesirable attribute of requiring radioactive substances.

E. Most drugs appear in the urine almost immediately after appearing in the blood.
   1. The authors have seen cases involving heroin in which, following an injection, the screen was negative.
   2. Thus, in any case in which a heroin overdose is suspected or in cases where the cause of death is not ascertained on routine handling of the case, analysis of the blood for drugs by GC-MS should be performed, even if the immunoassay screening tests are negative.
F. One of the limitations of immunoassay
   1. It can identify and quantitate only one form of a drug and not its metabolites.
   2. This becomes a great liability in drug overdoses due to drugs such as propoxyphene where the level of norpropoxyphene may be the determining factor as to the manner of death in a case where the cause of death is clear.

VIII. GAS CHROMATOGRAPHY (GC)

A. With gas chromatography (GC), one has the ability to analyze for a number of totally different chemical compounds simultaneously.
   1. GC is **extremely sensitive and produces accurate quantitative results.** It is able to detect drugs in blood in the ng/ml range with proper methodology.
   2. A GC separates a sample (a mixture of compounds) into its separate components while in a volatile state.
   3. The sample is introduced into the GC as a liquid, vaporized, and then carried by moving gas flowing through a column packed with a solid media coated with a thin film of liquid.
   4. As the sample moves down the column, the sample is separated into its different constituents by the differences in affinity the different compounds have for the moving gas phase versus the stationary liquid phase.
   5. As the sample emerges from the column, it will have separated into its components.
   6. As each individual component of the sample emerges from the column, they enter a detector.
   7. The detector produces a written record/picture of the time of emergence of the compound in relationship to the time it took to travel through the column as well as the quantity of material.
   8. The time a compound takes from the time it is injected to when it emerges is the **retention time.** This is characteristic of the specific compound.

B. While GC identification is very accurate, it is not 100%. Identification is based on the comparison of retention times to an internal standard, not a definitive physical identification as in GC-MS analyses.

IX. **HIGH-PRESSURE LIQUID CHROMATOGRAPHY (HPLC)**

In contrast to GC, in HPLC the sample is in a liquid state at the time of analysis rather than in a volatile state.

A. The liquid sample is carried by a mobile liquid phase over a stationary liquid phase (liquid bonded to silica particles).

B. Partition of compounds occurs due to interaction of constituents of the sample and the stationary phase as well as other factors such as partition coefficients.

C. HPLC identification is based primarily on the retention time of the drugs.

D. Since HPLC is performed at normal temperatures, it is more suitable for analysis of heat-labile drugs that may be destroyed at the high temperatures used in the GC.

E. Again, like GC, this test is not 100% specific.

F. A major advantage of GC and HPLC over the immunoassay methods is that both GC and HPLC can often quantitate both the drug being sought and its metabolites in a single analysis.

X. **GAS CHROMATOGRAPHY–MASS SPECTROMETRY (GC-MS)**

A. **This is the only method of analysis that is 100% specific.**

B. It consists of a gas chromatograph, which separates the drugs, and a mass spectrometer, which positively identifies them.

C. It determines the molecular weight of the drug to thousandths of an atomic mass unit and can characterize molecular fragments similarly.

XI. **CONFIRMATORY TESTING**

A. No scientist should go to court and testify a drug was **definitely present** in an individual or specimen based solely on a screening test!

1. To say that a drug is definitely present, **the presence of the drug must be confirmed by a second (confirmatory) test that is highly specific.**

2. This confirmatory test is absolutely necessary to confirm a positive screening test.

3. Simply repeating the initial screening test is not confirmation of the presence of the drug. All that one is demonstrating is the reproducibility of the original test.

B. The confirmatory test should not use a method of analysis subject to the same errors as the first test.

1. Thus, a test using one method of immunoassay cannot be used to confirm a test that utilized a different method of immunoassay.
2. **The confirmatory test has to employ a different principle of identification.** Confirmatory testing of immunoassay methods of analysis by TLC and vice versa is not valid because these methods have problems with both specificity and/or sensitivity.
3. There are three presently acceptable methods of confirming screening tests:
   a. High-performance liquid chromatography (HPLC)
   b. Gas chromatography (GC)
   c. Gas chromatography–mass spectrometry (GC-MS)
4. All three of these methods can also be used for screening, especially GC. In most modern labs, GCs are used extensively in the screening for alkaline drugs.
5. A positive screen by GC or HPLC still has to be confirmed. Confirmation with these two methods can be made by changing their columns rather than resorting to a completely different analytical method.
6. A positive identification by GC-MS does not have to be confirmed, as this method of analysis is considered to give absolute identification.
7. Confirmation of positive results is not necessary for most methods of analysis for alcohol.

XII. POISONS

A. Cyanide

Deaths from cyanide are relatively rare, most involving individuals who work in chemistry laboratories and have access to potassium or sodium cyanide.

1. Death is due to cellular hypoxia secondary to inhibition of cytochrome oxidase.
2. The minimum lethal dose is estimated to be 200 mg of potassium or sodium cyanide.
3. Collapse occurs almost immediately after ingestion, although there have been a few cases with delay of up to a half hour when taken on a full stomach.
4. Hydrogen cyanide gas is:
   a. Immediately fatal at atmospheric concentrations of 270 ppm
   b. Fatal after 10 min at 181 ppm
   c. Fatal after 30 min at 135 ppm

     5. Cyanide is normally found in the blood in low levels:
       a. 0.016 mg/l for nonsmokers
       b. 0.041 mg/l in smokers
     6. **Tests** on blood for cyanide **should be done as soon as possible,** as cyanide levels may either decrease or increase depending on the method of preservation and/or storage and time from collection.

B. Arsenic

Arsenic has over the centuries been the poison of choice.

     1. It is tasteless and odorless and can be readily concealed in food.
     2. It is generally administered in multiple small doses over a prolonged period of time.
     3. If given as a single large dose, it may cause convulsions, unconsciousness, and death. Alternatively, there may be vomiting followed by diarrhea, abdominal pain, and dryness and pain in the throat. Death may be rapid or may take a few days.
     4. With **chronic administration,** the victim develops weakness, abdominal pain, and diarrhea. A chronic neuropathy may develop. The patient may seem to waste away. Death may take weeks or months.
     5. If one thinks of the diagnosis, it is readily made on analysis of blood or urine. In cases of suspected chronic poisoning, the hair can be analyzed for arsenic.

C. Strychnine

Strychnine is obtained from the dried seeds of *Strychnos nux-vomica*.

     1. The mean lethal dose in an adult is 100 to 120 mg, although death has occurred at lower levels.
     2. Symptoms usually do not appear for 10 to 30 minutes, although they may be delayed as long as an hour or occur as rapidly as 5 minutes.
     3. The individual may experience symptoms of restlessness, apprehension, abrupt movements, or muscular stiffness of the face. Minor stimuli then trigger violent convulsions with the patient experiencing as many as ten episodes of **convulsions** separated by periods of nonconvulsion of 5 to 15 minutes. The convulsions last 30 seconds to 2 minutes. The patient is conscious during this time.
     4. Death usually occurs between the second and fifth attack within 1 to 3 hours after ingestion. Survival beyond 5 hours is usually associated with complete recovery.

5. Between convulsions, the patient's muscles relax. During the attack, all the skeletal muscles contract and the body arches in hyperextension so that it is supported by the heels and head (opisthotonos).
6. Strychnine can be taken orally, intranasally, or by injection.
7. It competes with the neurotransmitter glycine for specific CNS receptors. This results in loss of inhibition of postsynaptic neurotransmission and thus hyperexcitation of muscle.
8. Fatal blood levels range from 0.5 to 6.1 mg/l.

D. Lead
   1. Deaths from lead poisoning are relatively rare and involve chronic poisonings.
   2. They are seen most commonly in East Coast and Midwest slums and are due to ingestion by children of paint peelings from lead-based paints.
   3. There may be a vague history of gastrointestinal complaints, anemia, and weight loss.
   4. At autopsy the brain of such children is massively swollen and very pale.
      a. Eosinophilic intranuclear inclusions may be seen in hepatocytes and cells of the proximal tubules of the kidneys.
      b. Homogenous pink PAS positive material may be seen in the perivascular spaces of the brain.
      c. Smears of the blood show basophilic stippling of erythrocytes.
      d. X-ray may reveal dense bands of bone at the ends of long bones due to lead deposits.
   5. The diagnosis of lead poisoning is readily made on blood lead levels. Normal lead levels for adults are less than 0.20 mg/l.

E. Hydrogen sulfide
   1. This is a highly toxic colorless gas that is heavier than air; it has the distinctive odor of rotten eggs at low atmospheric concentrations (0.2 to 0.3 ppm) but cannot be detected at high levels (100 to 200 ppm) due to olfactory paralysis.
   2. The gas is most commonly encountered in sewers, septic tanks, and waste disposal plants where it is due to organic decomposition. It can, however, be produced in some industrial plants.
   3. Toxicity begins at 250 to 300 ppm; systemic symptoms beginning in 30 to 60 min at 500 ppm leading to unconsciousness and respiratory failure.

4. At concentrations between 700 and 1000 ppm, there is rapid loss of consciousness, respiratory paralysis, even death in a matter of minutes at the higher concentrations.
5. Most deaths occur at the scene.
6. Hydrogen sulfide is an intracellular poison that inhibits cytochrome oxidase even more than cyanide. Death results from respiratory arrest and hypoxia.
7. The autopsy findings are nonspecific. Greenish discoloration of the gray matter of the brain and viscera has been reported but not seen by the authors.
8. Toxicologic testing is difficult to interpret. Sulfide levels of 1.70 to 3.75 mg/l have been reported in fatal cases. Interpretation of these levels is difficult because of postmortem decomposition in storage coupled with postmortem formation from degradation of protein and rapid endogenous destruction.

XIII. DRUGS OF ABUSE
A. Cocaine
Cocaine has replaced heroin as the illicit drug of choice in many areas of the United States. It is being seen in greater frequency in individuals dying suddenly of heart disease, apparently acting as a precipitating agent.

1. Cocaine is snorted, injected, and, as "crack," smoked.
   a. Two to three (2 to 3) lines of cocaine (approximately 100 mg) give blood levels of 0.05 to 0.10 µg/ml.
   b. Intravenous injection of this same amount results in peak levels of 0.70 to 1.0 µg/ml.
   c. Smoking 50 mg of crack (16 to 32 mg of cocaine) gives levels of 0.25 to 0.35 µg/ml.
2. Cocaine is rapidly metabolized in the blood to **benzoylecgonine** and **ecgonine methyl esther**, nonactive metabolites. This metabolism continues after death, even in test tubes.
3. In the presence of alcohol, cocaine and alcohol combine to form **cocaethylene**, a compound as lethal as, if not more lethal than, cocaine.
4. There is for the most part no lethal level of cocaine. Some individuals die at levels that are recreational for other individuals. A level that is recreational in an individual one day may be lethal another day.
5. The mechanism of death in cocaine-related deaths is a fatal cardiac arrhythmia. Death can be caused by the toxic effects of the drug on the myocardium and/or coronary vasospasm.

   6. Cocaine:
       a. Acts on the cardiovascular system increasing the heart rate
           and systemic arterial pressure
       b. Blocks presynaptic reabsorption of norepinephrine in the
           heart with resultant coronary artery spasm
       c. Causes increased release of catecholamines from the adre-
           nal glands
   7. Thus, cocaine causes an increased myocardial demand for ox-
       ygen while decreasing the myocardial oxygen supply.
   8. **Acute myocardial infarction due to coronary vasospasm may
       occur even with normal coronary arteries.**
   9. Use of both alcohol and cocaine causes increased euphoria but
       a decrease in the psychomotor impairment seen with alcohol
       use alone.

B. **Methamphetamine**
   1. After cocaine, methamphetamine is the most commonly used
       illegal stimulant. It is sometimes sold as cocaine. It is extremely
       cheap and easy to manufacture.
   2. When methamphetamine is illegally manufactured, a small
       amount of its parent compound amphetamine is also pro-
       duced.
   3. Methamphetamine may be taken either orally or intravenously.
       a. Orally it takes about 30 minutes to act.
       b. Intravenously reaction is immediate.
   4. Like cocaine, in its usual form it cannot be smoked due to
       degradation of the compound by heat. But just as cocaine was
       purified to produce "crack," methamphetamine has been pu-
       rified to produce "ice," which can be smoked.
   5. Methamphetamine when ingested orally is rapidly absorbed
       (30 min) with peak levels in the blood at 1 to 2 hours.
       a. Duration of action depends on the dose but may exceed
           24 hours.
       b. Tolerance develops and larger and larger amounts are
           needed to get and stay high.
   6. Intravenous users may inject methamphetamine every 2 to 3
       hours during a binge.
   7. Methamphetamines have strong CNS-stimulating properties
       but after binge use, just like cocaine, there is physical collapse
       and depression. Chronic and/or heavy dosages may result in
       delusions, hallucinations, and paranoia.
   8. Flashbacks can occur months after cessation of use.

C. **MMDA, MDMA (ecstasy), phentermine, proplyhexedrine, and phenmetrazine,** just like methamphetamine, are all derivatives of amphetamine with more or less of the same actions.

D. **Opiates**

Opium is derived from the poppy plant, *Papaver somniferum*. It contains three alkaloids of interest to the field of toxicology: morphine, codeine, and heroin.

1. **Morphine** was first isolated in 1803. Due to poor absorption when taken orally, it did not become popular as a drug of abuse until the development of the syringe. Deaths due to morphine are uncommon because of the difficulty obtaining it.

2. **Codeine** was synthesized in 1832 and heroin in 1874. Codeine-related deaths are rare due to its great margin of safety.

3. **Heroin** (diacetylmorphine) has a greater euphoric action than morphine; it replaced morphine as the choice drug of abuse in the early 20th century.
   a. Death is probably due to acute pulmonary arrest following CNS depression.
   b. The drug is either injected too rapidly or the dosage is greater than the addict is used to (tolerant to).

4. The half-life of injected heroin is 2 to 4 minutes. It is deacetylated to 6-monoacetylmorphine (6-mam) in the blood and tissue.

5. This in turn is metabolized to morphine, principally in the liver. It is this compound that produces most of the actions of heroin.

6. In deaths due to an overdose of heroin, blood levels in themselves are rarely sufficient to make a ruling as to cause of death. Rather, it is the whole picture of the death.

7. In deaths occurring immediately after an intravenous injection, analysis of the blood by GC-MS shows levels of 6-mam in mg/ml, morphine in ng/ml.

8. If there is some survival, morphine is found in levels of mg/ml, 6-mam in ng/ml, and codeine in ng/ml.

9. As the survival time increases, 6-mam disappears and only morphine is present. In some cases, 6-mam may still be detected in vitreous.

10. Morphine is conjugated and excreted in the bile, appearing in approximately 30 minutes.

11. Morphine and 6-mam appear in the urine usually minutes after IV injection, although in some cases death occurs before this happens and the urine screening test may be negative.

12. Heroin is sold in glycine envelopes, capsules, or balloons depending on the geographical area of the country.
    a. On the East Coast, it is cut with quinine to give a bitter taste.
    b. In the rest of the country, it is cut with milk sugar or some similar compound.
13. The heroin is added to water in a "cooker," such as a bottle cap, and heated. It may then be "strained" through cotton and injected.
    a. Microscopic sections of the lungs may show refractile compounds such as talc used to cut heroin and cotton from the strainer.
    b. The liver shows a nonspecific chronic triaditis.
    c. Perihepatic lymph nodes are often enlarged.
    d. Pulmonary edema may be very prominent, although it may be absent grossly.
14. With the increasing purity of heroin now being sold, it is possible to smoke the drug just like crack cocaine or snort it.

E. **Fentanyl**
Fentanyl is one of a number of synthetic versions of the opiates.
1. Fentanyl was developed as an anesthetic agent. It has both anesthetic and analgesic properties.
2. It is approximately 200 times as potent as morphine with rapid onset of action and short duration.
3. Fentanyl, when injected, acts immediately on the central nervous system.
    a. It is metabolized to norfentanyl and despropiony fentanyl.
    b. Duration of action, in regard to respiratory depression, is approximately 30 minutes.
4. There are a number of legal analogues, e.g., sufentanyl, alfentanyl, lofentanyl with 2000–4000, 20–30, and 5000–6000 the potency of morphine, respectively. Another agent, carfentanyl, is used in veterinary medicine to immobilize wild animals. It is 3200 times as potent as morphine.
5. Of more interest than fentanyl are the illegal analogues that have been produced, the most famous of which is China White (a-methylfentanyl). It is 200 times as potent as morphine.
    a. Others are as much as 7000 times as potent.
    b. These agents may be injected, snorted, or smoked.
6. Fentanyl abuse is more common among physicians and nurses.
7. Fentanyl transdermal delivery patches are subject to abuse.

XIV. MEDICATIONS COMMONLY ASSOCIATED WITH OVERDOSE

A. **Tricyclic antidepressants**
1. This group includes a host of compounds including imipramine, amitriptyline, desipramine, doxepin, etc.
2. These compounds work on the brain to inhibit reuptake of serotonin, dopamine, and norepinephrine. Peripherally, they block reuptake of norepinephrine.
3. Peak blood levels occur 3 to 4 hours after ingestion.
4. Overdoses cause tachycardia, hypotension, and arrhythmias. Because of interference with sweating, they predispose to heat-stroke.

B. **Benzodiazepines**
1. These are antianxiety, hypnotic agents. Examples of these drugs are diazepam, lorazepam, alprazolam, and fluazepam. They have replaced barbiturates as hypnotics.
2. Most oral forms are extremely safe if used alone. Deaths from overdoses are uncommon and are associated with the presence of another central nervous system depressant — often alcohol.

C. **Propoxyphene**
1. This is a marginally effective analgesic with a narrow margin of safety.
2. Following a single dose, peak blood levels occur at 2 hours with its metabolite, norpropoxyphene, peaking in 4 hours.
3. With chronic use, the norpropoxyphene levels are 3 to 4 times the propoxyphene levels.
4. In an acute overdose, propoxyphene levels are generally higher or equal to norpropoxyphene levels depending on survival time.
5. The minimum lethal dose is 650 to 1000 mg.

XV. ETHANOL

Ethanol is the most commonly abused drug.

A. Medicolegally one uses blood levels, not plasma or serum levels. The latter are 1.18 times the blood levels.
B. One 12-ounce beer is considered equivalent to one 6-ounce glass of wine, which is equivalent to 1.5 ounces of 90 proof spirits.
C. Following ingestion on an empty stomach, peak blood levels occur in 45 minutes to 2 hours. **Table 21.2** gives the expected blood level depending on weight and alcohol consumption.
D. Vitreous alcohol levels reflect blood levels 1 to 2 hours prior. Because vitreous is essentially acellular, vitreous levels are 1.2 times their equivalent blood level.
E. Following ingestion of alcohol, impairment of visual skills occurs:

TABLE 21.2   Blood Alcohol Level (gm/dl) in Relation to Number of Drinks and Body Weight

Number of Drinks	Body Weight (lb)						
	100	125	150	175	200	225	250
1	.03	.03	.02	.02	.01	.01	.01
2	.06	.05	.04	.04	.03	.03	.03
3	.10	.08	.06	.06	.05	.04	.04
4	.13	.10	.09	.07	.06	.06	.05
5	.16	.13	.11	.09	.08	.07	.06
6	.19	.16	.13	.11	.10	.09	.08
7	.22	.18	.15	.13	.11	.10	.09
8	.26	.21	.17	.15	.13	.11	.10
9	.29	.24	.19	.17	.14	.13	.12
10	.33	.26	.22	.18	.16	.14	.13
11	.36	.29	.24	.20	.18	.16	.14
12	.39	.31	.26	.22	.19	.17	.16

   1. Impairment begins at levels as low as 0.03 g/dl.
   2. At levels >0.08 g/dl, there is marked impairment in nearly all individuals.
  F. Reaction time is consistently impaired at levels >0.07 g/dl.
  G. Nonalcoholics appear grossly intoxicated by 0.20 g/dl, begin to pass out at 0.30 g/dl, and begin to die when blood levels exceed 0.40 g/dl.
  H. Chronic alcoholics can mask their impairment to a degree and are more tolerant of higher levels. Individuals have been stopped while operating motor vehicles with blood alcohol levels >0.50 g/dl.
  I. For the average individual who is not an alcoholic, blood alcohol is metabolized at a rate of 15 to 18 mg/dl/h.
  J. Alcoholics can metabolize alcohol at a rate as high as 30 mg/dl/h.

XVI. **METHYL ALCOHOL AND ISOPROPANOL**
  A. **Methyl alcohol** is oxidized to formaldehyde and then formic acid.
   1. Acidosis is the primary toxic factor.
   2. Ingestion of as little as 70 to 100 ml can cause death.
  B. **Isopropanol** is metabolized to acetone.
   1. A lethal dose is approximately 250 ml.
   2. Lethal levels in the blood begin at around 150 mg/dl.
   3. In diabetic ketoacidosis with high levels of acetone, low levels of isopropanol may be seen due to conversion of acetone to isopropanol.

XVII. **PHENCYCLIDINE (PCP)**
  Phencyclidine is a hallucinogenic agent that:

A. Predisposes to violent behavior
B. May be injected, snorted, or ingested
C. Exhibits no correlation between blood levels and death

XVIII. DRUG AND CHEMICAL BLOOD CONCENTRATIONS
  A. The therapeutic, toxic, and fatal blood concentrations of various drugs that may be encountered in medicolegal cases are listed in **Table 21.3**.
  B. Toxic and fatal blood concentrations of various chemicals that may be involved in medicolegal cases are listed in **Table 21.4**.

General References

1. Karch, S.B., *The Pathology of Drug Abuse*, 2nd ed., CRC Press, Boca Raton, FL, 1996.
2. Baselt, R.C., *Disposition of Toxic Drugs and Chemicals in Man*, 5th ed., Chemical Toxicology Institute, Foster City, CA, 2000.

TABLE 21.3 Therapeutic, Toxic, and Fatal Blood Concentrations of Various Drugs

Drug Name	Dose in Milligrams	Therapeutic[a] (mg/l)	Toxic (mg/l)	Fatal (mg/l)	Half-Life in Hours
Acetaminophen	324	2.4–6.4 (6)	30–300	160–387	1–3
	1000	9.0 (1–3)			
	1800	26 (1)			
Alprazolam	1.0	0.019 (1.3)	0.1–0.6	0.12–2.1	6–27
(*Xanax*)	1.5–6/day	0.025–0.055			
	9/day	0.102			
Aminophylline	170 IV	4.5 (1)	>20	63–250	6.9 (<6 months)
	500 oral	1.4–7.7 (1–4)			4.1 (child)
					3–11 (adult)
Amitriptyline (A)	50 oral	0.016–0.035 (2–4) A	0.5–3.4	>2.0 A	8–51
Nortriptyline (N)		0.014 N	(A + N)		
(*Elavil, Endep*)	150/day	0.038–0.162 A			
		0.022–0.242 N			
Amobarbital	120 oral	1.8 (2)	8–21	13–96	15–40
	600 oral	6.4–12.3 (0.5)			(dose
					dependent)
Amoxapine	50	0.03 (1.5)	>0.3	0.9–20	8
(*Asendin*)	300/day	0.017–0.093			
Amphetamine	5–15 oral	0.035 (2)		0.5–41	7–34
	30 oral	0.111 (2.5)			
	160 IV	0.59 (abuse) (1)			
Brompheniramine	8	0.015 (3)	>0.05	0.2	15–22
		0.005 (24)			
Bupropion	32–55	0.06–0.125 (3)	?	?	4–24
	100	0.14 (3)			
Butabarbital	600	7.6–16.9 (0.5)	>10	30–88	>30
Butalbital	100	2.1 (2)	?	13–26	35–88
		1.5 (24)			
Caffeine	120	2–4 (1)	>40	79–344	2.3–12
	300	6–9 (1)			
	500	14 (0.5)			
Carbamazepine	420	6.5 (3.2)		35–70	18–65
(*Tegretol*)		4–8 optimal			
Carisoprodol	350	2.1 (1)	>30	39–110	0.9–2.4
(*Soma*)	700	3.5 (0.8)			
Chloral hydrate	1000 (oral)	2–12 (1)	50?	100–640	4 min chloral
(*Noctec*)		6.5–8 (2)			hydrate;
		3–6.3 (6)			6–10 hours
					trichloroethanol
Chlordiazepoxide	30	1.6 (4)	9–60	>20	6–27
(*Librium*)	55/day	2.3			
Chloroquine	50/day	0.022	>0.6	3–16	3–14 days
	300/day	0.176			
Chlorpheniramine	4 IV	0.01	>0.5	>1.0	12–43
	12 oral	0.017 (2)			
		0.010 (12)			
		0.004 (24)			

TABLE 21.3   Therapeutic, Toxic, and Fatal Blood Concentrations of Various Drugs (continued)

Drug Name	Dose in Milligrams	Therapeutic[a] (mg/l)	Toxic (mg/l)	Fatal (mg/l)	Half-Life in Hours
Chlorpromazine (*Thorazine*)	25 oral	0.001 (2.8)	>0.5	3–35	18–30 average
	150 oral	0.018 (3)			
	600 day	0.02–0.08			
	2400 day	1.1			
Chlorpropamide (*Diabinese*)	250	28.5 (3)	300–750	?	25–42
	500–1000/d	102–363			
Clonazepam	2	0.017 (1–4)	>0.1	?	19–60
	6/day	0.03–0.075			
Clorazepate (*Tranxene*)	15	0.16 (2)	?	?	2
	50/day	1.21–2.64			
Cocaine	17–48 oral	0.011–0.15 (0.4–2)	?	0.9–21	0.7–1.5
	2 mg/kg intranasal	0.161 (1)			
	2 mg/kg oral	0.210 (1)			
	32 IV	0.308 (5 min)			
	50 smoked	0.203 (5 min)			
Codeine	15	0.03 (2)	0.5	1–8.8	1.9–3.9
	60	0.134 (1)			
Desipramine	82 mg/70 kg/day	0.021–0.064	1.0	3–15	12–54
Diazepam (*Valium*)	10	0.148 (1)	>5	5–19	21–37
	30/day	1.03			
Digitoxin	0.05–0.3/d	3–39 ng/ml	?	>320 ng/ml	4–10 days
Digoxin	0.25 oral	0.001 (1)	2–9 ng/ml	15 ng/ml	30–45
	0.5 oral	0.0014 (2)			
	0.75 IV	0.013 (10 min)			
Diltiazem	90	0.130 (3–4)	>1	6.7–33	2.8–9.2
	120	0.174 (1.5–4.3)			
Diphenhydramine	50	0.083 (3)	>1	8–31	3–14
	100	0.112 (2)			
		0.014 (24)			
Doxepin (*Sinequan, Adapin*)	75	0.024 (2)	>0.14	0.7–29	8–25
	113/day	0.005–0.115			
Doxylamine	25	0.07–0.14 (4)	?	0.7–12	10
Ephedrine	19.4	0.081 (3.9)	?	3.5–21	5–7.5
	24	0.10 (1)			
Ethchlorvynol (*Placidyl*)	200	1.2 (1)	>50	14–400	19–32
	500	6.5 (1)			
Fentanyl	2 µg/kg IV	0.011	0.02	0.003– 0.03	3–12
		0.001 (1)			
Fluoxetine (*Prozac*)	40	0.015–0.055 (6–8)		1.3–6.8	1–3 days (7–14 days for metabolites
	20–60/d	0.025–0.473			
Flurazepam	15	<0.002 (0.5)	?	0.5–4	1–3
	30	0.002 (1)			

TABLE 21.3 Therapeutic, Toxic, and Fatal Blood Concentrations of Various Drugs (continued)

Drug Name	Dose in Milligrams	Therapeutic[a] (mg/l)	Toxic (mg/l)	Fatal (mg/l)	Half-Life in Hours
Fluvoxamine (*Luvox*)	50 100	0.008–0.03 (4.8) 0.021–0.06 (4.5)	>0.115	3.4–11	8–28
Haloperidol (*Haldol*)	20–200/d	0.006–0.245	0.01	1–2	14–41
Hydrocodone	5 10	0.011 (1.5) 0.024 (1.5)	?	0.13–7	3.4–8.8
Hydromorphone (*Dilaudid*)	4	0.018–0.027 (0.8–1.5)	0.02	0.02–1.2	1.5–3.8
Hydroxyzine	100	0.078(4)	?	4.2–39	13–27
Ibuprofen (*Motrin, Advil*)	200 400 800	26 (1.5) 17–36 (1–1.3) 49 (1)		>80	0.9–2.5
Imipramine (I) Desipramine (D)	75 150/d	0.037 I (4) 0.008–0.105 I 0.15–0.24 I&D (optimal)	>0.5	2.8–7 (I)	6–20
Insulin	Normal, fasting Normal, nonfasting Insulin treated	11 μU/ml (range 6–24) 27 μU/ml (range 7–37) 10–440 μU/ml (free insulin) 67–17,020 (total insulin)	?	>700 (free)	3.5–4.3
Isoniazid	350	1.2–4.8 (1) 0.2–2.7 (4) 0–1.4 (8)	>20	43–168	0.6–6.7 (genetically determined)
Ketamine	175 IV	1.0 (12 min) 0.5 (0.5)	?	7–27	3–4
Lidocaine	500 oral 70 IV	0.6–1.1 (1–2) 0.96 (.25) 0.4 (1)	>8	6–33	0.7–1.8
Lithium (as carbonate)	1500	1.66 mmol/l (1) 0.5–1.3 mmol/l optimum	>2 mmol/l	0.3–4.6 mmol/l	17–58
Lorazepam (*Ativan*)	2 10/d	0.018 (2) 0.009 (12) 0.140–0.24	0.3	?	9–16
Maprotiline	150 150/d	0.091 (8) 0.168–0.718	0.24–0.32 (seizures)	1.3–13	36–105
Meperidine (*Demerol*)	100 oral 100 IM 50 IV	0.17 (1.3) 0.31 (1) 0.52 (12 min)	?	8–20 oral 1–8 IV	2–5
Meprobamate	400 800 1600	7.7 (2) 12–19 (2) 8.6–27 (2)	>60	35–300	6–17

TABLE 21.3   Therapeutic, Toxic, and Fatal Blood Concentrations of Various Drugs (continued)

Drug Name	Dose in Milligrams	Therapeutic[a] (mg/l)	Toxic (mg/l)	Fatal (mg/l)	Half-Life in Hours
Methadone	15	0.075 (4)	0.1	0.4–1.8	15–55
	100–200/d	0.83 (4)			
		0.46 (24)			
d-Methamphetamine	0.125/kg	0.02 (3.6)	>0.10	2.0	6–15
	10	0.03 (1)			(urine ph-
	12.5	0.02 (2.5)			dependent)
		0.01 (24)			
	30	0.094 (3–5)			
Methaqualone	250	1–4 (2)	2–12	5–42	20–60
		1.1 (5)			
	600	7.0 (1)			
Metoclopromide	10	0.054 (0.9)	>2.0	?	3–6
Mexiletine	300	0.4 (4)	>2.0	21–45	8–17
	400	0.9–1.6 (2–4)			
	750/d	0.9–1.4			
		0.75–2 optimal			
Mirtazapine	20	0.032 (1.7)	>0.2	?	20–40
(Remeron)	20/d	0.007–0.046			
Morphine	0.125/kg IV	0.44 (0.5 min)	0.2	0.2–2.3	1.3–6.7
		0.02 (2)			
	0.125/kg IM	0.07 (10 min)			
Nefazodone	200	0.39 (1.3)	?	?	1–4
(Serzone)	400/d	2.0			
Nortriptyline	75/d	0.01–0.275	1.0	1–26	15–90
(Pamelor)	150–250/d	0.171–0.375			
Oxycodone	4.88	0.009–0.037 (1)	?	4.3–14	4–6
		0.016 (2)			
		0.009 (4)			
		0.005 (8)			
Paraldehyde	10 ml IM	77 (1.2)	?	115–480	3–10
		62 (2.3)			
Paroxetine	20	0.011	>0.2	1.4–4	7–37
	30	0.062 (5.2)			
Pentobarbital	100	1.2–3.1 (0.5–2)	8	10–51	20–30
Phenacetin	250	0.09–0.22 (1–2)	?	>100	0.6–1.3
Phencyclidine		0.007–0.24	0.09–0.22	0.3–25	7–46
(PCP)					
Phenmetrazine	75	0.13 (2)	>0.5	0.1–5	8
		0.06 (12)			
Phenobarbital	30	0.7	40	55–114	2–6 days
	30/d	8.1			
	600	18 (4.5)			
		10–30 optimal			
Phentermine	26	0.09 (4)		1.5–7.6	19–24
Phenylbutazone	200	16 (3)	>100	400	29–175
	400	60 (max conc)			

TABLE 21.3 Therapeutic, Toxic, and Fatal Blood Concentrations of Various Drugs (continued)

Drug Name	Dose in Milligrams	Therapeutic[a] (mg/l)	Toxic (mg/l)	Fatal (mg/l)	Half-Life in Hours
Phenytoin (*Dilantin*)	100 300–400/d	1.6–2.8 (2.4) 7.8–17.5 10–20 optimal	>30	45	8–60
Primidone	250 500 1000	4.9 (4) 6.7 11–15	>50	?	6–22
Procainamide	1000 1000 IM 1000 IV	4.5 (1) 5.9 (0.5) 16 (10 min)	>16	80–260	2–5
Promethazine	30 50	0.011 (2) 0.005 (12) 0.008–0.023 (3) 0.003–0.004 (12)	?	?	9–16
Propoxyphene	130 (as HCl) 800–1600/d for narcotic withdrawal	0.23 (2) 0.13–1.07	>1	1–17	8–24
Propranolol	80 160/d	0.097 (1.5–2) 0.46	?	4–29	2–4
Propylhexedrine		0.01	?	0.3–2.7	?
Quinidine	600	3.2 (2.25) 2–5 optimal	>8	45	5–12
Quinine	650	2.8 (2) 1.9 (8)	>10	6–24	3–15
Salicylamide	1000	3–32 (1) 0–22 (3) 0–15 (5)	?	27 (?)	26–35 min
Salicylate (acetylsalicylic acid)	1000 3000/d	31–114 (2) 44–330	>500	61–7320	13–20 min; 3–20 h for salicylic acid
Secobarbital	3.3/kg 600	2.0 (3) 1.3 (20) 3.4–5.3 (0.5) 2.7 (18)	5–12	5–52	22–29
Sertraline	50 100	0.0095 (6–8) 0.016 (6–8)		0.6–3	24–26
Δ^9Tetrahydro-cannabinol	10 mg = 1 cigarette 8.8	0.005 (2) 0.046–0.188	?	None	20–57 h infrequent user; 3–13 days frequent user
Theophylline	500 470 (syrup)	1.4 (1) 4.5 (2) 7.7 (4) 9 (1.5) 5–15 optimal	>20	63–250	3–11

TABLE 21.3　Therapeutic, Toxic, and Fatal Blood Concentrations of Various Drugs (continued)

Drug Name	Dose in Milligrams	Therapeutic[a] (mg/l)	Toxic (mg/l)	Fatal (mg/l)	Half-Life in Hours
Thioridazine	100	0.24 (1.7)	>2.4	0.3–18	26–36
	400/d	0.64			
Trazodone	100	1.1 (2)	?	15–23	4–7
(*Desyrel*)	150	2.1 (2–4)			
Triazolam	0.25	0.003 (1)		0.01–0.22	1.8–3.9
(*Halcion*)					
Valproic acid	400	32–42 (1.5–3)	?	720–1969	8–12
	1400–2520/	81–106			
	d	50–100 optimal			
Venlafaxine	50	0.071 (2.2)	6	6.6–89	3–7
(*Effexor*)	150/d	0.194			

[a] Numbers in parentheses are hours post dose.

Source: The data presented are adapted from Di Maio, V.J.M. and Di Maio, D.J., Interpretive toxicology: Drug abuse and drug deaths, in *Forensic Pathology*, 2nd ed., CRC Press, Boca Raton, FL, 2001, p. 536; and Baselt, R.D., *Disposition of Toxic Drugs and Chemicals in Man*, 5th ed., Chemical Toxicology Institute, Foster City, CA, 2000.

TABLE 21.4   Toxic and Fatal Blood Concentrations of Various Chemicals/Compounds

	Dose or Exposure	Therapeutic or Normal Level (mg/l)[a]	Toxic (mg/l)	Fatal (mg/l)	Half-Life in Hours
Acetone	Normal	<10	2500	?	3–6
	"Controlled" diabetes	<30			
	Fasting/ ketoacidosis	100–700			
Arsenic	Av. dietary intake 0.025–0.033 mg/kg/day	0.002–0.062	?	0.6–9.3	7
Carbon monoxide	Urban nonsmoker	1–2% CoHb	15–25%	>50%	4–5 (without O₂ therapy)
	Smoker	5–6% CoHb			
Chloroform	500 mg oral	1.5 (1)		10–194	1.5
	Anesthesia	20–232			
Cyanide	Nonsmoker	0.004	0.01–4.36	1.1–53 (ingestion)	0.7–2.1
	Smoker	0.006			
	Fire victim	0.17–2.2		1–15 (inhalation)	
Dicumarol	150 mg	17 (10)	22–192	?	21 (average)
Ether	Workers	18	>90	600–3750	?
	Sub-anesthesia	100–500			
	Anesthesia	500–1500			
Ethylene glycol		?	any amount	300–4300	3–5
Fluoride	Normal	0.01	?	2.6–56	2–9
	1.5–10 mg	0.06–0.4 (0.5)			
Halothane	Surgical anesthesia	80–260	?	33–650	43 (from fat)
Hydrogen sulfide	"Normal"	<0.05	any amount	0.9–3.8	?
Iron	Normal	0.27–2.93, serum 380–560, whole blood	2.76–25.5	18.8–50	?
Isopropanol			0.04 g/dl	0.10–0.33 g/dl	2.5–3
Lead	"Normal" (industrial society)	0.07–0.22	0.20 (children)	1.11–3.5	Up to 7 years
	"Normal" (taxi drivers)	0.16–0.49			
Mercury	Fish eaters	0.006–0.2	0.2	0.8–22	24 days inorganic mercury
	"Acceptable"	0.02			
Methanol	"Normal"	<1.5	?	>400	2–24
	Chronic bourbon consumption	27			
Nicotine	Nonsmokers	0–0.006	?	11–63	24–84 min
	Smokers	0.012–0.054			

TABLE 21.4   Toxic and Fatal Blood Concentrations of Various Chemicals/Compounds (continued)

	Dose or Exposure	Therapeutic or Normal Level (mg/l)[a]	Toxic (mg/l)	Fatal (mg/l)	Half-Life in Hours
Nitrous oxide	Surgical anesthesia	170–220 ml/l	?	46–180 ml/l	? (min)
Phenol	"Normal"	0.10	?	46–90	0.5
Strychnine			?	0.5–61	10–11
Thallium	"Normal"	0–0.08	1–8	0.5–11	2–4 days
Toluene	Workers	0.4–1.2	Sniffers 0.3–30	10–79	72
Trichloro-ethane	Exposure to 955 ppm	7–10 (1)		1.5–720	53
Trichloro-ethylene	Exposure to 100 ppm	1.0 (6)	?	3–110 (average 27)	30–38

[a] Numbers in parentheses are hours post dose.

Source: Data presented are adapted from Di Maio, V.J.M. and Di Maio, D.J., Interpretive toxicology: Drug abuse and drug deaths, in *Forensic Pathology*, 2nd ed., CRC Press, Boca Raton, FL, 2001, p. 536; and Baselt, R.D., *Disposition of Toxic Drugs and Chemicals in Man*, 5th ed., Chemical Toxicology Institute, Foster City, CA, 2000.

Index

A

Abdomen
    battered child injuries, 175
    blunt force injury to, 87–93
    gunshot wounds to, 135
Abortion-related deaths, 248
Abrasion(s)
    description of, 74–76
    ligature, 161
    Maltese cross pattern of, 147
    patterned, 110, 147
Abrasion ring, 140–141
Acceleration-deceleration injuries, 85
Accident(s)
    bicycle, 208
    choking death by, 156–157
    fire deaths by, 197
    hot tub drownings, 217
    incised wounds by, 117
    ligature strangulations by, 160
    motor vehicle, *see* Motor vehicle deaths
    smothering by, 156
    stab wounds by, 113
Acetaminophen, 273
Acetone, 279
Acetylsalicylic acid, 277
Acrolein, 195
Acute aortic dissection, 50
Acute coronary artery dissection, 46, 48
Acute epiglottitis
    in adults, 60
    in infants and children, 68
Addison's disease, 63
Adipocere, 28
Adrenal glands
    blunt force injuries to, 93
    disorders of, 63
Adrenal insufficiency, 63
Air embolism
    during pregnancy, 248
    during surgery, 252

Airplane crashes, 208–211
Albumin, 243
Alcohol
    blood alcohol levels, 271
    description of, 270–271
    dilated cardiomyopathy secondary to, 43
    drownings and, 217
    heat stroke and, 218
    hot tube drownings and, 217
Alcoholic liver disease, 62–63
Alleles, 20
Alpha receptors, 167
Alprazolam, 273
Alternating current, 227
Aminophylline, 273
Amitriptyline, 273
Ammunition
    bullet, *see* Bullet
    cartridges, 125–126, 130, 153
    centerfire, 125–126, 133, 142–143
    centerfire rifle, 142–143
    rimfire, 124–126, 134
    shotgun shells, 128–130
    velocity of, 133–134
Amniotic emboli, 246–247
Amobarbital, 273
Amoxapine, 273
Amperage, 227
Amphetamine, 273
Amyloid angiopathy, 55
Amyloidosis, 44
Anal intercourse, 183
Anesthesia-related deaths, 252
Aneurysms
    berry, 52–54
    syphilitic aortic, 50–51
Angulation fracture, 95
Ankle fractures, 97, 201
Anterior compression fracture, 95
Aorta
    acute dissection of, 50
    blunt force injuries to, 85–86